WHAT YOU DON'T KNOW CAN HURT YOU

WHAT YOU
DON'T KNOW
CAN HURT YOU

*A Study of Public Opinion
and Public Emotion*

By LESTER MARKEL

Public Affairs Press, Washington, D. C.

PREFACE

In his *American Commonwealth,* published in 1888 but still as timely as any work in the field, James Bryce wrote: "Of all the experiments which America has made, this endeavoring to govern by public opinion is that which best deserves study, for her solution of the problem differs from all previous solutions, and she has shown more boldness in trusting public opinion, in recognizing and giving effect to it, than has yet been shown elsewhere. Public opinion stands out, in the United States, as the great source of power, the master of servants who tremble before it."

More than 80 years later the promise has not yet been realized; it remains the great challenge for the future; if democracy is to succeed— or even survive—Bryce's words must be translated into action. This belief is the primary reason for this book, which attempts to deal with the challenge, to set out the problems in the opinion process and to suggest, non-dogmatically, some possible remedies.

The author's credentials are these: a long newspaper career, considerable activity in public affairs television, a persistent desire to find out, an uncynical skepticism. The book is based on these various experiences in the mass media, plus extensive reading in the literature on the subject—incidentally, much more illuminating than enlightening—and a goodly amount of original research. (All of this, I hear some say, suggests a "journalistic" approach. It does. I do not apologize for the adjective; in its true sense, journalism is the accurate reporting and the sound interpretation of current trends—and a most valuable exercise.)

If these pages have any value, it is this: they synthesize and analyze the previous work in the field; they offer some new observations and some personal variations on the theme, the pickings—some ripe, some, he suspects, not so ripe—of one who has labored for a half-century in the journalistic vineyards. Switching metaphors, the author dares to hope that, if nothing more, he has succeeded in indicating signposts that may serve to guide future travelers along a road heavily marked with detours and roadblocks.

There are in the book a large number of quotations: the author (becomingly and modestly) has felt it important to include the opinions of others as well as his own. Quotations from materials already published are designated by the reference numbers in the text and the corresponding footnotes at the end of the book. There are in addition a very considerable number of quotations from various

v

authorities—presidents, politicians, pollsters, public figures generally—interviewed by the author and his aides. Such quotations are original and do not carry reference numerals.

I am indebted to numerous people for their contributions to these pages: to my colleagues in journalism who over many years have informed and stimulated me, to those who provided expert advice in the preparation of various chapters, to those who assisted me in the research, and to those who read and commented on the manuscript.

I am especially grateful to the Twentieth Century Fund for supplying the monies which made possible the research for the book and to the Director of the Fund, Murray Rossant, who gave generous cooperation and useful counsel as the book evolved.

I give additional thanks: for aid in research, to Salim Lone, James Boylan, Dr. George Gallup, and Louis Harris; for reading the manuscript or sections of it, to Penn Kimball, Ithiel de Sola Pool, and Anthony Austin; for help in the preparation of the bibliography, to W. Phillips Davison (public opinion and the polls), Paul Lazarsfeld (structure of society), Sidney Hyman (the Presidency), Robert Bendiner (the Congress), James Boylan and John Hohenberg (the press), and Jack Gould (television).

L. M.

CONTENTS

1: Public Opinion: Paramount Issue

Almost daily the problem grows in proportion and in urgency—this problem of informing and spurring public opinion. For years the issue has been evolving, until now it has become a topmost national concern—a matter of prime import for the future of the country, for the welfare of the people, for the course of democracy itself.

In recent years the complexion of the world has changed; old philosophies, old methods, old attitudes no longer apply; man's affairs today are unlike any of the past, so much larger and more complex are they. As never before, new ideas, new approaches, new actions are needed.

The problem is composed of various elements—what we are told, what we are not told, the impact of these reports (and non-reports) on the national mood, the ebb and flow of opinion, the towering problems of communication—all adding up to a paramount issue.

Developments of recent months have sharply accented the issue: the administration's attacks on the press, the press attacks on the administration, the credibility gap that confronted President Johnson and plagues President Nixon, the media's own credibility gap (almost as great), the Nixonian pre-emption of prime television time, the tangled question of subpoenas for newspaper men, the duel over the Pentagon Papers, fought all the way to the Supreme Court, the growing tensions between the Congress and the President over executive privilege.

Clearly then this is a new world in which we are living. Yet we have not yet learned to adjust ourselves to it. Public opinion lags at a time when its relevance and its urgency cannot be over-estimated.

*   *   *

This is the basic proposition from which the book flows:

In a democracy, policy, eventually, if not immediately, is made or unmade by public opinion.

Such are the promise and the peril of democracy — promise in that we, the people, if we exercise our potential power knowledgeably and responsibly, can achieve a wise national program; peril in that, more often than not, we do not assume this responsibility.

In a dictatorship it is different. The Fuehrer must heed the public mood; he tries to mold that mood by fiat and propaganda. He does not wait upon parliaments or committees; he does not hesitate because of any basic freedoms. For a short while, the dictatorial method may seem more effective, but in the long run, as history repeatedly reveals (Hitler, 12 years; Mussolini, 21 years; Stalin, 29 years) it does not prevail.

If public opinion is informed, policy is likely to be enlightened; if it is uninformed, it is likely to be unenlightened.

The executive constantly takes readings of public opinion; the Congress tries frantically to keep its ear close to the ground. The leaders in a democracy must take account of public thinking, for political reasons and, more importantly, for determination of what is possible and what is impossible in the way of legislation. Therefore the true functioning of democracy depends in large degree on the knowledge and wisdom of the electorate.

American public opinion is not sufficiently informed to meet the need of the times.

Because of military service overseas, of investment and trips abroad, we have learned about other lands and other peoples—and so we may be better informed now than at any other previous period in our history. Nevertheless, in view of the world's increasing complexities, we are not knowledgeable enough and concerned enough to carry out the assignment democracy requires of its peoples.

Thus a huge responsibility is put on those entrusted with the task of informing the public.

Public opinion is molded by the government, by the mass media, by our schools, by dialogue with neighbors. Each of these elements must make its contribution if we are to have the enlightened viewpoint which is the ultimate objective.

*   *   *

These, in general, are the four divisions of the book:

In Part I "public opinion" is defined; the methods used to gauge it (especially the polls) scrutinized; its present state analyzed, the "public" dissected. "There is much mystery about the tides of opinion but there is this certainty: that the tides are there and affect deeply our national course."

In Part II the forces that mold public opinion are appraised, the "outside" and the "inside" influences — the "inside": family, tradition, education; the "outside": government, the educators, the directors of the mass media, the poll-takers. "Public opinion is an elusive and tricky current; to steer through it requires a master mariner."

In Part III the impact of public opinion on public policy is considered; certain case histories are analyzed and the lessons for the future drawn. "We are motivated much more by emotion than reason."

In Part IV the defects in the public opinion process are indicated and suggestions made for remedies. "What we don't know can surely hurt us."

*　　*　　*

In the Preface it is suggested that the issues discussed in these pages are as urgent and as relevant as any among the large number with which the nation is confronted today. In the chapters that follow there will be found recurring evidence in support of that statement. For example:

The nation, as rarely before, is confused and uncertain. This bleak mood is reflected in "public opinion," which often illogically swings, which is easily swayed, which does not have the information required for sound judgment.

The "credibility gap" between government and people seems to grow wider almost daily. There have been serious doubts, for example, that the truth has been told about Vietnam; the suspicion mounted with the publication of such documents as the Pentagon Papers.

In general the political scene is a shadowed one. As a result of the advent of television, charisma too frequently in politics is rated more highly than character, issues are obscured even though they are presented in "living color," there is danger of serious misjudgment at the polls.

All of this adds up to deep misgivings about the functioning of

democracy. In a world wracked by ideologies, nationalisms, ruth-
less ambitions, a world faced with gaps of all kinds—credibility,
moral and ethical gaps—what is needed is not a theoretical but a
working democracy.

*   *   *

At the outset two questions arise: Is democracy "of, by and for"
the people a really viable institution? Assuming that a better informed public opinion can be achieved, what will that mean to the
democratic process? The quick answer to the first is: "Yes, if—;" to
the second, "a great deal." Obviously these questions cannot be
adequately discussed until their full implications are explored, so no
attempt is made to answer them here. (A summing up based on the
observations in the various chapters will be found in Chapter 22.)

Suffice it to say here that, having set down the dark entries in the
national ledger, this observer retains his optimism because he believes
that democracy is still the best of all political systems evolved by
man; and because, knowing that somehow in the past we have always muddled through, he is confident that we shall see it through
this time, provided that national is put above self interest and that
calm concern is substituted for blind fear.

*Before beginning the discussion of these large issues, the background
should be made clear. This is done in the chapters that follow.*

Part I

BACKGROUND

These chapters are designed to set out the background of the book's theme; to answer particularly these four questions: What is meant by the phrase "public opinion?" Can that "opinion" be accurately measured? What exactly is this "public" that opinionates? How does the complicated process operate?

The definitions include those of Bryce, Lippmann and Markel; the uses and abuses of the polls are catalogued; the "Elite," the "Non-Elite" and the "Middle American" are identified; our startling ignorance is revealed.

2: What Is "Public Opinion" Anyway?

Few phrases in the political lexicon are as resounding and as often invoked as the phrase "public opinion." Yet it remains obscure, another of those labels which are constantly yet blindly applied. "Public" is not easily defined and "opinion" often is not, as it seems to imply, considered viewpoint but snap judgment or sheer emotion. The Romans had two words for it: "Vox Populi." We fully endorse the concept, even though at times the "Vox" is Babel and the "Populus" a vague corpus.

The phrase remains elusive even though there has always been a vast concern and an abundance of material about the subject—books, articles, and surveys, by communicators and non-communicators, by certified and uncertified accounters, by "experts" in the social science areas, and by the pollsters, whose operations have had an almost unholy escalation and who have achieved an astounding and disturbing influence.

The explorer hunting for clues is likely to become lost in a jungle of tangled theories. One school holds that public opinion is composed of stereotyped judgments and that so-called rational conclusions are, in fact, only expressions of sentiment. Another school contends that public opinion is a considered and logical group judgment and that, even if at times it verges on the emotional, it does represent the basic views of the nation.

Again, there is the concept that public opinion represents the viewpoint of that small segment of the population called "the Elite" and that the public, lacking a mind of its own, adopts the conclusions of these leaders. In a contrary concept, the people are given a much higher rating; to them are attributed a basic common sense and a morality that eventually produce enlightened opinion. So one tries to sort out the hodge-podge of theories in an effort to arrive at a basic understanding.

The attempts to arrive at a definition reach far back into history. The early Roman jurists referred to a "consensus populi," indicat-

ing that even in those days there were Lyndon Johnsons. Pragmatic
philosophers in the eighteenth and nineteenth centuries paid tribute
to the power of public opinion. Jean-Jacques Rousseau, the French
humanist, defined "l'opinion publique" as "the common will." He
contended, as did David Hume, of the 18th Century English School,
that even the most despotic governments must pay heed to public
opinion.

Jeremy Bentham defined public opinion as a "system of law
emanating from the body of the people"; he called it "the only check
to the pernicious exercise of the power of government." But, even
though all three of these observer-philosophers agreed that public
opinion was a potent force, they provided few clues as to its operation.

Two definitions call for special attention because each in a way
constitutes a landmark—those of James Bryce and Walter Lippmann.

Bryce, in his *American Commonwealth*, defined public opinion as
"the power exerted by any . . . view, or any set of views held by an
apparent majority of citizens." Even though he said of the United
States, "In no country can it be so well studied," he did not suggest how it could be studied or measured.

In 1933 Walter Lippmann (in his *Public Opinion*, the classic modern
work: very philosophical, and at times remote and indefinite) offered
this definition: "Those features of the world outside which have to do
with the behavior of other human beings, the pictures of themselves,
of others, of their needs, purposes, and relationships, are their public
opinions. Those pictures which are acted upon by groups or by individuals acting in the name of groups are Public Opinion with
capital letters." [1]

Yet opinion is surely more than a picture, which is the product of
imagination and prejudices; and certainly it implies some process of
cerebration. Moreover, how can "pictures of themselves," etc., be
public opinion? The phrase suggests the musings on an analyst's
couch. But that would be strictly private not public opinion. It
is all still obscure.

Then came the social scientists with a new set of definitions. Thus,
V. O. Key, Jr.: "Public opinion may simply be taken to mean opinions held by private persons which governments find it prudent to
heed. Governments may be compelled toward action or inaction by

such opinion; in other instances they may ignore it, perhaps at their peril; they may attempt to alter it; or they may divert or pacify it. So defined, opinion may be shared by many or by few people." [2]

In sum, there are almost as many definitions as definers. So now this observer throws his weather-beaten hat into the ring and offers this:

"Public opinion in a democracy is a collective viewpoint powerful enough, if the power is exerted, to influence public policy. It may be the viewpoint of a majority of the people, or, in the absence of an effective majority, the viewpoint of an effective minority."

Some Caveats

The reader can take his pick, but he is urged to keep these caveats in mind:

The public in a democratic society with almost universal communications is a dynamic and shifting body and not, as sometimes suggested, a homogeneous and stable one. Its viewpoint is subject to change, often swift change.

A distinction must be made between two kinds of majority opinion: active and passive. Opinion is active when a majority of the public, bound together by common belief, moves to influence government policy through electoral decisions, through pressure upon its representatives or other direct means. It is passive when a numerical majority holds common beliefs but does not act upon them. (This last is often referred to as the "mood of the country." The phrase is a favorite with commentators and they feel they can use it freely and with impunity because there is no way of checking its accuracy.)

An active majority opinion is rare except at election time. In most instances, it is a minority which has the power to influence government policy because of its importance or the intensity of its opinions and which exerts that power. Yet, to be truly effective, an active minority must have at least the passive acceptance of its objectives by the inactive majority. Thus, in the long run, the public prevails.

Confusion and contradiction about its meaning have raised questions as to whether there is any such force as public opinion. Yet even though there are persistent statements that public opinion does not really exist, political leaders believe that it does; they try to fathom it and they are guided by their findings. Thus any debate about its reality is wholly academic.

Assuming, as we must, that there is "public opinion"—or "public emotion"—can it be definitely measured? This is the second large question and mostly it involves the issue of the validity of the polls. It is discussed in the next chapter.

3: The Polls: Always Potent, Sometimes Puzzling

The public opinion poll has become almost synonymous with public opinion itself. Since its official debut in the 1936 Presidential election, the polling profession or science or business (or whatever it is) has grown by huge leaps and often outside bounds.

The electorate at large treats polls with wide-eyed reverence. Political leaders check them as intently as the sages of old examined the entrails of lambs to guide them to decisions. Candidates turn to them in the hope of learning where they stand and how they can improve that standing. More than fifty polls, on an average, are inserted annually into the *Congressional Record,* an indication of the magic they possess for Capitol Hill. Madison Avenue depends on polls to tell it what arguments, accents and adjectives will be most effective in advancing its clients' canned goods or causes.

Polls, both public and private, powerfully influence political campaigns. In 1968 Governor Romney's decision to bow out of the Presidential race even before the New Hampshire primary was based on surveys showing him far behind Nixon. President Johnson's announcement that he would not seek re-election was made the day the Gallup Poll reported his popularity at an all-time low. (A coincidence, but the climax of a trend.) In the same year Governor Rockefeller decided to seek the Republican Presidential nomination because private surveys had convinced him that he could win in a popularity contest with Mr. Nixon.

In the 1960 Presidential campaign private pollsters persuaded John F. Kennedy to adopt a strong position on civil rights and to meet the religious issue head-on. Likewise Edward Brooke, a Negro, became convinced as a result of surveys that he had more than an even chance of winning the 1968 Senatorial contest in Massachusetts if he confronted the race issue directly in a series of television appearances; his conclusion proved correct.

Yet, despite their widespread acceptance, there is great controversy over polls. The critics contend that they are not true measures of public opinion; that they deal with complex issues in simplistic and unscientific terms and that they have a dangerous "bandwagon" effect—that is, they influence voters who want to be on the winning side; but as British elections have revealed (see page 246) a bandwagon sometimes turns out to be only a caboose. The poll-takers offer refutation rhetorically and arithmetically; before analyzing their rejoinders the facts about polls should be considered.

The Variety of Surveys

There are two general categories of polls: the public polls, which are intended for publication and the private polls, which are not. Public polls are of two kinds: those conducted by commercial pollsters (some of whom are also engaged in marketing research) and published in newspapers as circulation bait; and the university polls designed, say their practitioners, to probe much more deeply and knowledgeably into human behavior and the social and political aspects of an issue. (Maybe, but a lapse of two years between survey and report is not uncommon and therefore there is a likelihood that they will be at least somewhat out of date; a statute of limitation might well run here, even though the university pollsters say their objective is to study human behavior rather than to predict.)

Private polls are also of two varieties: the commercial poll, designed to help manufacturers decide what to sell and how to sell it; and the political poll, commissioned by candidates to help them determine courses of action in seeking nominations, in running campaigns and in appraising the moods of their constituents.

The private commercial polls are outside the main concerns of this book because they are not published and therefore have no direct impact on the public. It might be noted, however, that the task of the pollsters in this area is much simpler and less open to cavil than their performance in public affairs. Undoubtedly polls can be useful in determining advertising programs. But there is this important difference between commercial and public affairs polls: the former put simple questions to evoke definite answers about products; moreover, queries about what is desired in the way of a soup or a soap cannot be compared to inquiries about what should be our role in the world or how the dilemmas of inflation can be resolved.

The candidates' private polls, since they too are not made public—except when they are deliberately "leaked" by hard-pressed politicians—are also outside the range of this book. (Parenthetically it should be noted that even though they are not likely to be as accurate as the soup and soap surveys, they can provide clues as to what issues should be emphasized and where attention in a campaign should be concentrated.)

Our concern is rather with surveys in the area of public affairs, because they constitute the only statistical and allegedly "scientific" method presently available for measuring public opinion and because they receive extensive publicity and have wide acceptance.

The best known public pollsters are Louis Harris, whose polls are syndicated in about 130 papers and who also does work for *Time/Life,* and Dr. George Gallup, whose polls appear regularly in the *New York Times* and about 125 other daily papers across the country and who polls for *Newsweek.* Other eminent pollsters include Oliver Quayle, who does work for N.B.C. and on occasion for politicians, Roper Associates, which rarely undertakes public polling, and Daniel Yankelovich.

In view of the great influence of polls and the sharpness of the debate over them, it is vital to any study of public opinion that these surveys be sorted out and their methods, accuracy and value appraised. (Such an analysis has been made for the purpose of this book. The broad conclusions are stated in this chapter; a detailed analysis appears in Appendix I.)

Appraisal of the Polls

Generally, our research tends to indicate:

• Of the three elements involved in a poll, the first, the sampling methods, are generally accepted as sound, but there are doubts about the second and the third, the questionnaire and the questioners.

• Even though the standard sample consists of only 1,500 interviews to gauge national sentiment on an issue, it is estimated that, if approved methods are followed, 95 times out of 100 the sampling error will be no greater than two percentage points either way.

• Many critics feel that the questionnaires are at times inadequate and insufficient attention is given to some of their inherent difficulties.

They must be so framed that they will be understood by college graduates and high school dropouts by bankers and housewives alike. They must not be too long or too complicated; on the other hand, there is danger in oversimplification because a complex issue cannot be covered in a few abbreviated queries.

• The critics contend, with some reason, that the half hour allowed by some pollsters for an interview is not sufficient to elicit sound opinion; that there is no opportunity to put the "informational" questions which reveal the amount of knowledge possessed by the interviewee and the depth of his feeling about an issue.

• There is also the question of whether the interviewer himself— or probably herself—has the background to pursue the proper queries, and to pin-point defects or ambiguities in the answers. The interviewers must be of first-rate caliber if a poll is to have full value. For the most part, however, interviewers are housewives who do polling as a part-time, pin-money job; they are likely to have college degrees, but this is not necessarily proof of perspicacity or even intelligence.

• Among the important potential pitfalls for interviewers there is the matter of prestige. I am convinced that few people, being human, are willing to admit ignorance, even to a stranger whom they are unlikely to encounter again. Unless the interviewer is both persistent and perceptive, he is likely to be misled by interviewees who instead of responding "I don't know" protect their egos with firmly positive answers. Sometimes the proportion of "don't know" answers runs as high as 20 percent.

• No small part of the defects in the opinion process can be charged to the press—television and radio as well as newspapers. The media are obsessed with the idea of "instant news" and apply pressure on the poll-takers for quick findings, even though there is agreement that a good poll requires careful preparation, good procedure and sound analysis.

Election Polls—Why?

When questions of accuracy are raised, the pollsters will point to their election surveys, the most widely publicized of all their activities. They contend that in election polling (as distinct from primary election surveys) they have been eminently successful; that in public issue polls they use the same methods and procedures as in election surveys; and that therefore the public affairs surveys are as trustworthy as the election polls.

The fact is that with election polls the pollster uses more safeguards than he does with public affairs polls. He increases the size of the sample and he is much more cautious in his reporting of results. Indeed, Seymour Lipset, a critic of the polls, accuses the pollsters of "cooking the data" for their election predictions. "The pollsters" he says, "juggle the figures, estimate varying turn-out possibilities, compare the late responses with earlier ones, read over a number of interviews to get a feel for different types of respondents, bring to bear all past experience and know-how on how various groups have acted in different situations, and finally, nervous and perspiring, come up with some figures which may diverge considerably from the raw, unmanipulated data." [1]

Moreover, election surveys and public affairs surveys are not at all comparable. Election polls involve a simple query: which of two or three men do you favor? An issue poll, on the other hand, involves questions about complex problems—questions seldom susceptible to yes or no answers. As Bryce puts it, "The choice of one man against another is an imperfect way of expressing the mind of a constituency." The election returns do not indicate popular sentiment on specific issues. Moreover, many problems come up between elections. "The action of opinion," says Bryce, "is continuous, that of voting occasional, and in the intervals between the elections, changes might take place materially affecting the views of voters." [2]

Usually there is little social purpose served by election soundings; now and then, it is true, they may act as warnings that renewed efforts are needed to defeat an undesirable candidate. In general, though, it can be said that the electorate can well wait until the returns are in to find out who are the victors; that the delay can inconvenience only the gamblers; that there is always the danger that polls may bring about a "bandwagon vote" (a desire to be on the winning side) and that a bad showing in the polls may make it difficult for a candidate to raise money. (Hubert Humphrey was a victim of this kind of handicap in 1968).

Dr. Gallup feels that election polls have a definite value, especially from a technical point of view. "They have made us improve our methodology," he told me. "You stand naked in the public light. I believe that if the social scientists had to meet some such test, they would be generations ahead of where they are now." Both Messrs. Gallup and Harris vehemently deny the "bandwagon theory," insisting that if the theory were valid, election predictions would be wrong because they would result in massive switching to the leading candidate—and that this does not take place is revealed by the British election of 1970.

Another rejoinder the poll-takers make to criticism of election polls is that the press, which has a fervent (even though unscientific) hankering for surveys of all kinds, insists upon them, putting them almost in the same category as predictions of horse races, with the favorites rated and the "best bets" supplied.

The Pollsters' Reply

Whatever the criticisms of them, the fact is that the polls provide virtually the only "scientific" method of gauging the mood of the citizenry. There is no doubt that they perform useful functions for both the public and the policymaker; they indicate, if only in a general way, the public's desires, and it is urgent that the *Vox Populi* be heard, even though it be only in whispers. Polls can serve as alerts to the danger that opinion may be headed in a wrong direction; they can be used to counter powerful special interest groups that claim greater support than they possess and so to protect the many from the manipulations of the few; finally, they can stimulate discussion of important issues.

The pollsters contend, with considerable logic, that the primary function of polls is to provide information—for the executive and the legislature—as well as the public. They insist they are not suggesting that the President and the Congress blindly follow the polls but rather that they use the findings as aids toward arriving at wise decisions. I asked Messrs. Gallup, Harris, and Roper to comment on this vital point.

"A Congressman," Dr. Gallup says, "is like a general who is in charge of a battle. The intelligence division doesn't tell the general what to do, but it gives him the kind of knowledge he needs to make a good decision. If there were no polls there would still be many voices claiming to be speaking for the public—all sorts of groups, every variety of person, ranging from the topmost elite to the lowest lobbyist. That is why some sort of documentation is valuable by way of counter and corrective."

And Mr. Harris adds, "Leaders do not necessarily have to follow public opinion, but they do have an accountability to public opinion in the end, because in a democracy, we live by the consent of the governed." He acknowledges that polls can be disturbing "if they are viewed as a permanent fix on American public opinion"; he urges that they be viewed as "single snapshots at one point in time of a constantly moving picture, a kaleidoscope of people reacting to their national crises and challenges." And Elmo Roper: "We have to take it on faith that, as inaccurate expressions of public opinion as they may be, polls are probably more accurate than most newspaper editorials."

Nevertheless, the fact is that both government and public have come to look upon the polls not as indicators but as conclusions.

Potential Remedies

The summation in general then is that the polls provide an essential service, but that there are serious imperfections in the polling process that call for remedial action. If democracy is to depend ultimately on public opinion, there is grave need for better methods of assessing that opinion.

The pollsters, even though they have recognized the shortcomings of their surveys, have made only laggard effort to correct them. Various codes of ethics have been accepted, both by individual pollsters and by the polling organizations. The American Association of Public 'Opinion Research has adopted for its members a code of "disclosure standards" which calls for: identification of the survey sponsor; exact wording of the questions; definition of the population sample; size of sample; allowance for sampling error; identification of findings based on parts of the total sample; a statement as to whether interviewing was done in person, by phone, mail, or on street corners; and information on time of interviewing in relation to events.

Other conditions might well be added: that the polling budgets be ample to the need; that the importunities of the press be resisted

more sternly by the pollsters; that the press itself recognize its responsibility in insuring both the accuracy and the accurate presentation of polls; that the public be educated to recognize polls for
what they are. Polling is still more of an art than a science and even
if polls have their uses as straws in the wind, it is perilous, even though
it is done constantly, to mistake the straws for the wind itself.

There are those who believe the answer is a government-supported
poll. Elmo Roper and Burns Roper, his son, contend that, by
mobilizing the economic and social resources of the federal government, such surveys would have the needed funds and could provide
the in-depth approach of the university survey in a much shorter
time. Burns Roper has proposed such a publicly financed, continuing
opinion-polling operation, covering national and international issues.

He suggests that, even though the operation would be financed by
the government, the work might well be assigned to a reputable outside organization and the findings issued independently of the government.[3]

Elmo Roper advocates a small committee to administer such polls,
with a number of consultants from the social sciences. He believes
that, if surveys of this kind revealed popular opposition to measures
which legislators considered desirable, the legislators would then make
an attempt to persuade the citizenry to their views. "Perhaps the
greatest use of such polls," he says, "would be in charting areas of
public ignorance. Pollsters do not do much of this today because
there is no money in it."

The pollsters say if they had the required funds they could do a
better job. This seems to me an insufficient alibi for inadequate work
in an area as sensitive and potentially important as this. It is probably
true that commercial pollsters have lost money on public affairs polling although recently lucrative contracts with the newsweeklies have
probably righted the balance sheets for Messrs. Gallup and Harris.
But, even if the red-ink problem has not been solved for them,
they derive a tremendous indirect benefit from the publicity attached
to public affairs polling—publicity likely to bring them commercial
clients.

The government-supported poll is probably only a dream because
it is most unlikely that Congress would ever approve the proposal
unless it had control of the process, in which case it would be of

little value. Yet the objective of such a poll is surely valid. The present dialogues are too one-sided; government leaders have access to the media so that they can barrage the public with their ideas, but the public has only limited means of letting the government know how it feels.

* * *

In concluding this chapter, it is useful to restate the fundamental proposition: that we have a democracy, that no other system (certainly not Communism, certainly not Fascism) has been proved better, but that democracy is not functioning as it should. Most of us, it must be assumed, want to effect a government "of the people, by people, for the people." But "of the people" is the hitch, the rub, the conundrum. A huge conundrum, the sum of three questions: How do our national leaders determine what the people want? If and when they are able to make such determinations, shall they try to implement them without questioning them? If they do question them, how do they persuade the voters to their views?

(These questions are discussed in later pages, particularly in the chapters dealing with the Presidency and the Congress.)

The first is the basic question and the one out of which flow the second and third. It involves, of course, the polls and other possible solutions to the problem which Woodrow Wilson described in these terms: "I do not know what the people are thinking about; I have the most imperfect means of finding out, yet I must act as if I knew. I'm not put here to do what I please." And Bryce noted: "The next stage in the development of democratic government would be reached if the will of the majority of the citizens were to become ascertainable at all times." [4]

Who then is the "public" of "public opinion"? What sort of people are we? And what can be expected of us? This is the theme of the next chapter.

4: "We The People": A Quilt-Work Profile

Because democracy ultimately depends on the viewpoints and actions of the electorate, a prerequisite for any inquiry into American public opinion is a survey of the American people.

This might be a primary division: the "Elite," the "Have-Nots" and the "Middle Americans." Admittedly, these classifications may be too arbitrary; moreover, there is a constant shifting from one group to another because in a democracy such as ours there is freedom of movement despite the lines drawn by Dun and Bradstreet or by the Social Register. Nevertheless, the three categories seem to be approximately accurate; roughly it can be estimated that the "Elite" comprise 10% of the population: (20 million people), the "Have-Nots," 30%: (60 million), the "Middle Americans" 60%: (120 million).

The "Have-Nots," because of their economic status and uncertainty about life in general, do not play a positive role in public opinion. It is true that in the form of protest or violence they have a significant negative role and so make a political impact; but they are almost totally preoccupied with the task of finding the wherewithal of existence. They live at or below the poverty line (a sliding scale from $3,000 to $3,500 a year set by the Department of Health, Education and Welfare); many of their names are on the welfare rolls; they are the poor whites and ghetto-bound blacks who, despairing and for the most part ignorant, provide ready tinder for the demagogue's torch.

The Middle Men

The "Middle American," who has come lately into large political and psychological view and made considerable impress on the national scene, calls for close scrutiny. The category is divided into "Lower Middle" and "Upper Middle" groups.

The "Lower Middle Americans" are the less skilled industrial workers, farm labor and service employees, numbering possibly 40 million and the nation's elderly citizens living on fixed incomes, totalling possibly 30 million. Of the "Upper Middle Americans," the largest segment, possibly numbering another 40 million, consists of the skilled workers who earn between $9,000 and $15,000 for a family of four; having moved up from the lower to the middle rank, they now have the expectation of further upgrading. A smaller group, possibly 10 million, is in the upper income bracket; in it are found small entrepreneurs and the lesser professionals in medicine, law, etc.

Studies made by the Labor Department indicate that the majority of "Upper Middle Americans" were once renters of homes and are now owners. They have moved from beer to whisky, from public to private transportation.[1] The wife, perhaps even more than the husband, "senses the chaos. Often enough, inflation determines the diet she feeds her family. She worries about safety in the streets; she worries about her children being bused; about the sex education to which they are subjected; about the drugs her children might pick up at school; about the smut for sale in the drugstore newsstand and on the neighborhood movie screen." [2]

The "Middle Americans" are likely to be found in the nation's heartland rather than on its coasts, but they live in Queens, New York, and Van Nuys, California, as well as in Skokie, Illinois, and Chillicothe, Ohio. Generally they are not the poor or the rich, yet many wealthy business executives are "Middle Americans." (Many general practitioners, too, are "Middle Americans" and they have great influence in their communities.) In their ranks there are few blacks and few of the nation's intellectuals. "Above all, 'Middle America' is a state of mind, a morality, a construct bound together by a roughly similar way of seeing things." [3]

Mr. Nixon calls the "Middle Americans" the "Silent Majority." (The adjective is surely wrong; Mr. Nixon's "Silent Majority" is an unsilent, raucous group.) Surveys made by Louis Harris Associates in January, 1970 and January, 1971 reported that, while some 57% of the public considered itself part of this group, some 9% indicated that if the 1972 elections were held at that time they would vote for George Wallace on a third party ticket rather than for Mr. Nixon. In terms of a three-way Presidential race, this would mean a reduction of the "Silent Majority" for Mr. Nixon to a figure below the 50% mark.

The possibility of a conservative third party remains a worry for Mr. Nixon. A Harris survey in 1968 indicated that if Wallace had not been in the contest, Nixon would have won by a margin of 53 to 47%, whereas the actual results were 43.1% for Nixon, 42.7% for Humphrey, 13.6% for Wallace. The Wallace threat remains.

In another Harris poll taken in January, 1970, those surveyed were asked to choose among 26 situations they considered important to their happiness; 95% wanted "green grass and trees around me," 92% wanted "neighbors with whom I feel comfortable," 84% "a kitchen with all the modern conveniences," 81% "good schools nearby." These personal goals signify a "marked shift away from the old ethic of continued hard work and success, stressing instead a desire for peace and middle class satisfactions."

This survey disclosed that the viewpoint of the "Middle American" is conservative, as reflected in his attitude toward morals: 75% oppose premarital sex; 73%, including 68% of the young, consider marijuana "a very serious problem" and feel strongly that it should be legalized. Distrust of the "new permissiveness" extends to the "new culture, to what is going on in books, music and movies"; 54% feel the "present styles in hair and dress are a sure sign of moral decay."

The average "Middle American" holds a resentment against both the "Elite" and the "Have-Nots." He feels that the "Have-Nots"—the blacks and the browns in particular—have spoiled the neighborhoods, destroyed the school systems and heavily overloaded the welfare rolls for which he is heavily taxed. The "Elite" are condemned as "the Establishment" that owns and operates the important communications media, backs movements for social reform and advocates foreign and economic policies contrary to the traditional ideas to which "Middle America" clings. Bond issues endorsed by the "Elite" for better schools and public transportation are regularly turned down by "Middle America."

The "Middle American" was acclaimed in early 1970 by Spiro Agnew, who was then riding a wave of popularity. (According to a Gallup poll at the time, Mr. Agnew ranked only behind Mr. Nixon and Billy Graham as the "nation's most admired man.") At that time an editorial in the *Wall Street Journal* offered this analysis:

"Mr. Agnew's popularity is mirrored by apoplectic convulsions among the 'Elite.' No doubt the 'Elite,' generally, view the Vice President as rallying 'the rednecks' against the 'thinking people.' The heart of the Agnew phenomenon is precisely that a class has sprung up in this nation that considers itself uniquely qualified ('the thinking people') and is quite willing to dismiss the ordinary American with utter contempt ('the rednecks'). Mr. Agnew has merely supplied a focus for the inevitable reaction to this arrogance. Mr. Agnew's targets—the media, war protesters, rebellious youth— are representatives of a class that has enjoyed unusual moral and cultural authority through the 1960's. And now there is being witnessed the movement against that class—the 'assaulting' of 'the aristocracy.' " [4]

But after a year of the Nixon regime, despite the gesture to them in the social and cultural areas, the Middle Americans began to have deep doubts arising out of inflation. This was the group which had experienced a sudden rise in wages and in its standard of living and had confidently embarked on extensive gambles on the future in the way of mortgages and installment purchases. When unemployment increased, money became tight and the cost of living spiralled upward, the Middle American was heavily hit.

The political reaction was evident in the polls. A Harris survey, taken on the eve of Mr. Nixon's announcement of his "New Economic Policy," asked voters how they would rate his job "in keeping the economy healthy." The result was 73% negative, 22% positive, 5% not sure. The President discovered that, for the average man, even for the Middle American, economics, personal economics, is much more potent than ideology.

The "Elite"

"Elite" is a word to conjure with and puzzle over; it applies to a varied and constantly changing group. By definition, the "Elite" are really the "chosen people." The word is taken from the French "elite," meaning the "select"; the French word, in turn, is derived from the Latin "eligere," meaning "to choose." (Not that all members of the "Elite" groups are well-informed or deeply concerned.) Yet there are essential differences between those officially elected to office and those unofficially elevated to elitedom; the first are selected by the voters, the second achieve high station because of their competence or eloquence or wisdom or because, by crashing the headlines, they nominate themselves.

The "Elite" are those members of the public who, through personal power and prestige, have access to both the policymakers and the general public; they communicate their ideas to government through acquaintance with officials and to the general citizenry through the mass media. Thus they possess the potential power to influence government policy and/or public opinion. They can be likened to a group the French call "The Notables," defined as men who have the confidence of their neighbors and who, even though they may have different political ideas, are sought out for advice by the non-notables because they have succeeded in their own affairs.

A random list of the "Elite" would include: in newspaper circles: editors and publishers, columnists and reporters; in television and radio: network and station heads and commentators; in the business world: the chairmen and presidents of large corporations, their directors of research and others in high posts; in education: presidents and past-presidents of universities and prestigious scholars; in the public groups: heads of large trade organizations, world affairs councils, women's clubs, farm groups and other nationally organized voluntary associations and, at times, the leaders of Rotary, Kiwanis and similar groups that occasionally arrange discussions of public affairs. The "Elite" are found in local as well as national ranks. Ministers, doctors and even pork-barrel sages qualify as shepherds of community opinion.

In the formation of opinion, the "Elite" obviously play a key role. This is true especially in the area of foreign affairs because of the complexity of the issues and the feeling on the part of a large majority of citizens that such problems are remote from their lives (an illusion, as Vietnam proved.) And it is also true of complicated domestic problems, notably those matters involving economics.

The influence of the intellectual "Elite" in general and the academics in particular waxes and wanes according to the political complexion of the administration in office in Washington. Under John F. Kennedy, the Galbraiths, Sorensens and Schlesingers wielded considerable power. Under Nixon, with a policy compassed toward the Middle American, the influence of the intellectuals has receded; for the most part consultants are likely to come from the business rather than the academic world. (Such academics as Henry Kissinger—and Daniel Moynihan for a while—are exceptions; they are "adaptable" academics, meaning, to my mind, that their infatuation with power exceeds the pull of their principles.)

One grouping in the "Elite"—the "Eastern Establishment"—rates special attention because of the broadsides fired at it first by Vice President Agnew and since at frequent intervals by other non-Eastern politicians. I do not doubt that there exists an Eastern "liberal" viewpoint held by Eastern editors and television commentators. Nor do I doubt that this viewpoint, even though it is found in minority groups in other sections of the country (especially on the West coast), does not represent the view of the greater part of the nation. Whether this is unfortunate or not is beside the point; there is the fact and it cannot be wished away.

The "Eastern Establishment"

What are the geography, the viewpoint and the impact of this "Eastern Establishment"? Here are comments by Messrs. Gallup and Harris (especially prepared for this book) based on the many polls they have taken:

Question: Is there an Eastern liberal point of view?

Gallup: "The best and the only objective evidence of this is the vote in Presidential elections. The East (the New England and Middle Atlantic states) has increasingly given greater support to liberal candidates. In 1968 the East was by far the most liberal (Democratic) area in the United States, judged by the vote cast for Hubert Humphrey.

"The East has by far the largest percentage of Catholics—who in politics have tended to support the liberal-labor viewpoint. The Jewish vote is predominantly Democratic and liberal. And now Northern blacks constitute an almost solid voting bloc for liberal candidates. These three groups make up fully half of the voting population of this area of the nation. White Anglo-Saxon Protestants (WASPS) are a definite minority in the East. On all issues involving a liberal-conservative split, the East consistently gives the liberal viewpoint a higher percentage of the vote than do other areas of the nation."

Harris: "After considerable rumination on the subject, I think I would conclude that, in a loose way, there is an Eastern Establishment. It does not have any formal structure as such; it is not a secret 'battalion' passing the word to its captains or its family members; nor is it capable of commanding all of its resources to come to bear on a particular event or situation. Still, if it is viewed as a state of mind among people located in key power centers in the eastern sweep from Boston to Washington, then there is such an Establishment. Its roots are partly economic, partly the media, partly academic-based, partly political, and partly social.

"If the Eastern Establishment has an academic home, it could well be Harvard, although any prestige college or university in the region is likely to have its Establishment group. If it were concentrated in a city, it would probably be New York, with its concentration of corporate headquarters, the financial center of the country, the home of national publications and television and radio, the home of the largest foundations, and its vibrant sense of being at the nerve center of the most powerful superpower in the world. In many ways, New York is the seat of real power, rather than Washington. Boston and Philadelphia have styles all of their own, but they fit the establishment world of the East."

Question: What does the liberal viewpoint stand for?

Gallup: "The liberal viewpoint stands for internationalism in foreign affairs. It is likely to be held by those who are the most critical of our involvement in the Vietnam war. Those who hold this viewpoint are also the most pro-labor, most inclined to favor aiding the poor, most in favor of persons who want greater government support for programs dealing with social welfare problems, and the most inclined to be pro-black."

Harris: "The people who populate the Eastern Establishment are characterized by a sense of being able to view the nation and the world through literate and presumably objective eyes. A singular mark of the Establishment type is capacity to observe the best or the worst of events or times while at the same time not losing a sense that something ought to be done about it.

"The moral imperative of the Establishment usually is to see that change takes place, but that, above all, it be orderly and well-grounded, rather than ad hoc, poorly prepared, and patently untidy. In a fundamental sense, the Establishment probably prides itself as fulfilling the traditional role of true conservatism in society: to preside over change but at the same time not to lose the reins of essential control over the kind, the quality, and the pace of change."

Question: Does the Eastern viewpoint represent majority sentiment in the country?

Gallup: "The nation is fairly evenly divided between conservatives and liberals. Hadley Cantril and Lloyd Free, in the book *The Political Beliefs of Americans,* found that the public embraced conservative views on questions of basic political philosophy, such as the relationship of the states to the nation and reliance upon individual initiative rather than government help. On the operational side, however, these same people took a liberal view of governmental social welfare problems, such as housing, urban renewal and aid to education. In short, they found that we have a nation of 'ideological conservatives' and 'operational liberals.'

"The moderately conservative vote in the 1968 Presidential election (Nixon, 43.3%) plus the extremely conservative vote (Wallace, 13.6%) add to 57%, the total conservative vote in that election. In the previous election in 1964, the conservative candidate, Republican Barry Goldwater, polled only 38.7% of the vote. When we ask the public in our own surveys how they classify themselves—as 'liberals' or 'conservatives'—the results usually show a fairly even division between the two."

Harris: "The Eastern Establishment is likely never to be a mirror reflection of the country since by definition it is different both in make-up and style from the rest of the country. But it will always be reflective enough of the rest of the country to be capable of leveraging change which will indeed affect the rest of the country. In a sense, the Eastern Establishment is more inclined to make its business to clinically understand the rest of the country and the world rather than to ape it or to reflect it as such."

In summing up, Harris says: "If there is an Eastern Establishment, it has not really become a definable target to large numbers of Americans. But this does not mean that any part of the establishment, such as the big TV networks or Eastern papers, cannot be given a hard time at any given point in time as, indeed, Wall Street, the Ford Foundation, the corporate headquarters world, or any other parts of the establishment can become a target."

The theme is not a new one. For example, a study entitled *Megalopolis: The Urbanized Northeast Seaboard of the United States* sponsored in 1961 by the Twentieth Century Fund and conducted by Dr. Jean Gottmann concludes that "this huge complex of cities, suburbs and rural sections is the major decision-making center of the nation and the dynamic hub of international relations." Megalopolis possesses a "personality of its own" and, according to Dr. Gottmann, has developed a supremacy in the politics, arts, communications and economy of the country. The power centers in this area of 40,000,000 are New York, Washington, Boston, Philadelphia and Baltimore. Dr. Gottmann predicts that other megalopoles will in time grow in the industrial Midwest between the Great Lakes and the Ohio River, and on the California Coast." [5]

In 1964 the Twentieth Century Fund financed a follow-up to Gottmann's study written by Wolf von Ekhardt, columnist for the *Washington Post*. Ekhardt's work confirmed Gottmann's and added that "on the average, the Americans living along the Atlantic seaboard from north of Boston to south of Washington are the richest, best-educated, best-housed and best-serviced group of any of similar size in the world." [6]

Arnold Hano, writing in the *New York Times* Magazine, contrasts the American West with the American East. "The Westerner," he says, "is a pragmatist, a doer. The Easterner is a dogmatist, a nondoer. The Easterner knows it all by now; he does not have to say anything or run around to prove anything . . . . His intellectual grain goes far deeper and he hones it to a far sharper edge than the Westerner." The West is "suspicious of the intellectual." For example, when Theodore Roosevelt went out "to rough it" in the Dakota badlands, the Westerners treated the bespectacled Easterner with disdain; to them, he was "Four Eyes," but when he flattened a drunk one day in a Montana bar, suddenly he became "Old Four Eyes." "Vigor, Movement, Violence," writes Hano, "are values prized out West, marks of the doer, of the man who scorns theory and plumps for the left hook."

As Hano sees it, Western pragmatism "does not make for stability"; instead "it makes for a helter-skelter approach to life, a trial and error experimentalism that continually comes up with crackpot solutions and crackpots to implement them." For example, it is difficult to imagine the East electing a tap dancer to the Senate. Hano contends that the West is unsure of its image, while the East "full well knows what it is." Nevertheless, "the West provides a social environment in which people seek progress in new things, new ideas . . . it has always been that kind of place." Wyoming's territorial legislature was the first to give women the right to vote, in 1869; Montana was the first state to do so. People out West involve themselves "furiously" in political affairs. Oregon was the first state to make wide use of the initiative, referendum and recall. Utah consistently leads the nation in percentage of eligible voters who go to the polls.[7]

The center of conservative voting strength in Congress is of course the South and the Midwest. For decades anti-intellectualism has been a mark of the "American heartland." In the Presidential campaign of 1952 the most bitter charge made against Adlai Stevenson was that he was an "egghead." In the wake of that election *Time* wrote that Dwight Eisenhower's victory "discloses an alarming fact long supposed: there is a wide and unhealthy gap between the American intellectuals and the people." And it is that gap which the Republican Right has been trying to exploit.

Now that we have defined—or attempted to define—both the "opinion" and the "public" of "public opinion" the question arises, how well-informed is the public? The following chapter offers an answer.

5: What We Know (Some), What We Don't Know (Much More)

Assuming, as we must, that an informed public is an essential requirement of an effective democracy, the question arises: how well-informed are we as a nation? The quick answer is that there is a dangerous ignorance in a number of vital areas.

Alfred O. Hero, of the World Peace Foundation, has estimated that "possibly as few as 15 percent of American adults display a significant degree of interest in world affairs, and that many of these interested citizens possess only rather trivial or peripheral information on international relations." [1] Lloyd Free and Hadley Cantril concluded that only 26% of those interviewed in a national poll could be called well-informed; two-fifths of the public "appear to have too little information about international matters to play an intelligent role as citizens of a nation that is the world's leader." [2]

In foreign affairs opinion is particularly uninformed or misinformed. Even late in 1967—by which time there had been many demonstrations against the war and much evidence that the nation wanted out — there was no clear idea among most of the public and even among the elite, as to what course to pursue. The years since 1967 have been marked by the same low level of information and uncertainty about objectives.

In October of 1964, three out of every ten persons surveyed in a Gallup Poll were unable to give any reasons for the U. S. presence in Southeast Asia. Only two out of five adult Americans in 1967 had heard or read or followed any of the discussions about the foreign aid programs, according to a survey made in March 1967 by the Institute for Social Research. Sixty percent could not identify U Thant and the one quarter had never heard of NATO.

In domestic affairs, the picture is somewhat better but still far from bright. Two months before he was nominated in June 1952 Adlai Stevenson was unknown to 60% of the public. In August 1952, about 55% of the public did not know the name of the Republican Vice

Presidential candidate, Richard Nixon. A poll taken by Dr. Gallup in January 1961 indicated that only one of the five of those interviewed could name the man appointed Secretary of State by President Kennedy (Dean Rusk). A national survey conducted in November, 1965 by the Opinion Research Corporation of Princeton for CBS revealed that 41% of those interviewed were unable to name either of their U. S. Senators.

In the national current events test given by CBS News in January, 1965, 73% of the national sample failed the entire test when they were graded on 10th grade standards. A month after the Presidential convention in 1968, according to a Roper Poll, 28% of the public could not name the Democratic Vice Presidential nominee (Edmund Muskie) and 33% could not name the Republican (Spiro Agnew!) When these pollees were asked what issues concerned them most, 32% could not think of any.

A light note is supplied by James Michener in his book *Presidential Lottery.* Michener was interested in the movement for the abolition of the Electoral College and did some man-on-the-street interviews on the issue. One citizen said, "Every boy and girl should go to college and if they can't afford Yale or Harvard, why, Electoral is just as good if you work." A woman in Philadelphia said, "I've heard some very nice things about Electoral. It's here in the neighborhood somewhere. I think it's that bunch of red-brick buildings about three blocks farther down." And she pointed towards Independence Hall. A sportsman said, "The guys at the bar poor-mouth Electoral something awful. Wasn't they mixed up in a basketball scandal or something?" [3]

In a Congressional survey done for this book, members of the Congress were asked for an estimate of the nation's information level. Out of a sample of 109 Members only 11 rated the public as "well-informed," 58 rated it as "fairly well-informed," and 26 as "poorly informed." [4]

A Harris poll in 1969 cited various events and asked in each case if those polled felt they were "very well informed by the news media." These were some of the results: 83% felt they were well informed about the moon shot, 72% about the assassination of Robert Kennedy, 58% about the heart transplant operations, 45% about campus protests, 31% about the Vietnam peace talks in Paris, 28% about the invasion of Czechoslovakia, 27% about the Middle East conflict.

These findings lead to the conclusion that much of the important news in the mass media is likely to be read only by that relatively small segment of the public which is already well informed and to go unread by the large majority of citizens who do not have the required background or impulse to inform themselves.

The situation might be figured thus: only twenty out of every hundred persons are really even reasonably well-informed; only one out of five feels any duty to be well-informed; half the voters do not understand the basic implications of domestic problems; three out of every ten voters are unaware of almost every major issue in foreign affairs. In other words, I would place 20% of the population in the moron category; another 20% are ignorant and unwilling to learn; some 40% do not know, but are willing to learn, provided that the lessons are easily digested. Which leaves the enlightened at 20%.

I asked Dr. Gallup whether, based on his years of polling, he considered the American people well-informed. The answer was an emphatic negative. "The British public," he said, "is much better informed than the American, even though formal education in England has not reached the proportions it has here. Most college graduates think their education ended on the day of graduation and many of them have not picked up a book since." The great need is adult education and public television, Dr. Gallup feels, can make an important contribution toward that end.

Louis Harris, also asked about the state of public information, replied:

"The American people do not have a solid textbook case of knowledge and fact on which their opinions are based. What is viewed as public opinion is not a well-thought-out logical series of conclusions. Rather, most public opinion represents people's emotional reactions to events of the day. Therefore, in public opinion research, we are measuring and analyzing emotional responses and feelings far more than completely rational positions.

"Nonetheless, the public generally is more sophisticated, more serious, and more selective in its judgment on most issues of the day than the country's leadership realizes. Consistently, editors, television program planners, and those in public office assume a lower level of taste, understanding, interest and sophistication than we have found the public to have. In this sense, the people are way ahead of their leaders."

In this connection Richard Neustadt has observed: "One should never under-estimate the public's power to ignore, to acquiesce and forget, especially when the proceedings seem incalculable or remote from private life." [5] We are not likely to be aroused to a crisis until it is upon us; the sagacious few will take note of a cloud gathering in the skies, sometimes no bigger than a man's hand, but for the large majority, it will go unnoticed. When the crisis is plainly revealed, that majority will join in the effort to meet it, but once the emergency is over they will lapse into accustomed ways without concern as to whether the victory or, for that matter, the future has been assured.

There is a growing and distressing demand for digests and tabloid tid-bits. Since articles are rarely read in full, there are excerpts and condensations in which both flavor and perspective are lost. Moreover, too many among us are addicted to the approach by emotion rather than reason. It is much easier to acquire an opinion than to grasp the implications of a fact. And the opinions increasingly are there to be had—from the newspaper and television exhorters, from the for-god's-sakers, from the columnists and commentators. It is so simple, so time-saving, so easy on the brain and the feet to get an opinion ready-made from the Soap-box Sinatras and the Seven-O'clock Svengalis. Dr. Gallup has expressed to me the hope "that someone will start what might be called the Hour-for-Hour Club of America. Members of this group would agree that for every hour spent on entertainment, an hour would be devoted to becoming better informed."

There is in addition the pervasive problem of apathy. It is described by John Gardner, the former Secretary of Health, Education and Welfare who now heads the Common Cause movement: "We know our lakes are dying, our rivers growing filthier daily, our atmosphere increasingly polluted. We are aware of racial tensions that could tear the nation apart. We understand that oppressive poverty in the midst of affluence is intolerable. We see our cities sliding toward disaster. Yet we are seized by a kind of paralysis of the will. It's like a waking nightmare." [6]

The National Commission on Causes and Prevention of Violence, of which Milton Eisenhower was chairman, cited these as internal threats to the nation: "Haphazard urbanization, racial discrimination, disfiguring of the environment, unprecedented interdependence, dislocation of human identity and motivation created by an affluent society." As the commission concluded: "The greatness and durability of most civilizations have been finally determined by how they have responded to the challenges from within. Ours will be no exception." [7]

The high rate of illiteracy does not help the situation. A survey in the fall of 1970 conducted by Harris Associates indicated that at least 13% of the adult population (those over 16) lack the reading ability necessary for day-to-day living. Harris says this figure is conservative and would be 24% if it included those who refused to be interviewed. This survey generally supports an earlier Harvard study which suggested that as many as half the adult population cannot read well enough to master a variety of ordinary reading materials.

Some Perilous Illusions

As a result of the faults in the information process and the substitution of emotion for logic, there are certain illusions that operate dangerously among us.

There is the illusion that, even if we are not, we deserve to be loved. We picture ourselves as a combination of Santa Claus and Lady Bountiful. Too many of us are inclined to look upon foreign aid not as insurance for us (which it surely is) but as charity. The fact is that a good part of the world does not love us; there is the resentment that any recipient of charity has toward the benefactor; there is envy of our position as the Number One Nation; there are fears we shall bring on World War III or drag the rest of the world into another depression.

Then there is the go-it-alone illusion. The old brand of isolationism is dead; and it is now generally accepted that we are part of the world. But there is a new kind of isolationism—the belief that, even though we are the top nation, we can play a lesser role in global affairs; the belief that so long as our defenses are strong we do not need allies and diplomacy and all that "Old World tripe." But what is overlooked is that in the modern world, politics, ideology, trade, are all parts of one huge complex.

There is the illusion that we have the "know how"—and that is enough. We surely have the "know how"; Hitler learned that and the Kremlin must know it, too. But "know how" is not enough; there must also be "know what," so that we recognize the problems that confront others and act wisely in international affairs. "Know how" may win a war for us, but only "know what" will win a peace.

Then there is the "quick and easy" illusion. We are a nation addicted to slogans and verbal nostrums; one year it is ammoniated toothpaste that will bring us salvation, the next year it is hormones or the Bessarabian Air Force Exercises. Our faith in "cures" is matched only by our false optimism; we cling to our rosy lenses. The Russians may invade Czechoslovakia but if they send the Bolshoi Ballet over here as a gesture of friendship we are likely to forget about the Czech affair. Moscow constantly plays upon this tendency toward optimism.

It should be recognized that there are basic reasons for these illusions and the public ignorance that underlies them. Foremost among them are the absorption of the average man in his immediate affairs, his suspicion of any proposal that might change his way of life, his reluctance to partake of information unless it is encased in sugar coating, the conviction that he is making up his own mind, the influence of environment and education.

Nor should the task of acquiring and digesting information about the many and pressing issues of the day be underestimated. In domestic affairs it is difficult enough; such issues as the complex problems of the national economy, the deep stresses of the racial conflict, the large implications of Supreme Court decisions—all these and many like them require much reading and more thought if they are to be fully grasped.

In foreign affairs the assignment is even more difficult—to unknot such tangled issues as East-West relations (once the "Cold War," and now the "cool confrontation"), West-West relations (the differences among the Allies), East-East relations (the dissensions in the Communist camps) and North-South relations (the relationships between the developed and the developing nations).

Moreover, highly complicated scientific and technological factors are involved in many of these issues. In the defense area, for example, there are the problems of the ABM, of nuclear testing and the like. To form sound judgments in such matters requires knowledge of the Soviet Union's intent, the extent of radiation danger, the effectiveness of detection devices, and similar intricate computations. These undoubtedly are formidable problems, even for the experts.

Experts and Inexperts

Incidentally experts should not be overestimated. Naively we have come to believe that expertise in one field qualifies a man as a sage in all fields. In foreign policy great reliance is placed on military and business leaders even though they may be as ill equipped to discuss international politics as they are unaware of the psychological factors involved in the opinion process. The fact that a man has made a name in industry or in philosophy or in education does not qualify him as a sage in foreign policy.

Outstanding examples from the past are Henry Ford, whose peace ship was really a Model T, and Albert Einstein, who was pre-eminent in mathematics but an innocent in the area of politics. Today, as an example, there is Dr. Benjamin Spock, who, having had large (and well-deserved) success in concocting formulas for babies, is now propounding prescriptions for foreign policy. I am not trying to restrict the freedom of a Ford or a Spock to say what they please; I am only criticizing the media for playing up their non-expert opinions as expert ones.

The expert undoubtedly has an important role to play in government but it is nevertheless a subordinate role. He can supply political counsel but he cannot take the place of a political leader; he may draw up a program for action but he cannot supply the inspiration and imagination that are essential to political leadership.

Yet, admitting the difficulty of analyzing information, nevertheless the average citizen must somehow be persuaded to make a greater effort to inform himself. He need not be an expert to have the feel of a proposal and come to a general conclusion. Long ago Aristotle argued that citizens did not have to be experts to exercise sound judgment in public affairs. Time has proved him right: official thought is often stimulated by imaginative suggestions from individuals or groups of citizens and public opinion is needed to rally support for charges in old and sterile policies.

As for the feeling that international affairs are remote from the life of the average person, this is a giant fallacy. Foreign policy issues involve domestic problems also. Vietnam has cast a huge shadow over social problems; the racial question enters into the bloodstream of our relations with the Afro-Asians; moves in international finance have great impact on the domestic price structure. "Foreign news" is a misnomer; it is not alien, it is immediate, it is local. An obscure event in Southeast Asia may, years later, result in the deaths of thousands of American youth, as Vietnam has demonstrated; developments in Europe's Common Market can deeply affect a factory on Fourth and Main Streets. Paris, Ohio, is ultimately linked to Paris, France. No longer is any nation an island unto itself.

And, as a corollary, the government and the media must play their parts, in making information more available and understandable for the average citizen—much less classification and much more clarification.

If we are to have an enlightened public opinion, the deep and dangerous illusions must be dispelled, the fog in the grey area of the 40% (those who are willing to learn if the task of learning is made simpler) dissipated. It is an essential assignment but not an easy one, as the chapters that follow demonstrate.

6: The Opinion Process: Complex and Confusing

Public opinion can be divided into the categories of general and specific. General opinion evolves out of environment, upbringing, education, religion etc., and remains fairly stable for the large majority of people. Specific opinion results from the impact of events. Because of its news aspect, this book is mainly concerned with specific rather than general opinion.

Two groups are involved in the opinion process: the public at large and the "Elite"; they operate at different levels and very distinct ways.

Some waves of opinion originate with the public at large; a dramatic event will produce a wide and emotional response and a demand for immediate action; then, as the voices of the "Elite" are heard and heeded, realism may begin to prevail over emotion and the popular mood may change. (At times, however, emotion runs so strong that no preachments by the "Elite" are effective, as in the case of the racial issue.)

Other waves of opinion are generated first among a few of the "Elite," then involve other "Elitists," then engage the attentive citizenry and finally reach the majority of the citizenry.

Quick Reaction — or Slow

Thus, three kinds of opinion process can be identified: (1) cases in which a startling development or event produces an almost immediate reaction; (2) cases in which the "Elite" take the lead but a considerable period elapses before the general public is persuaded; (3) cases in which opinion clings for a long time to an emotional position.

Three examples of the first category—instances of almost immediate response to a dramatic happening—are the Pentagon Papers, the Pueblo incident, and the moon landings.

Extracts from the Pentagon Papers, a study of the origins and course of the Vietnam War, were published in several leading papers despite the "classified" label. The public response came quickly; critics of the government's Vietnam policies found in the documents confirmation of their belief that the war was wicked and that President Johnson had deceived the country. The episode soon took on wider aspects as it became clear that there were involved in it various basic issues—classification, national security, press responsibility. And the debate continues. (A full account of the Pentagon Papers case will be found on pages 204-11).

The Pueblo incident is another example of the instant reaction of public opinion — or emotion. On January 23, 1968, the U.S.S. Pueblo, an electronic spy ship, was captured by the North Koreans, who charged that it had intruded into their waters. The Pentagon, however, declared that the Pueblo had been boarded when it was twenty-five miles off the coast and denounced the act as a "grave provocation." Throughout the country there were shock and anger, followed by demands that the government take swift action.

After the first outbursts of indignant patriotism there came calmer counsels and doubts about the credibility of the government. (For example, while the Pueblo was boarded twenty-five miles from the coast, it was in fact only thirteen miles from the coast when it was first approached by the North Koreans — a fact that the Pentagon had chosen not to mention.) The national temperature fell. Washington did not try to rescue the Pueblo and its crew but initiated negotiations. What had been daily headline news for about a month moved into the inside pages.

The surge of elation over the moon landings also illustrates the impact of single dramatic events. In periods of discouragement, the astronauts' exploits gave the nation lifts that it sorely needed, persuading it that man was capable of great exploits and that therefore he might be able to cope with the large problems on earth.

Examples of the second category—instances in which the opinion process takes months and even years—are the nation's attitudes toward the United Nations and, domestically, such issues as poverty and pollution.

The founding of the United Nations in 1945 took place amid a great blaze of expectation; here was an organization through which future wars could be prevented and a shield behind which, undisturbed, we could enjoy life, liberty and happiness. Soon, however, the clouds of disillusionment gathered, not so much because the United Nations had failed but because the hopes for it had been so grossly inflated. But there is slowly developing, spurred by "Elitist" argument, a feeling that possibly the U.N. can perform a unique, even an urgent, function.

The issues of pollution and poverty provide examples of this same slow evolution of opinion.

Evidence of sentiment against pollution and the demands for correction are found in the news columns every day. The immediate results have not been as extensive as might have been expected in view of the wide publicity the issue has had. But that was almost inevitable because there are short-term urban problems—crime in the streets and filth in the slums, to cite two — that call for solution before money will be provided to meet these other, seemingly more distant needs, pressing as they may be. Nevertheless the idea first advanced by the "Elite" has registered and later, if not sooner, there will be a clear call for implementation.

There is likewise the re-examination of the causes of poverty. Until recently there was the widespread assumption that if people were poor it was because they were indolent and had not availed themselves of the abundant advantages in this Great Land of Opportunity — the belief that poverty was the individual's not society's fault. But now, as a result of "Elitist" argument, the idea is gaining headway that poverty is not inevitable but avoidable — and moreover intolerable — because it is a threat to the nation's future.

The third category in the opinion process — the persistence of emotional attitudes for long periods — is best exemplified by the nation's attitude toward Communism.

For years the country had a great fear of Communism, not only of threats from abroad but of subversion within; and the government did little to allay this apprehension. But gradually the realization came that the Communist states were here to stay and that somehow we had to reach an understanding with them. When popular opinion took this softer view of the "Red Threat" the government finally acted, no longer fearing a political reaction against a compromise with Communism.

An Analysis and Some Conclusions

For the purposes of this book, two studies were made in an effort to obtain light on the processes of opinion-formation: an analysis of the opinion trends of recent years, and a survey in depth of seven contemporary case histories — Vietnam, which illustrates how emotional opinion can be; the racial problem and the campus revolts, which indicate how extremism on one side can produce extremist reaction on the other; China, which reveals how the government can misread opinion; the Los Angeles and Wallace elections, which show the impact of a well-hidden backlash; the ABM debate, which indicates the dilemmas that develop out of disagreements among the experts; and the "Sexplosion" which is an illustration of how a vociferous minority can create a misleading impression about the attitudes of the public at large.

In tracing these trends, the polls have been used as indices rather than as conclusive evidence. Despite the reservations about them, the fact remains that they offer virtually the only "scientific" way of measuring opinion. Other clues to opinion have also been taken into account, such as commentary in the mass media, public demonstrations, and elections in which issues are sharply joined.

Here, then, are the main conclusions of the studies with documentation out of the analyses of the case histories and other sources:

Public opinion is often little more than public emotion. Prejudice and tradition enter heavily into it, making it, not infrequently, unreasoning, volatile, impulsive.

Abundant evidence of this is found in the reaction to the Vietnam conflict. The horror of war was realized as never before when television brought the stark events into the nation's living rooms — films showing the burning of villages, the desolation of the peasants, the callousness such as that of the Songmy massacre which made inhumans out of human beings. There were increasing demands that we "get out," but the question of *how* was rarely discussed, indicating a reluctance to face the facts.

The strong play of emotion is also revealed in studies of the confrontation between students, critical of American society and hopeless about their future, and their elders, resentful of "ingrates" and angry at "revolutionaries"; and of the civil rights issue, in which feelings are so deeply ingrained that one is led to the conclusion that equality of the races cannot be legislated but will come only with changes in basic viewpoint and in mores.

Emotion, too, deep emotion, has marked the debate over the "sexplosion." The "new freedom" in sexual affairs has been loudly proclaimed, almost as a modern crusade. Yet the polls indicate that the nation as a whole clings to conventional views of sex and that, while the "new morality" is making inroads in minority groups, the "old morality" persists among the large majorities.

Strong feeling (or "opinion") arises in most cases out of personal rather than public concern. General principles are likely to be endorsed but when a situation strikes home, the reaction is wholly different.

The civil rights movement provides a striking illustration of this tendency. When whites are asked whether they believe generally in the equality of the races, the response is overwhelmingly in the affirmative. But when the questions are put in specific terms—when whites are asked whether they would like to see their children go to a school in which more than a majority of the children are black or when they are asked whether they would welcome Negroes as neighbors—the response is decisively in the negative.

The debate over the Anti-Ballistic Missile provides another example of the dominance of private concern over public sentiment. In the beginning little thought was given to the issue, but then the problem struck close to home. ABM systems, it was announced, would be set up near fifteen cities, one of them Chicago. In November 1968, John Erskine, a physicist, warned that the proposal would increase the possibility of a Soviet attack on the city. The reaction was immediate, it soon spread to other cities and it became so vehement that the President decided to restrict the system to two sites.

Demonstrations are not an accurate measure of public opinion; often they represent only the views of a minority. Moreover violence by one side produces an even more violent reaction by the other opposing side.

Despite the publicity the demonstrators receive, the polls indicate that those who demand *unconditional* withdrawal from Vietnam do not have majority support; that the "revolutionaries" on the campuses comprise only a minority of the student body; and that the rioting blacks are the lesser part of the Negro community.

On the other hand, violent demonstrations produce harsh counter-actions. At times the Vietnam protesters have created support for the war. As Senator Frank Church has pointed out, "When people see hippies and violence, a lot of them are alienated." The racial conflict provides the most conspicous example of backlash effect. The "Black Power" movement has stirred up among lower and lower-middle class whites so much fear and resentment that the integration process has been slowed down to a substantial degree.

Because public "opinion" is so often the expression of prejudice or fear, a demagogue can play frighteningly upon it. For such appeals to emotion television provides a powerful tool; here indeed the "medium is the message."

The classic example of course is that of Senator Joseph McCarthy. Five difficult years were needed to overcome McCarthyism; not until the people were alerted by Edward Murrow's magnificent broad-casts did they begin to question McCarthy's thesis and his veracity.

This kind of appeal to prejudice was demonstrated in the Los Angeles election of May 1969. Samuel Yorty, the incumbent, defeated Thomas Bradley, a Negro Councilman, by playing on the fears of his white, "Middle-American" constituency; he pictured Bradley as a symbol of rebellion and violence and tied him to the hard-core national issues of lawlessness, black and left-wing radicalism and disorders on the campuses. (Incidentally, this election indicates that often there are much larger undercurrents of bias than appear on the surface; a great number of voters told the poll-takers they were "undecided," even though, as it turned out, most of them were not uncertain but unwilling to reveal their prejudices.)

The same kind of tactic was used in the Alabama gubernatorial run-off primary in May, 1970, between the incumbent Albert Brewer and George Wallace. Wallace "dished out his politics the way many of his Alabamans like their whiskey and religion," as the *New York Times* put it. Repeatedly he spoke to the white fears: "Quit busing our children all over town, and give our schools back to the folks in Alabama." This blatant appeal to racism succeeded; for the first time in Alabama history, the runner-up in a primary contest became the victor in a run-off.

Public opinion, when it is clearly and forcefully asserted, has an impact on public policy. However, when there are no clear clues to opinion, the Executive and the Congress move on their own; and at times the assumptions they make about public sentiment are erroneous.

The outstanding example of this in recent years is Vietnam. When public opinion indicated clearly its desire for disengagement, the government took large notice, as evidenced by President Johnson's action in halting the bombing, his announcement that he would not run again and the decision by President Nixon to withdraw.

Government policy was indubitably influenced by the reaction to the American intervention in Cambodia during the first few days of May, 1970. The widespread protests were sharply intensified when, on May 4, the National Guard killed four students at Kent State University during a meeting protesting the invasion. So intense was the public outcry that by June 30th the administration had pulled out of Cambodia all our ground troops and our air force.

The impact of public opinion on public policy was also demonstrated by the legislative response to the campus troubles. Because of the protests against the student rebels a number of states passed laws designed to deal with the protesters; and the Congress made it a crime to travel from one state to another to incite riot.

In the absence of definite opinion, the government may follow a policy based on what it assumes is a public attitude without realizing that the viewpoint has changed. The most notable instances of this are found in studies of national sentiment toward Communism.

The viewpoint of Americans about Communism during the 1950's was molded in large part by those two militantly anti-Communist figures, Senator Joseph McCarthy and F.B.I. Chief J. Edgar Hoover. Under their tutelage much of the nation came to believe that Communism was a giant, monolithic force centered in Moscow and dedicated to the subversion of the Western democracies. These attitudes persisted long after the unmasking and death of McCarthy — so long in fact that successive administrations felt free to make strong anti-Communist policy. (There was hardly a protest against the intervention in Korea or against the government's stand against China's admission to the U.N.)

But events slowly modified the public's harsh attitude toward Communism. In the late 1950's Peking challenged Moscow for leadership of the Communist world; the two countries engaged in bitter invective and their duel finally flared into armed clashes along their borders. Moreover, countries of the Soviet bloc in Eastern Europe began to assert their independence. So the American public gradually discarded its picture of Communism as a monolithic world and discerned cracks even in its disparate parts.

Despite signs of this shift in opinion, the State Department persisted in its anti-Communist policy, presumably because of its basic conservatism and its fear that another McCarthy might arise to play havoc in its hallowed halls. And Presidents Kennedy and Johnson went along with the policy-makers in Foggy Bottom.

Some elements in Congress however, became aware of the shift in opinion. A group of Senators—notably J. William Fulbright, Jacob Javits and Alan Cranston—advocated the lifting of trade embargoes against Communist China, the extension of communication, both formal and informal, and the admission of Red China to the community of nations. Finally the Nixon administration took notice of this shift in sentiment and in 1970 made some timid moves toward establishing a relationship with Peking.

Then came a surprising break-through. In April, 1971, a team of 15 American table tennis players accepted an invitation to engage in a ping-pong tournament in China and spent seven well-publicized days there. Three American newsmen were granted visas to cover the match—another first.

On July 15th, President Nixon announced, to the nation's complete surprise, that he had accepted an invitation to visit China and would do so within a year, in an effort "to seek the normalization of relations between the two countries and also to exchange views on questions of concern to the two sides."

The nation is divided; geographically, between, between East and West; ideologically, between liberals and conservatives; racially between colored and white; chronologically, between generation and generation.

The Geographic Gap; between East and West, largely coincides with the Ideological Gap — a division between the liberal East and the conservative Middle and Far West. (The South is changing so rapidly that its ideology is hard to pinpoint.) This is revealed sharply in attitudes about such issues as the Vietnam War, the mass media, sexual freedom and other questions of "morality."

The Racial Gap shows no sign of decreasing. Integration has retro-
gressed, segregation widened. Mr. Nixon's edict against school busing
to achieve integration is a political reflection of widespread opposition
in the South to almost any form of compliance with the Supreme
Court's rulings.

The Generation Gap became sharply delineated in the differences
between students and elders and is found generally in questions of
conduct and ethics.

*   *   *

The two surveys done for this book show both pluses and minuses
in the national opinion ledger. On the one hand, they reveal striking examples of the effective mobilization of public sentiment —
the adverse reaction to President Roosevelt's court-packing plan; the
response to President Kennedy's appeal to the nation to seek out
"New Frontiers;" the rejection of Mr. Nixon's Supreme Court nominations; the sharp reaction to the Nixon decisions to move into Cambodia.

On the other hand, the studies reveal instances in which opinion
has been badly informed or uninformed or based almost wholly on
emotion — the conflict over civil rights, in which the white view of the
blacks and vice versa clearly indicate that neither side is understanding or communicating with the other; or the debate over the Anti-
Ballistic Missile about which only the experts have the facts; or
the campus revolts in which unreason has confronted unreason.

*So much for conclusions about the opinion process. Now, what
about the forces that operate on that opinion? It is necessary to
differentiate between the two kinds of influence—"inside" and "outside." This is done in the following chapter.*

7: Influences and Impacts: "Inside" and "Outside"

In the molding of public opinion, there are "inside" and "outside" influences; the "inside influences" are the attitudes and pre-dispositions acquired in childhood and shaped by early education, religious ties and the like; the "outside influences" are, prominently among others, higher education, political and social leadership and the mass media. There is continuing debate over the relative impact of the two.

The "Inside Influence" Theory

Those who contend that the interior forces have greater effect on opinion than the exterior influences hold that the early years are the most critical and that after them an individual's attitudes remain fairly stable. Childhood influences come mainly from two sources: the family and the school. According to Harwood Childs, Professor of Politics at Princeton, "It is in the family that the small child usually receives his first impressions, forms his early habits, develops early prejudices, likes and dislikes, desires, wishes and goals. Moreover, the parents and family have virtually a monopolistic control over the stimuli affecting the child, especially during the early years." [1]

The exponents of this theory still refer to a study by the Survey Research Center of Michigan which revealed in 1952 that 82% of young people who listed their preferences as Democratic had Democratic parents and 73% of the children who listed their preferences as Republican had Republican parents. Party preferences, it is asserted, are well established by the age of seven or eight. When asked why they favor the Republican party, respondents are likely to answer: "Well, I was just raised a Republican;" "My father was a Republican"; and "I'm from a strong Republican family." Similarly, "I'm a Democrat, that's what my folks are"; "Well, my father is a Democrat, and I'm one by inheritance, sort of."

To the family is also attributed a large role in determining interest and participation in politics; children who grow up in a family

47

in which political questions are discussed are likely to absorb an interest in politics. A later study by the Survey Research Center reported that respondents whose parents had a keen interest in politics felt a sense of involvement in the 1958 campaign more than twice as often as the children of parents with low political interest.[2]

Where the parents leave off, early education, according to this theory, continues the process of forming social attitudes; the elementary and secondary schools "propagate the historical lore of the people, the myths, the beliefs, and the faiths and thereby aid in the process of political indoctrination," setting patterns that persist for a long period.[3]

The adherents of this first school are inclined to downgrade the impact of the "outside influences"; these, they contend, are rejected unless they reinforce opinions already held by people. Joseph Klapper, head of the C.B.S. research staff, makes this point emphatically: "By and large, people tend to expose themselves to those mass communications which are in accordance with their existing attitudes and instincts. Consciously or unconsciously, they avoid communications of opposite hue. In the event of their being exposed, nevertheless, to unsympathetic material, they often seem not to perceive it or recast and interpret it to fit their existing views or to forget it more readily than they forget sympathetic material."[4] (But—a large but—the mass media, even the most partisan of them, in reporting the news give some space to views opposing their own. Thus, except in the case of sheer propaganda, the opposition gets a hearing even if at times it is a scant one.)

The "Outside Influence" Theory

To the "inside influence" concept there is one diametrically opposed: the view that the "outside influences" tend to predominate. It is conceded that upbringing, education and training, especially in their religious aspects, constitute a powerful force; but even if this force is dominant in the early years, later in life, as it encounters increasing pressures from all sides, it wanes. The more education a person has, according to the same Michigan survey, the more likely it is that he will break away from his parents' political party. (As evidence, there is, of course, the "generation gap.") With increased education, the individual develops "a greater sense of citizen responsibility, a greater inclination to participate in politics," and to inform himself about current concerns.[5]

This conviction is reinforced by polls designed to gauge the political impact of the new 18-to-20-year-old voter. These surveys challenge the theory that it is the "inside" rather than "outside" forces which have the greater influence on opinion. A Harris survey published in January, 1971 indicates that the younger voters will not follow the patterns set by their elders. On the basis of three separate surveys in which the attitudes of the 18-to-20-year-olds were compared with those of persons over 50, the conclusion is that the young group feels significantly more strongly than the older about cleaning up pollution, liquidating our involvement in Vietnam, speeding up racial integration, beefing up Federal poverty programs and reaching accords with Russia.

This survey also finds that the younger group are "far less worried about campus protests and college administration permissiveness, much less distraught over the drug and pornography problem, less inclined to oppose welfare or demand that recipients be made to go to work, and significantly less inclined to give high ratings to President Nixon and Vice President Agnew."

After weighing the arguments on both sides, one—or at least this one—concludes the "outside influences" are stronger. For, potent as they may be, the early forces are countered not only by education but also by two other important factors: the "peer impact"— the influence of friends whose ideas may be different from those of an individual's parents, conversations over the telephone or the backyard fence or during lunch in the factory cafeteria; and the "Elite" opinion—the influence of leaders, official and unofficial, and of the mass media. One other factor plays a part in the process: mobility, social or occupational. As individuals move upward on the economic or social ladder, they tend to become more conservative; those who move down a few rungs tend to become advocates of change.

Thus the persuaders, hidden and open, in government and out, the mass media or "Elite" can have great impact provided always that they do their jobs responsibly and effectively.

The Large Role of Education

Education is an important force in shaping viewpoints and thus in molding opinion; as an "inside influence" operating, during the formative years, in elementary and secondary schools; and as an "outside force" operating, when earlier influences have begun to slacken, in the colleges, the universities and adult programs.

American education, I strongly believe, does not on the whole prepare youth for citizenship—meaning interest, discussion and action in public affairs. There are in my view two kinds of education; "positive" and "negative." "Positive education" teaches students to think rather than merely to repeat; it imbues the pupil with a sense of curiosity and a habit of tolerance. "Negative education" rigidifies minds; it turns the student into a parroter of conventional knowledge, creating "fact factories" in which the teachers' words are merely echoed. The first might be termed "root education," the second "rote education."

If students are told only that the ghettos present a tremendous challenge while the sociological factors which give rise to the slums are not identified, no thinking takes place; if the teacher provides for students only a superficial picture of alien peoples and fails to supply the background needed for understanding, feelings of contempt and superiority will result; if teaching about the role of the U. S. in the world does not include discussion of the relationship between past policies and present difficulties, this is "negative education."

The student's viewpoint is shaped by a school's atmosphere as much as by its curriculum. The classic example is that of the British public schools (private schools in American usage), which for centuries have molded the minds of the nation's leaders and the permanent civil service. In the United States the picture is more complicated; here there have evolved two separate strains of leadership: the private school–private university sector, and the public school–public university sector. In the private segment, a traditional kind of leadership is shaped, much as in Britain, but it is in the huge public school complex that the typical American outlook is created.

In the public school-public college sector the teaching assignment encounters difficulties. Efforts to deal frankly with contemporary issues are hampered by outside forces; for example, conservative pressures after World War II prevented free discussion in the schools of the meaning of the United Nations and of international organizations in general; they imposed serious limits on the consideration of such crucial issues as the relations between the United States and the Soviet Union and between the United States and Communist China. Because of these kinds of pressure, many schools and universities have failed in their approach to the race problem; an indication of this is the fact that most of the books used as texts in the schools do not give proper recognition to the contribution of the Negro to American society. Now, having ignored the colored races far too long, there is an effort to allay guilt feelings by romantic embellishment of the facts. This, too, is dangerous.

The assignment is made more difficult because of the philosophies embraced by the new generation—philosophies which Fred Hechinger, education expert of the *New York Times,* has described thus: "If the modern youth movements have any patron saints (leaving aside the radical pro-Mao and pro-Guevara lunatic fringe), they are probably Rousseau (and the Noble Savage) and Thoreau (and the concept that the government that governs least is the best). On that score, there is actually a merging of the ideologies of the left with those of the right; the latter have always extolled the rugged individualist who refused to pay taxes; whereas the former extol doing one's own thing, which means not to pay taxes to support the Establishment.

"Perhaps as a result of the influence of Madison Avenue and television, it is a generation that adroitly manipulates slogans and substitutes them for knowledge. 'Make Love Not War,' 'Don't Trust Anybody Over Thirty,' etc.; all of them are slogans in no way rooted in reality. One of the radical student leaders last year described himself as a neo-Marxist but added that he had not read Marx."

There is virtual agreement among the experts that the mere addition of classrooms, books, teachers, and students is not the answer; that education itself must be reshaped, its methods and its goals re-examined. The student restlessness suggests that if our educational institutions are to make a significant contribution to an informed opinion, they must alter their viewpoint and their curricula so that both will be brought closer to reality. On the other hand, too much "relevance" must also be avoided. In attempting to meet the demand for the specialization which arises inevitably out of the increasing complexity of life and the requirement for particular skills, the universities have been developing too many IBM rather than Renaissance Men, too few humanists with the well-rounded approach.

The technician who has had a general education will bring to his special problems a better organized and less rigid mind than the one who has been educated only for particular skills. A "liberal" education is essential if the graduate is to live a full or even adequate life. ("Liberal" is used here in the best sense of the word, meaning a broad, open-minded and informed approach.)

The Study of Current Events

The role of the school is vital in the opinion-making process, whether it be by design or default. Too often now it is by default; it must be by design. As one whose career has been devoted to journalism, to the coverage of public affairs and analysis of the problems that arise in such coverage, I offer these suggestions for the part education could play in the opinion process:

The past should be related to the present, so that each shall be better understood and the future shall not be a vast darkness.

The student has been too prone to dismiss the past as useless "because it happened the day before yesterday"; the teacher too likely to ignore the present because it is "too ephemeral, too journalistic." Neither viewpoint is logical and both are harmful.

In the elementary and secondary schools there should be more serious attention given to current events. Little is being done toward that end at the present time; newspapers and periodicals are used in the schools but in a marginal way; there is dabbling in remote corners of the news, rather than the seeking of light in the main corridors, concentration on an item on page 29 that happens to illustrate an obscure point rather than on the first page where the great currents of events are delineated.

This kind of proposal is not welcomed by most teachers; they plead that they have neither the time nor the background to give such courses. I accept this, but there is an effective alternative method: each high school might assign one teacher to current events with the duty of reading the contemporary periodicals, keeping in close touch with news and once a week briefing the teachers in the school on contemporary happenings.

In the colleges the study of current affairs should have special attention. Of incalculable value are such programs as the Great Issues Course which was originated by Dartmouth; vital contemporary issues were explored by leading experts, political, journalistic and academic; the student then analyzed the day-by-day coverage in the various media, thereby developing his analytical skill and at the same time acquainting himself with the background of immediate issues. Similar objectives were the aims of a course inaugurated some twenty years ago at Amherst College. Known as "American Problems," this course, a classic of its kind, was required of all students; fundamental problems were set out, the basic documents relating to those problems studied and the students asked to assay these issues in terms of both past and present events.

In these ways the student can reach sound judgments about current problems—approaches to thinking that are essential to the development of civic responsibility. He will learn how to appraise developments in areas ranging from the finest of the arts to the crassest of politics.

It is discouraging that the Amherst course has been abandoned in most of its key approaches and that the Dartmouth Great Issues course has been discontinued—discouraging because these developments indicate that false ideas about "relevance" have sprouted weed-like on the campuses. The student concern on this point is largely justified because much of the college curriculum has been remote and unrelated to the present. But courses must have depth as well as breadth and perspective must be retained. As a current example, there is the rash of "black studies." Now there is no doubt that Negro history has been neglected; but the remedy is not to isolate it but to integrate it. In this manner, the whole student body, rather than a segment of it, will become acquainted with the contribution of the blacks.

Particular attention should be paid to the problem of communication.   –

I profoundly believe that one of the fundamental problems of the world is the problem of communication—domestic, community, national and international; that understanding results from good communication, misunderstanding from faulty communication. In every-day affairs there must be dialogue out of which comes a modus vivendi. In community matters, there is a like need; as a case study, there is the conflict between blacks and whites, neither side understanding the problems and prejudices of the other. In national affairs there must be communication between the leaders of the nation and the people, otherwise, "credibility gaps" will develop. In international affairs difficulties among nations arise because of like failures in understanding; a better flow of information may solve some, if not all, of the problem.

There is great need, then, to study the philosophy, the impact and the machinery of communication in the hope that better understanding among peoples and nations will be achieved. I believe that the universities should deal in fundamental ways with this problem of communication; the performance and the impact of the mass media should be appraised; the interaction between national leaders and people studied. The assignment should be undertaken with the full help and expertise of the academic departments, notably those of psychology and sociology.

I include sociology because I am thinking of what such courses might be rather than what they are now. I am dismayed about many of the social science texts used in our colleges; they are neither scientific nor socially significant; for the most part, they are couched in fancy-foggy language which, one suspects, is camouflage for concealing foggy thinking. That is why outstanding teachers in the social sciences do not use text books or treat them only as supplements to other more contemporary and pertinent materials—newspapers, news weeklies, daily news broadcasts, TV documentaries dealing with public affairs.

Of the 25 million adults involved in education, only 1,080,000 are studying current events, public affairs and citizenship.[6] If education is to play a major role in the development of an enlightened opinion—and it is essential to the opinion process—it must be made more contemporary and, again it needs to be said, more relevant.

Adult Education

Even though adult education is a factor of increasing importance in the opinion picture, it is an amorphous thing and difficult to classify or to measure. In general, it can be said that it consists of two categories: formal and informal, one usually taking place in classes, the other in public groups.

Classes for adults range from sewing instruction to advanced degrees in the liberal arts. Most of the education programs are given in educational institutions which of course consider the teaching of non-adults during their regular hours as their prime responsibilities. High schools have literacy classes for those deficient in reading skills and history lessons for those so inclined. Most large universities offer similar courses on a more advanced level although in some cases, in conjunction with the community, they have programs of a therapeutic nature.

But these formal programs in adult education have no clearly identifiable purpose and no clear direction; they are diffuse and, because rewards and recognition are limited, they rarely attract to their teaching staffs those of the greatest capability. The Ford Foundation tried a few years ago to pull these efforts together but gave up the attempt as too complicated. Adult education can play an important role in bringing about a better-equipped citizenry. But until it is more effectively organized and more professionally staffed, it will be a minor influence.

Informal adult education operates through groups which bring people together to discuss matters of public concern. The impact of these associations is also difficult to measure—as difficult almost as to calculate their number. Yet they might be grouped in three categories: the "educators"; the "activists"; the "occasionals."

The "educators" are divided into the "Elite" and "Not-so-Elite" groups. The "Elite" organizations, highly selective in membership, are oriented toward the policy-makers and have few channels to the public. The "Not-so-Elite" organizations have virtually open memberships and the audience they seek is the general public.

The "activists" are groups with causes and are much larger vocally than numerically; their goal is ideological confrontation. Prominent among these are the Students for a Democratic Society, the Black Panthers and the John Birch Society.

The "occasionals" are not addicted to crusades or to particular causes; they are the Rotarians, the Elks, and the fraternal associations basically concerned not with cosmic, but with community matters.

But larger events are introduced every so often for discussion at luncheon lectures.

These groups, even though some of them are limited in membership and others are limited in discussion of public affairs, do have a definite, even though sporadic, influence on opinion.

Such then are the "inside" influences which have a "background impact" on opinion. Much more immediate and much more potent are the "outside" influences and to them the major part of this book is devoted.

The discussion of the "outside influences" begins, naturally, with the Presidency, the most potent—or at least potentially the most potent—voice in the nation. The job and its ordeal are described in the following chapter.

Part II

THE GOVERNMENT

In these chapters the role of the government in the opinion process is described—the part played by the President, the Congress, the Washington agencies generally. Questions such as these are raised: What are the qualities of Presidential leadership? How can better communication be established between President and People? Between President and Press? Between President and Congress? Whom does government influence and who influences it?

8: The Presidency: Pressures of the Oval Office

The Number One Voice in the nation is the voice that emanates from the Oval Office in the White House. In the process of informing and persuading the voters, no individual plays a larger role than the President of the United States. His decisions are the most reverberating made in any executive office anywhere; they affect world as well as national affairs, and, not infrequently, they write momentous pages of history.

Effective communication between President and people is a difficult undertaking because, even though the President may have the qualities needed for leadership, his task is of such proportion that the observer wonders how he can give to it the time and the energy it requires. When the dimensions of the judgments are considered — such as John Kennedy's ordeal over the Bay of Pigs operation or Lyndon Johnson's and Richard Nixon's tortured decisions about Vietnam — it is hardly surprising that President after President has spoken of the "agonies" of the office. (Not that too many politicians have displayed great reluctance to undergo these tortures.)

The Presidential assignment is a four-fold one: as Chief Executive, as Principal Propagandist (the word propaganda is used in its prime and non-invidious sense), as Ceremonial Figure, as Party Leader.

The first two functions obviously are the priority ones; the other two are essential to the leadership role but to a lesser degree. The ceremonial aspects of the Presidential assignment are exceedingly time consuming; in a single year, Mr. Johnson, by his own account, entertained and consulted with eighty-five other heads of state. In addition to the receptions and what-not, there are the hours of conversation with miscellaneous foreign visitors. Domestic politics also require constant attention; the party, in selecting him as standard-bearer, pledges its allegiance to the President as the Chief. He must nurture this allegiance to obtain support of his Congressional proposals, for confirmation of his appointments and, in general, for execution of his political programs.

These two latter functions should not be minimized but, inasmuch as this book is basically concerned with the task of leadership, it concentrates on the first two — the making and implementation of programs and the effort to rally the nation behind them.

The Human Side

The pressures on the individual required to carry out the various Presidential functions are almost inhuman. Relaxation is a word missing from the White House dictionary. The degree of tension depends on whether the President is a worrier, an introvert or an extrovert. Woodrow Wilson was so much the brooder that the struggle over the League of Nations made of him a prematurely old and broken man. On the other hand, Herbert Hoover, despite all the attacks on him as the architect of the Great Depression, lived to a hearty old age; he was convinced he had been right and, being an ardent fisherman, he was endowed with patience and confidence in the ultimate catch. Franklin Roosevelt was the complete optimist; the ordeal of his struggle against physical infirmity seemed to have steeled him for any external crisis and armed him with the courage to attempt almost any experiment.

Harry Truman, after the first breathless week of his accession — when he felt, as he put it, as though the heavens had fallen in on him — acted without hesitation before a decision and without worry afterward. He had no doubts about himself; in a talk with me the day after he had ordered the atom bomb dropped on Hiroshima, he said, "It was necessary, otherwise we would have sacrificed 100,000 American lives in landing on the Japanese Islands." (Did he, after making that decision have a sleepless night? No. He had only one sleepless night in his life. Which? The night before his daughter Margaret made her debut.)

Dwight Eisenhower also made his Presidential decisions without prolonged soul-searching. He was a military man and military men recognize, from the beginnings of their careers, that the job calls for life-and-death judgments; it should be remembered that he was the commander who gave the D-Day orders, a most difficult and delicate calculation, involving thousands of lives.

John F. Kennedy seldom vacillated. When events turned out badly he was likely to give vent not to self-pity but self-blame. For days after the Bay of Pigs fiasco he remarked broodingly: "I don't see how it could have happened." On one occasion he said: "It is much easier to make the speeches than it is to make the judgments, because your advisers are often divided. If he takes the wrong course, the President must bear the responsibility; his advisers merely move on to new advice."

Lyndon Johnson as President was a monumental worrier. He often reacted sharply to the unfavorable reception of a speech or a negative poll. He was concerned especially about the political implications of any development. But despite the intensity of his feelings, he never brooded for very long.

Richard Nixon, I suspect, is much more introverted than he shows on the surface. His unease was plainly evident in his first debate with Mr. Kennedy in the 1960 elections, in his outburst after his defeat for the governorship of California, and in his angry reaction to Senate rejection of two of his Supreme Court nominees. For a while at least the attainment of his ambition and the glamor of the Presidency seemed to have brought him a degree of calm. But whether this serenity is likely to survive the multiple and monumental problems that will confront him during the remainder of his administration is difficult to prophesize.

Mr. Nixon, I confess, remains a mystery to me, to most of the people who know him, and possibly to himself. I asked a White House correspondent who has known the President intimately since the first day of his Vice-Presidency to tell me, off the top of his head, what sort of person Mr. Nixon is; he thought for a few moments and said, "I really cannot tell you." As for Mr. Nixon's own view of himself, there is a story, probably apocryphal, that tells of his waking up during the night and saying to himself, "If I were President, this is what I would do." In the morning he realized that he was the President; this came to him as something of a shock.

Somehow I feel, insignificant as the incident was, that the dressing up of the White House guards, or at least the attempt to do so, was an indication of what was going on in the Nixon mind. Could it be that, in order to assure himself that he was the President, he was trying to add as much pomp as possible to the office? To the same effect, there is the unprecedented order given to the White House guards that Mrs. Nixon be referred to as "The First Lady."

The mystery about the man was intensified by his turn-abouts during 1971.

In his campaigns and in the first period of his administration, this is the picture that emerged from Mr. Nixon's public appearances and the press reports about him: a conservative, a cautious conservative in thought as well as in act—one who stops, looks, and looks again—and listens intently before he makes a move. Political considerations, notably those involved with 1972, loom large in all his calculations. Yet—

For a year and a half Mr. Nixon talked de-escalation and played it cool in Indo-China. Then, in April 1970, he ordered an invasion of Cambodia to destroy the supply bases in enemy sanctuaries—a move as adventurous as it was startling.

For years, the whole Nixon career had been built on a platform of anti-Communism. Then on July 15, 1971, he disclosed that he proposed to go to Communist China on "a journey for peace, peace not just for our generation, but for future generations on this earth we share together."

All along Mr. Nixon had been completely conservative in economic matters—balanced budget, free economy (wage and price freeze? never!) and all the rest. Suddenly he let it be known that he was a sort of Keynesian (meaning he favored government spending, without concern about a balanced budget, to help the economy.) In August 1971 he proclaimed a "New Economic Policy," freezing prices and wages for ninety days and in effect devaluing the dollar.

All this was done even though some of it seemed politically inexpedient; at one stroke he alienated both labor and the extreme conservatives; he acted more like a Democrat than Lyndon Johnson himself. Yet in the same period he made a gesture to the Southern whites —reversing the policy of school busing to achieve integration and he made an overture to the Catholic vote by promising aid for parochial schools.

These were the acts of a man who does not hesitate to switch positions, to take chances that are vast gambles—or of a man whose popularity had been steadily declining and who sought by almost any means to reverse the trend. (According to a Harris poll in March, 1971, "with few exceptions the trend from the earlier 'honeymoon' period in 1969 on the direction of Mr. Nixon's leadership has been downward." In February, 1971, only 28% of those polled thought Mr. Nixon was doing a "good to excellent" job of inspiring confidence in the people, while 54% judged his performance only "fair to poor.")

Mr. Nixon's great interest is in foreign affairs. He has very definite ideas about foreign policy and he depends on Henry Kissinger, his foreign policy adviser, to bat things up to him, but there is no doubt that he has many ideas of his own. Theodore White reports that Nixon once made this comment on the function of the Presidency as he saw it: "I have always thought this country could run itself domestically without a President. All you need is a competent cabinet to run the country at home. You need a President for foreign policy; no Secretary of State is really important. The President makes foreign policy."[1]

Mr. Nixon has doubtless discovered, as his predecessors did, that the process of decision-making is a difficult one, requiring of a chief executive all his qualities of head and heart. Eleanor Roosevelt proposed what seems to me the ideal formula for Presidents: "I do not worry about the past, because I cannot do anything about it. I worry about the future, because *that* I may be able, even in a small way, to influence."

The Task of Leadership

Obviously, the leadership function is as complex as it is difficult. In appraising this function, the meaning of the word "leadership" should be clarified. It clearly does not mean the Fuehrer principle. In a totalitarian state there is the *diktat* and the lock-step march; fiats are substituted for elections. In a democracy there must be understanding and conviction; there cannot be blind support of a policy proclaimed from above.

The ideal leader explains, appeals, and, most of all, inspires. He does not wait to be forced onward from behind; he chooses the course which he judges to be right and he holds to it despite the political and editorial winds. Harry Truman once said to me: "A leader is one who can persuade the people to do what they don't want to do and like it."

At home the support of popular opinion raises a President's stature with the Congress; abroad it is accepted as proof that he is truly representative of the nation. If he does not have it, he commands only limited respect from other leaders. Before his meeting with Soviet Premier Kosygin, President Johnson remarked grimly: "If I had heard about him, in his own papers and from his own people, what he's read about me from mine, I'm not sure I'd get in the same room with him."

The ability to persuade is vital in virtually all areas of the Presidential operations — in the Chief Executive's relations with the people, with the press (which is presumed to speak for the people), and with the Congress. And it is, of course, a major safeguard against the credibility gaps which have been casting deep shadows over the White House.

The first test of a President's ability to persuade—his relations with the people—is discussed in the following pages.

9: President and People: The Call for Leadership

Presidential contact with the people is made through two main channels: directly, through television addresses to the nation or reports to the Congress on the state of the Union; indirectly, through press conferences or televised dialogue with selected correspondents.

"Fireside" And Other Chats

Franklin Roosevelt's initial "fireside chat" on the banking situation in 1933 marked the beginning of a new era. (Harding, Coolidge, and Hoover had used the radio sparingly.) Radio was the perfect medium for F.D.R., with his warm voice, his compelling delivery, and his unique way of emphasizing the personal pronoun to inspire confidence. On the radio he explained the programs of the New Deal to the people simply and effectively. There were only twenty-seven such "chats" in the course of his four administrations. (There might have been more except for Mr. Roosevelt's fear of over-exposure.)

Mr. Truman was the first president to use television, in October, 1947; Americans could now see their leader as he spoke; with gestures, facial expression and visual aids, he could accent his text. But there was always the danger that the image might detract from the words.

Even though Mr. Truman's televised addresses were in effect filmed radio speeches, they had a large impact. Jack Gould, reporting on Mr. Truman's announcement of U. S. involvement in the Korean War, delivered from an unadorned lectern, wrote: "For the first time in a period of national emergency, the person at home not only heard the fateful call for sacrifices to preserve his freedom, but also saw the grave expressions of the President. In millions of living rooms . . . history was personalized last night."[1]

General Eisenhower took full advantage of the new techniques. As the conveyer of the famous grin, television had substantially helped the General in his Presidential campaign; in office he consciously molded his audio-visual presentation to the fireside form. James

Hagerty, his Press Secretary, called in professional consultants: Robert Montgomery, the actor-producer, who advised the White House on lighting, camera angles, backgrounds, delivery and the like; and the advertising ageny of Batten, Barton, Durstine and Osborn, which arranged programs showing the President in discussions with members of his Cabinet.

Various devices were employed to emphasize the "Eisenhower sincerity." His speeches were written in a homespun style and delivered, with the aid of teleprompters and cue cards, directly into the eye of the camera. When the President wanted to emphasize the "spontaneity" of what he was saying, that portion of the script was printed in large type so that he could read it without his glasses. The efforts of the Eisenhower-Hagerty-Montgomery communication team were highly successful.

President Kennedy needed no Hagerty to convince him of television's potential. In 1959 he referred to the medium as a force that had changed the political scene; moreover, he was convinced that his television debates with Richard Nixon had contributed considerably to his victory. He used the technique of the television address nine times during his term of office, an average of three speeches a year, one more a year than Mr. Roosevelt's annual average on radio. Mr. Kennedy spoke from either a lectern or a desk, dividing his attention equally between his notes and his audience; and on occasion he introduced graphs and other visual material.

(Both the style and the content of Mr. Kennedy's talks were greatly admired. His inaugural address, for example, won wide applause. Once I remarked to Theodore Sorenson, a Kennedy adviser and confidante, that somehow that speech reminded me of the Gettysburg address; and, lo, Sorenson reported that they had checked the Lincoln speech, discovered that, out of 336 words, 300 contained only a single syllable and that they had adopted the Lincolnian Biblical style.)

President Kennedy's addresses did not have the informality of the Roosevelt "fireside chat," even though he introduced a rocking chair as a principal prop in a December, 1962, broadcast—an hour-long review of his first two years in the White House in which he answered questions put to him by three Washington correspondents. His was the best Presidential image of the early television era; but he was concerned about wearing out his welcome in the American home and he appeared on TV only when he felt he had really something urgent to report.

Less than a week after the assassination of John Kennedy, Lyndon Johnson addressed the people. In his message, directed to the nation's living rooms from a deep leather chair, he indicated that he intended to make full use of television to reach the voters. He did not share Mr. Kennedy's fear of over-exposure and took frequently to the air. Somehow he had convinced himself that, even though he did not have the Kennedy style or appeal, he did have great ability, possibly greater than Kennedy's, to communicate with the people. He was mistaken. He had definite problems with television; his TV image was against him because he was ill at ease and showed it; he seemed to have a kind of perpetual half-smile on his face, even in the most serious moments. In sharp contrast, in person-to-person conversations he was as persuasive as any man I have ever known. Once I listened to him talking over the telephone to Martin Luther King for a half-hour, trying to justify his position on the Vietnam War. It was a most eloquent performance and you were almost converted, even though you felt both premises and logic were wrong. But his unease with any prepared speech was clearly evident.

Mr. Nixon does not have a personality that registers warmth on the television screen, yet he has scored success with content if not with manner. A rather bland figure, with less capacity for public inspiration that his three predecessors, Mr. Nixon has nevertheless managed to make an impression through a shrewd sense of timing and a capacity to take full advantage of the new technologies of communication.

In addition to the direct TV address, the President speaks indirectly to the nation through his press conference — an important or potentially important institution. (The press conference is dealt with fully in Chapter 10.)

The Curtain of Isolation

There are, then, various and effective ways in which the President can communicate with the people. But there is another large and largely unanswered question: How can the people communicate their desires and their moods to the President?

Such communication is increasingly difficult because the Chief Executive has become more and more isolated and the gilt-edged curtains around him have become higher and higher. There are various reasons for this: the Presidential task has grown almost unbelievably in complexity; there has been a great tendency, as a result, to turn to kitchen cabinets (in which too many cooks are likely to spoil the Executive broth) rather than to the Congress or members of the cabinet. Moreover, concern for the safety of the President since the Kennedy assassination has led to rigid protective measures and these in turn have contributed to more isolation.

"The Presidency," in the opinion of Tom Wicker of the *New York Times,* "is probably more isolated today than any comparable political office has been since the days of absolute monarchy. The vast growth of its responsibilities and involvements since World War II has not only overburdened its occupant but forced him to rely more and more on staff reports by 'experts' and other second-hand sources of information. This is the heart of the problem, and it is compounded by the inevitable workings of bureaucracy, the tendency of staff men to become yes-men, the reluctance of even high-level advisers to take a chance on being overruled, the vested interests that officials and experts develop in seeing to it that actions and policies they have supported appear to be successful." [2]

George Reedy, who was Press Secretary to Lyndon Johnson, adds this description of the White House atmosphere: "The quality of life within the White House walls is unforgettable. It is governed by one overriding rule—the overwhelming drive to stand in the closest possible proximity to the President when he is in a good mood. When the Presidential storm flags are flying, the picture is quite different. Then the President walks alone. Such moments drive home the true pathos of the Presidency, a position so lonely that its occupant can only have sycophants or followers, not friends. Unfortunately, the mood of the walk is also the mood in which far too many decisions are made." [3]

Reedy speaks of the White House as "wrapping Presidents in a blanket of its own making," so that it separates a man from political reality the day he enters the mansion. He makes this suggestion: "I think we should consider turning the White House over to a king or presiding President, and then name a manager, working out of a nearby office with the doors always open, to handle our affairs. The setting of a Royal Court purged of all emotions save awe and ambition—and that is what the White House has become—is not an appropriate place for the government of a free people." [4]

The President must see people. It is, of course, true that Presidents entertain a great deal. The Nixons had 45,313 guests to the Executive Mansion during their first year there; of these about 5,000 came to dinner, some 26,000 to teas or receptions, some 5,000 for Sunday worship services, 2,500 to picnics on the South Lawn, 575 to partake of breakfast. This broke the hospitality record of 26,000 guests set by Lyndon Johnson in 1968, even though he had the reputation of being the most get-to-gether President of all time.

But these guests are not *the people* and, even if they were, ceremonial affairs held in the midst of pomp and gold-braided splendor are hardly occasions for talking and listening to the average citizen. Some of the gap between President and people is filled at White House meetings with members of the Congress, assuming that the Congress does more or less represent the people (a large but generally valid assumption). However, these gatherings are usually devoted to discussion of legislation or party matters and seldom to talk about what the man in the street thinks and feels.

The President is thus isolated both from the people and the Congress. The problem of "getting through to the President" is listed as Topic A among White House observers because this isolation almost inevitably tends to result in some misreadings of the public mood. A Harris poll taken just before the invasion of Cambodia indicated that by a margin of 59% to 39% the country favored "staying out of Laos and Cambodia even if a Communist take-over could be prevented only by military involvement." The public reaction to the invasion took Mr. Nixon entirely by surprise and only the pledge of quick withdrawal stopped the gathering storm.

Then there was the extraordinary affair of Secretary of Interior Walter Hickel, who had seen Mr. Nixon only twice in the sixteen months since his inauguration. After the Cambodian invasion Mr. Hickel made repeated efforts to see the President but could not arrange an appointment. Finally, in the belief that Mr. Nixon's inaccessibility held grave dangers, Mr. Hickel sent a letter to the President protesting that he was ignoring his own appointed Cabinet members and failing to make contact with community leaders.

"Permit me to suggest," Hickel wrote, "that you consider meeting, on an individual and conversational basis, with members of your Cabinet. Perhaps, through such conversations, we can gain greater insight into the problems confronting us, and most important, into the solutions to these problems." He added that since students form so large a body of protesters, it was vital to understand them. "We are in error if we set out consciously to alienate those who could be our friends . . . I suggest that in this vein you meet with college presidents to talk about the very situation that is erupting." [5]

While it has never been established who leaked the letter, it was clear that the President was upset over its disclosure. Nevertheless Mr. Hickel continued to speak up for those he considered alienated from the decision-making processes, especially youth; on September 25th he made a speech in which he denounced the "rhetoric of polarization." Two months later he was asked to resign on the ground that Mr. Nixon had to have a positive relationship with the members of his cabinet.

Another example of the Nixon isolation is his attitude toward influential blacks. Three Negro Congressmen—William Clay of Missouri, Augustus Hawkins of California and Louis Stokes of Ohio—sent a letter to the President on February 18, 1970, saying, "the patience of many black Americans is exhausted. Since you assumed office, you have travelled to all corners of the earth emphasizing your concern for many problems, but you have not come to black America." The Congressmen concluded by requesting a meeting with the President. Two months later they received a letter from a staff aide, saying in effect: "Don't call the President, he'll call you." On January 22, 1971, twelve members of the Black Caucus notified Mr. Nixon that they would boycott his State of the Union address because of his consistent refusal to hear the pleas and concerns of black Americans. Finally, on March 25th, Mr. Nixon met with the 13 members of the Black Caucus—a meeting that took place a year after they had first asked for it.

"The evidence accumulates," Robert Semple, Jr., of the *New York Times* reports, "that the flow of information may not be so perfect as the White House pretends and that information, when it is received, is sometimes pigeon-holed or prematurely dismissed. Some of the young White House staff never expected immediate access to the President, but hoped their views would be more quickly acted upon. And department agency heads have increasingly complained that the lines to the White House are snarled. The Treasury and Budget Bureau officials have been particularly caustic, charging that some decisions are made without full review by the agencies responsible for finding the money." [6]

Presidents as Pollsters

All this indicates that Mr. Nixon should establish new methods to learn what the country is thinking. Other Presidents have set up listening posts, each of his own invention, but none of them really did the trick. Mr. Eisenhower depended largely on his intuition to guide him in public relations, even though he had has own method of making surveys of public opinion. Friends would report to him on what taxi drivers were saying. Once he told me with glee of an encounter one of his friends had had with a driver who did not like Ike because "some Navy chap named Rich — or Rick—something had invented an atomic submarine and Eisenhower had stolen the idea from him." (The Rick—or Rich—referred to was in fact Admiral Hyman Rickover, the nuclear submarine pioneer).

Mr. Truman, like President Eisenhower, put much reliance on intuition in dealing with the people. But, unlike Mr. Eisenhower, he was a political animal, with an instinct developed over many years of political jousting and he had a sixth sense about the public's manner of thinking. He scorned polls and other mechanical, unhuman devices.

President Kennedy had a different approach, which might have been expected in view of the variances between him and his two predecessors in temperament and training. He told me he did not pay great attention to public opinion, although he was a poll-watcher; that he felt he was doing the right thing and was proceeding on that assumption. The pressure of the lobbies bothered him and he tried to counter it with press conferences and direct talks to the nation.

In his first Presidential years, Mr. Johnson had a deep faith in polls; at the drop of a reportorial hint he would produce for the visitor a wondrous collection of statistics purporting to show where he stood in popularity in all fifty states (and abroad too) and on almost all important issues. There was a constant stream of reports, some commissioned, some voluntary, from the chieftains of the Polling Tribe—Gallup, Harris, Roper and Quayle. But when the polls started to go against him, Mr. Johnson's faith in them began to falter.

Mr. Nixon also ponders the polls, but not with the erstwhile Johnsonian intensity; he supplements them with other gauges, particularly personal estimates. The findings of the standard surveys, including those done by Gallup and Harris, are served up to him regularly; in addition he has his private polls, done presumably by the appraisers who service the Republican National Committee. All these surveys are designed to test public sentiment on issues as well as candidates.

Mr. Nixon seems to rate highly the personal contacts he makes in his frequent travels around the country, evidently believing that he can catch the mood of the nation by (as Mr. Johnson used to put it) "pressing the flesh" of the people at airports and other gatherings. Correspondents who travel with him are skeptical about this "osmosis opinion." They point out that most airport crowds are recruited by advance men or the local Republican organizations and hardly constitute what the pollsters would qualify as a "scientific sample."

The President also has set up other listening posts. Herbert Klein, his Director of Communications, mans one of most important stations of this information network; he has broad contacts with editors and publishers throughout the country and, because of the nature of his job, he keeps in close touch with small town television and radio broadcasters.

The telegrams and mail to the White House are carefully monitored and analyzed by Klein and others. They are taken quite seriously; for example, when Mr. Nixon appealed, in November, 1969, for the support of the "silent majority," several television commentators did some unfavorable instant analysis. There followed a slew of telegrams to the White House, denouncing the newscasters. This led, it is reported, to the decision to launch a counter-attack on the media in the person of Vice President Agnew.

Mr. Nixon, like Mr. Johnson, periodically sends some of his trusted aides to sound out opinion on campuses, at business meetings, at Wall Street gatherings and the like. This was a regular assignment for

Daniel Moynihan when he served as domestic policy consultant. Henry Kissinger, Mr. Nixon's foreign policy consultant, has taken on many of these chores.

Every morning the President receives a 12-to-20-page packet containing a summary of the news prepared by Patrick J. Buchanan, who has a staff of three or four people who watch the television newscasts, read newspapers, news magazines and other current materials. (Columnists, it is reported, get special attention.)

In general it can be said that no President has been too successful in gauging the mood of the country; in most instances decisions in the final analysis are made on the basis of hunches, informed or otherwise. But on the other hand, no one, including Messrs. Gallup and Harris, would contend that it is easy to measure the mood of a nation as diversified and as often distracted as the United States.

This, then, is the nature of the first of the three vital relationships of the President — the contact with the people. The second is the relationship to the press, which is the theme of the next chapter.

10: President and Press: A Delicate Relationship

A President's approach to the news and his relations with the press often provide clues to his character and his methods.

Franklin D. Roosevelt had a good relationship with the press. He met the members of the Fourth Estate on their own terms; he called them by their first names, he respected their weekends, he entertained them at Sunday night scrambled-egg dinners. Few Presidents were more adept at flattery—and few newspapermen are as prone to flattery, as full of their own importance and as jealous of their prerogatives as the White House correspondents.

President Truman did not have this same intimate relationship with the press; he was more remote, less personal than Mr. Roosevelt. Moreover, after the war, the President had a new press corps to deal with—larger, more competitive, lacking the unity of a group in the midst of crisis and including more representatives of foreign newspapers.

General Eisenhower had a much easier relationship with the media. He was as amiable as he was frank in his dealings with correspondents, even though at times there were complaints that his answers to reporters' questions were needlessly vague.

Mr. Kennedy was much more reserved, at least in public. Privately he occasionally used the phone to criticize a reporter or an editor for a story he did not like—or to express appreciation of a story he liked. His critics felt that he frequently tried to manage the news and/or newsmen. He granted interviews to selected reporters and was on intimate terms with certain correspondents; he would swim in the White House pool with one, dine at the home of another.

As a Senator, Mr. Johnson had warm, highly personal relations with the Washington correspondents. But as his Presidential problems piled up and the credibility gap widened, this relationship changed almost completely. Mr. Johnson felt that the press, and especially the columnists, had become unfair to him; he was very thin-skinned about it and the end result was the deep muddle in which he found himself. Moreover, Mr. Johnson endangered his press relations by being overly secretive about his plans.

Mr. Nixon, unlike most of his predecessors, came to the White House with a poor press image. He had handled his press relations badly in the 1960 Presidential campaign and disastrously in his unsuccessful 1962 California gubernatorial race, when he accused newsmen of "kicking him around." The press does not forget—and he knew it. During his 1968 campaign he offered no apologies but devoted his efforts to developing a picture of a "new Nixon," well informed, efficient, successful. All through the campaign he worked hard at proving himself to a critical press.

As President, Mr. Nixon still keeps the press at arm's length. He seldom sees individual correspondents on or off the record. He seems to be trying to by-pass the Washington correspondents and to appeal directly to the people, through television addresses or news conferences, and to the leaders of opinion. In addition, he has been making approaches to the "Elite" of the mass media—the publishers and the editors—through top level briefings and through mailings to editorial writers and by-line commentators. Mr. Nixon evidently feels he has a better chance of getting across by direct means than by having his views filtered through the Washington reporters. "The President," says one of his aides "feels that the White House press corps has not been giving a faithful representation of his Administration." [1]

Herbert Klein, the President's communications commissar, who devised the strategy, says it is "no reflection on the Washington press corps, which has to follow things minute by minute. We're looking at the long range and trying to provide a full supply of facts to those who are editing or writing editorials. The more resources they have to decide on an issue the better. It's difficult for people out there (away from the East) to get all of the background on all of the issues. We've made a major effort to give them a factual presentation." [2]

Mr. Nixon is far from non-partisan in his dealings with the press. His regional briefings have generally been held in cities distant from the "polluted" Eastern seaboard. When he came to New York to brief the *Daily News,* one of his few Eastern supporters, he made no effort to establish contact with the *New York Times* or the *New York Post*. At times reporters from the *New York Times* and the *Washington Post*—papers which have expressed opposition to some of his policies—have not been invited to press conferences.

The Press Conference

More than any other method of communication, the press conference reveals the manner and the mind of a President. Each Chief Executive adapts the format to his own personality; from Wilson to Kennedy the dialogues between President and press have been almost completely transformed. (Whether these changes have been for the national good is another question. As the conferences have grown in size and as the techniques of handling them have become more complex, the illumination has lessened.)

Woodrow Wilson initiated the press conference as a means of dealing collectively with many requests for interviews. He met newsmen on a regular basis (either twice a week on Mondays and Thursdays or once a week on Tuesdays), fielded their questions and often provided them with "off the record" information. Mr. Harding, an old newspaper man, continued the twice-weekly format but stipulated that questions be submitted in advance. Mr. Coolidge was not at all the "Silent Cal" of legend during his semi-weekly news conferences; he spoke at length at these meetings, expressing freely, usually off the record, his ideas on impending legislation.

In his early days in office Mr. Hoover liberalized the press conference, allowing more direct quotations and less rigid control of background information; but as his troubles mounted his availability decreased. Franklin Roosevelt opened up the press conference; although he insisted that direct quotations had to be authorized, he allowed much more freedom in the use of background statements. Also, to ensure exposure for topics considered urgent or viewpoints the President wanted to express, Steve Early, the Press Secretary, resorted to planted questions.

Although President Roosevelt seemed to enjoy the convenience and the intimacy of the Oval Room for news conferences, the growth of the press corps made a change of place imperative and in 1950 the meetings were moved to the Indian Treaty Room in the Executive

Office Building across the street from the White House, where there were seats for 250 reporters who would rise and identify themselves before asking questions. The poor acoustics of the Indian Treaty Room led to the introduction of microphones and then came another innovation—electronic recording of the sessions.

At Mr. Truman's first news conference, five days into his Presidency, he announced that, due to the burdens of the office, he would reduce the number of meetings from two to one a week. Unlike President Roosevelt, who had seen the conference as an educational tool, Mr. Truman rarely provided background information, dismissed many questions with one-line answers and discouraged follow-up queries with a succinct "no comment." He initiated pre-conference briefings by White House aides and relied heavily on the prepared introductory statement.

President Eisenhower greatly extended the electronic form of the press conference, opening it to radio and television coverage. The sessions were held less than twice a month and modified to suit his style. His opening statement usually consumed half the time and his answers to questions were lengthy, in sharp contrast to Mr. Truman's replies. Mr. Eisenhower—or, more accurately, Eisenhower plus James Hagerty, the most active of recent press secretaries—made other significant changes: the press was permitted to hire a professional stenotyping firm whose transcripts, available within a few hours of the conference, were recognized as authoritative; moreover, the exact Presidential words were brought directly to the people through tape recordings.

Thus the stage was set for the most important step: President Kennedy's institution of the live-telecast press conference on January 25, 1961. The first such conference was transmitted by four TV cameras, plus the usual microphones, from the State Department auditorium; 418 reporters attended the session and the television and radio audience was estimated at 24 million. Both the President and Pierre Salinger, his Press Secretary, considered this direct method of communication an important forward step in the furtherance of Presidential aims. Mr. Kennedy was convinced that "he must go directly to the people to sell the programs of the New Frontier."

But there were difficulties with the live telecast. With the intro-

duction of the TV camera, the complexion of the conference changed
perceptibly. The correspondents became self-conscious performers and
in its new setting, larger and more amphitheatrical than the Indian
Treaty Room, the half-hour session turned into a kind of free-for-
all; correspondents competed to capture the eye of the President.

Moreover, the planted question was increasingly used—a technique
more easily employed because Mr. Kennedy dropped Mr. Roosevelt's
reporter identification rule and those who asked questions remained
anonymous to the public.

Other changes resulted from Mr. Kennedy's decision to broadcast
the conference live. Since he was risking his prestige he had to be
better prepared than his predecessors. His pre-conference briefing became a most elaborate institution, presided over by Salinger. The
process began with the gathering of information from departments
several days before the broadcast, continued through an advisers'
breakfast or lunch on the day of the telecast and ended with a report
of the latest developments presented to the President by the Secretary of State just before Mr. Kennedy walked to the podium.

Like Mr. Truman, Mr. Johnson elected to disregard the news conference procedures set by his predecessors; he avoided the live broadcasts in the State Department auditorium and instead chose to brief
the press as the spirit moved him — perhaps on a walking tour of the
White House grounds, in the midst of a visit to the New York
World's Fair or at his Texas ranch with a bale of hay for a lectern.
When he decided to hold more formal press encounters, he used
different locales—the White House projection room, the International
Conference Room at the Department of State, the East Room of
the White House.

Salinger, who was retained by Mr. Johnson as Press Secretary, believed that a President should experiment until he found the setting
in which he felt "most comfortable." But Mr. Johnson was never
totally comfortable with live coverage of his press conferences; his
style was much better adapted to informal meetings with a few reporters—the kind of relationship he had had with the press while he
was Majority Leader of the Senate. So Mr. Johnson used the informal, often impromptu, press conference more often than the formal
sessions.

Mr. Nixon prepares thoroughly for his press conferences. Before one of these sessions he is likely to clear his schedule, cloister himself in the Executive Office Building and devote his day almost exclusively to the preparation of answers to possible questions. He has displayed great agility as a parrier, but this kind of *legal*demain is more likely to evoke admiration than affection. Moreover he has become so sure of his skill as an extemporizer that he seldom relies upon prepared texts. At times the results have been unfortunate, as in the case of his remark that Charles Manson was a "murderer," said straight-out, without an "alleged" or any other qualification.

Despite careful rehearsals and Mr. Nixon's ability to make his points in an orderly, lawyer-like fashion, there is a general feeling among the correspondents that the President's answers are often inadequate and the real issues are dodged. But the President does not seem concerned about this; his target is the vast unseen audience.

The press conference puts tremendous emphasis on the adroitness of the President; like Mother Goose's Jack he must be nimble and he must be quick. Otherwise, he will find to his dismay that what makes the headlines is a Presidential slip.

Faults Of The System

In its present form the press conference has serious defects. Many White House correspondents seem less interested in putting the President's views on the record than in barging into the record themselves, even if their questions, prepared in advance, have no relevance to what has gone before. These meetings should be made less hit-and-miss, more logical. The President, in an opening statement, might set the agenda, to indicate how his mind is running on current issues. The reporters, for their part, should not derail the train of dialogue on an important issue with trivialities or efforts to use the conference for discussion of local problems.

Possibly questions could be submitted in advance so that the President would not be talking off the top of his head. Half the conference might well be devoted to the President's replies to these advance questions, the other half to the present free-for-all. Thus both the demand for "access" to the President by the press and the needs of logic would be satisfied. Incidentally, cabinet officers also should hold press conferences regularly and in general be more accessible to newsmen.

*   *   *

In surveying the various Presidential attitudes towards the press, this conclusion emerges: unless there is a good relationship between the two, both parties, and especially the country, will suffer. By "good" is meant not a milk-and-honey affair, but something workable, always recognizing that the attitudes of President and press are quite different; that the administration will always show optimism and the press skepticism.

The relationship between President and press is part of the larger issue of the relationship between government in general and the press. This phase of the opinion process is dealt with in the ensuing chapter.

11: The Larger Contest: Government and the Press

The relationship of the Presidency and the press is only one aspect, although a most important one, of the larger issue of the relationship in general between the government and the press. That relationship, which has large bearing on the flow of the news and therefore on the information process, has always been a delicate one, and it becomes more complicated almost daily.

There is inherent conflict between the two. On the one hand, the government tries to put the best face possible on developments and this often results in the fuzzing of issues or in the unjustified withholding of information. On the other hand, the press quite properly considers it its duty to keep close watch on government, to penetrate the curtains of secrecy, to resist the efforts, official and unofficial, to mold the news.

Secrecy comprises methods and devices used by government designed to suppress news through concealment or prohibition. *Pressures* are attempts by the executive departments and the Congress to influence the direction of the news through formal procedures, such as subpoenas or contempt citations, or informal behind-the-scenes efforts at intimidation or persuasion.

Direct government efforts to withhold or suppress the news take the form of classification (call it concealment) by either the executive departments and agencies or the Congress; or censorship, the suppression of news in time of war. Indirectly, news can be withheld from the public when the President invokes executive privilege to deny information to the Congress. (Executive privilege is discussed in Chapter 13.)

These practices have come under increasing scrutiny and criticism. In 1966 the Congress took note of charges that the secrecy disease was assuming epidemic proportions and enacted the Freedom of Information Law — a measure which stipulates that federal agencies, when requested, shall give out information in the "public domain". Theoretically, any citizen is supposed to have access to a great deal of information, *but—*

• The act places restrictions on large areas of classification and executive privilege.

• The act specifically exempts "foreign policy data" which the government feels should be kept secret, "inter-governmental communications" and similar kinds of information.

• The exemption clauses are often interpreted so broadly that almost any data can be kept from the news media and thus the public. The Foreign Operations and Government Information Subcommittee of the House reports that executive agencies tend to suppress even routine information because their personnel "want to protect their jobs."

An analysis of the act leads to the conclusion that its title is a misnomer; it should be called the "Restriction of Information Act."

In the light of this background, the various means used to achieve secrecy can be examined.

Classified Information

There are two kinds of concealed information: the stamped and the unstamped. The first is designated "secret," "top secret" or "topmost secret," filed away in restricted compartments and denied for use in any way by the press or the public. The second is fully as secret but here the suppression takes place without any formal labelling.

A correspondent reports: "You may not believe it, but occasional newspaper stories in the form of clippings are stamped 'Top Secret' in State, Defense, etc., files. To read your own printed story would thus be a violation of security because some idiot placed the 'Top Secret' stamp on it. Over-classification is a Washington disease. The insinct is to classify, 'sanitize' and conceal whenever possible."

An outstanding case of concealment is that of the record of the Tonkin Gulf hearings held by the Senate Foreign Relations Committee in August 1964. Secretary of State Rusk, Secretary of Defense McNamara, and the Joint Chiefs of Staff testified before the committee. After two years elapsed, Senator Fulbright, who had become suspicious about the administration version of the Tonkin episode decided, with the support of the committee, that the record of the hearings should be made public. After "sanitizing" by the executive branch, the document was released, but the deletions made for "security reasons" were so heavy that the hearings did not give the true picture. Had the record been put out in full, the press and the public would have been alerted to the concealment and could have been on the lookout for future half truths.

As for unstamped classified material, sometimes the government withholds information from the public on grounds of security or of diplomatic expediency. This was confirmed by George Christian, White House Press Secretary during the Johnson administration, when he appeared on NBC's "Meet the Press" soon after his return to private life. "There were instances," he said, "where the full story was not told immediately, such as during sensitive negotiations." He reported, for example, that discussions with North Vietnam looking toward ending the United States bombing of that country and setting up peace talks in Paris were kept secret for about two weeks. Even though such action might be justified because of the delicate diplomacy involved, it nevertheless represents a form of government suppression of news.

The maneuvers of the Central Intelligence Agency have been the most secret of secret operations and classification has prevailed there to the nth degree, raising suspicions that some of the actions have been highly questionable. In June, 1970, John A. Hannah, Director of the Agency for International Development, acknowledged that the aid program in Laos was being used as a cover for operations of the CIA—operations so large, it was revealed in August, 1971, that the CIA in Laos had an army of its own of over 30,000. Hannah said that he disapproved of the practice but contended that Laos was the only country in which it was taking place and that it stemmed from a 1962 decision to the effect that such activity was in the "national interest." This disclosure was most unusual; rarely does an official of the executive branch acknowledge publicly that his organization is being used for under-cover work abroad.

Then there was the revelation that under a secret agreement entered into in 1967, the United States has been paying Thailand $50 million a year, plus arms assistance, for sending a combat division to South Vietnam. At hearings held by the Senate Foreign Relations Subcommittee on Security Arrangements, State and Defense Department officials admitted the truth of recurring reports about such an arrangement. The Thai government had denied these reports and the State Department had clamped down on any information bearing on the transaction.[1]

As for exemptions under the Freedom of Information Act, in addition to those involving foreign policy and inter-governmental communications, there are these categories: information and financial data supplied by contractors to the government; material compiled for investigatory purposes; personnel files and medical data concerning government employees; and bank reports, tax returns and patent applications. These exemption clauses have been construed at times so broadly that they have been used to cloak such items as the fat content in hot dogs, breakdowns in transportation safety and studies of water pollution by federal installations.

Some critics see a sinister pattern in these practices, contending that such secrecy seems aimed, as Ralph Nader has charged, at "protecting incompetence and cloaking surrender by regulatory agencies to special interests," especially powerful corporations.[2] In reply, officials say they are dependent on private interests for essential information and advice. "If I give you this stuff," a representative of a government agency explained when a correspondent asked him for certain data, "then the companies we get it from would stop giving it to us — and we need it." Other officials insist that the disclosure of some raw data could be misinterpreted by the public, with consequent injustice to the companies.

This kind of suppression was encountered by the *New York Times* when it attempted to get information from the government's Renegotiation Board, which oversees cost overruns by government contractors. The *Times* asked for a list of contractors guilty of such practices and an accounting of settlements between those contractors and the government. For a year, the Board refused to supply the data; then the *Times* went to Herbert Klein, Mr. Nixon's coordinator of information, who said the material could not be disclosed because of the financial data exemption of the Freedom of Information Act. And so it remained classified.

Anyone to whom information is denied can appeal for administrative review within an agency, but the review process can take weeks, months, even years. For the press, to which delay often amounts to denial in the case of a timely news story, review procedures are of little benefit. Under the Freedom of Information Act, an agency can be taken to court and required to show why the information should not be released, but this entails even more delay and considerable expense.

The mass media have been slow to make use of the Freedom of Information Act, mainly because of the cumbersome procedures and the delays. Sam Archibald, former staff director of the House Information Subcommittee, argues that the law will not really begin to work until newspapers sue the government for withholding information. "If newspapers wanted to mount a publicity campaign on certain government agencies' non-disclosure policies—if they would put some of their printer's ink where their mouth is," the law would work, he insists.[3]

There are many examples of the suppression of trivial and/or embarrassing information. The Forest Service refused to allow access to records showing that it had bought a piece of land in Arizona for $133,000 which it itself had assessed at $1,200; data on testing of various brands of hearing aids were withheld by the Veterans Administration, the reason being that the manufacturers of the devices would be annoyed; during the Kennedy administration, a government study of birth control was kept from the public and released only after the press got wind of it (it turned out to be a harmless list of organizations concerned with the issue); for a long time the Defense Department refused to release the names, addresses and the occupations of draft board members to concerned citizens.

Executive departments are not alone in withholding "secrets" for no apparently good reason. Many Congressional committees hold executive (that is, private) sessions on subjects that do not warrant "secrecy ranking." For instance, the Senate Committee on Interior and Insular Affairs held an executive session in which the claims of Alaskan natives were discussed. In August, 1971, there was an executive session of a Congressional investigation concerning Latin America. Nothing of importance was discussed, but nonetheless the secrecy lid was applied.

In the course of a conspiracy trial that opened in New York in February, 1970, there were persistent efforts to hamper the newsgatherers. The case involved thirteen members of the Black Panther party who had been indicted ten months before on charges of plotting to kill policemen and to dynamite department stores and other buildings. Nearly all of the defendants were indigent; bail for most of them had been set at $100,000 each, which meant that they had no possibility of release while awaiting trial. For eight months before the trial the defendants were held in prison and reporters were denied access to them. As a result, accounts of the case reaching the public came from the police, the prosecutors or the defendants' lawyers; no first-hand reporting was possible. (Eventually the Panthers were acquitted—a refutation of the charge that a black man could not get a fair trial in this country.)

The Shield of Censorship

Censorship is another of the methods used by government to suppress news; it usually relates to the inhibition on the publication of military news and the press has accepted it as a matter of course, even though, as in the case of the Vietnam War, correspondents often have serious reservations about it. The official reports from both Saigon and Washington have tended to be very much on the optimistic side during both the Johnson and Nixon administrations; but the correspondents, when they return from the front and are free to tell the whole story, have indicated that things are going far from well.

It became clear early in 1970 that a full-fledged military effort was taking place in Laos; the North Vietnamese and the Laotian Communists had been carrying on an important operation which the American command had been attempting to counter with airplanes and "advisers." Yet the shield of censorship was thrown over the campaign and it was played down in the official reports as an undertaking in which we were only tangentially engaged. The result, when the truth became known, was the development of a large credibility gap about the military's reports.

Censorship also can in effect be achieved by setting the conditions and circumstances of reporting the news. Because transportation has been denied, correspondents have often been unable to report personally on developments in the bush and outlying regions. For their daily stories, consequently, they have had to rely on briefings from the Army's press officers. This means that the reporters receive their information — on the progress of the fighting, or the status of Vietnamization, or the rate of Communist infiltration—from military

men who, not surprisingly, do their best to achieve favorable re-
portage.

The press officers are greatly interested also in the images created
at home by the correspondence from the war zone; they are particularly concerned about the 140 unit newspapers and 18 magazines published for servicemen, which the troops send to their families
or from which they quote in their letters.

The effort to gloss over the ugly aspects of the war is well illustrated
by a directive to press officers issued in late 1969 by the U. S. Command in Vietnam. Entitled "Let's Say It Right," it altered or
banned twenty-two terms which had been used frequently in briefings.
Instead of "search and destroy," officers were to say "search and
clear;" a Vietcong tax collector was to be called a "V.C. extortionist;"
U. S. withdrawals were to be described as "U. S. redeployment." Another directive suggested that service papers stop emphasizing "hard
combat news" and instead print "reports of progress of our efforts in
the fields of Vietnamization, pacification and civil action."

*   *   *

These various instances of suppression of important facts, of
attempts to color the news, of deliberate misinformation have added
considerable width to the credibility gap. Senator Stuart Symington of Missouri feels that urgent need of "a proper measure of accurate information" to enable the people "to determine whether their
government is wise and right." He reports "continuing failure to reveal, explain or justify the true dimensions of our activities abroad;
dimensions which are far better known by our adversaries than by
the American people—and in some cases, by the American Congress."
As a result "Executive secrecy surrounding the conduct of foreign
policy and its associated military operations is, I am convinced,
endangering not only the welfare and the prosperity of the United
States but also, and most significantly, the national security."

The Senator gave these examples: waging a war in Laos for at
least six years but denying in public and in Congressional hearings its
existence; insisting that the Philippine contingent in Vietnam was
"volunteer" when in fact it was mercenary; maintaining secret nuclear
stockpiles in unnamed countries. The consequences of this secrecy,
he says, is that "key foreign policy activities have not been properly
debated in Congress, for we simply have not known enough to play

our traditional and constitutional role in the formulation of foreign policy and the direction of the country." [4]

There is no doubt that secrecy through classification and censorship require complete overhauling—a need sharply indicated by such examples as those encountered in the Vietnam war and in the case of the Pentagon Papers.

Governmental Arm Twisting

Government pressures on the press are exerted in three ways: through formal legal procedures, such as subpoenas or citations for contempt; efforts, through threats or favors or persuasion, to manage the news in the government's direction; direct assault on the integrity and believability of the press, such as the attacks by Mr. Agnew and other members of government.

Pressure By Subpoena

Several outstanding cases in the first category merit detailed examination:

In April, 1970, a resounding controversy arose out of an effort by the government to subpoena newspaper and television reporters and demand their notes, tape recordings, news film and unedited files as evidence to support a government case against the Black Panthers and the Weatherman faction of the Students for a Democratic Society.

These moves brought vehement protest from the media on the ground that reporters have traditionally had the right to withhold the names of confidential informants and that denial of this right would impede the free flow of information by drying up news sources. Subsequently, Attorney General Mitchell put out an apology, saying that there had been an apparent misunderstanding between the Justice Department and the press: "The department has had in the past, and continues to have today, a policy of negotiating with the press prior to the issuance of any subpoenas." As for the scope of the subpoenas: "The point of these negotiations is an attempt to balance the rights of the press with the rights of the grand jury making an

investigation." Mr. Mitchell said that in some instances after negotiation the government had dropped its requests.[5]

Despite Mr. Mitchell's back-tracking in the Panther and Weatherman cases, the issues raised in such controversies are far from
simple. Involved are these kinds of questions: What is the duty of
the reporter if he is told confidentially that a crime is about to be
committed? If he witnesses a criminal act? If he receives private information that contradicts public testimony? What is his obligation
to his informant, to his craft, to the public?

Reporters assert the right to withhold the names of confidential informants; 12 states have given them statutory right to do so under
specified conditions. The picture is unclear; attorneys have the
privilege in common law of asserting the sacredness of their dealings
with clients; but journalists (like physicians, priests, psychiatrists and
teachers) operate in a kind of gray area. The law in this regard is so
vague that neither side has ever wished to test it in court, for fear of
losing.

Abraham S. Goldstein, Dean of the Yale University Law School,
argues that the issue has not been resolved:

"The outrage with which the news media greeted recent efforts
by federal prosecutors to subpoena reporters' notes and TV tapes
and the hasty retreat beaten by Attorney General Mitchell have
obscured from view just how unsatisfactory the ultimate resolution
was. The public was left with the impression that Mitchell had
violated the right of newsmen to keep their notes and tapes confidential and that indignation had brought him to heel. Yet, in the
Federal system and in three-fourths of the states, reporters have no
more right than any other citizen to withhold information demanded
by the subpoena of a court, grand jury or legislative committee.

"The paranoid tendencies latent in a mass society are running
unusually strong these days and make all the more essential a clear
standard which strikes the proper balance between the demands of
confidentiality and those in the public interest. Newsmen occupy
the uneasy position of espousing the right of access to the government's files while denying government access to theirs. In so doing,
they are putting the need to protect their sources and their news
gathering procedures above the state's right to a full investigation
or a fair trial. For these situations, a judge should be authorized,

each time the privilege is asserted, to decide whether or not the investigative or adjudicative interest is great enough to override the public interest in confidentiality and freedom of the press." [6]

The problem is a delicate and difficult one and legislation is needed to clarify procedures when there is seeming conflict between the First and Sixth Amendments. In cases in which the reporter's information would result in apprehension and conviction of criminals, my view is that the media should cooperate with the government. There are times when the right to publish or to withhold confidential information clashes with the public interest; and in such cases, I feel, the role of reporter must yield to the role of citizen.

Unselling "The Selling of the Pentagon"

Now and then Congress also tries to uncover news sources. A case celebre of that nature involved the CBS documentary entitled "The Selling of the Pentagon."

The program, first broadcast on February 23, 1971, reported that the Pentagon had a propaganda machine which cost the nation's taxpayers at least $50 million a year, possibly even $200 million. Films were shown of Pentagon colonels on lecture circuits defending the Vietnam war policies despite a Defense Department prohibition against such speeches, industrialists being lavishly entertained and permitted to fire real weapons, pilots rehearsing fabricated stories for relaying to correspondents. The documentary also included portions of Defense Department films designed to alert Americans to the dangers of Communism, one such film portraying the Communist takeover of an American town.

The program produced a tremendous reaction. CBS received many requests for repeat showings, which it agreed to readily; as Jack Gould wrote in the *New York Times* of March 7, " 'The Selling of the Pentagon' was an hour of hard-hitting reporting that was impeccable in its integrity, absorbing in its revelations, and a priceless guide for electronic journalism." And the television industry awarded the documentary an Emmy for an outstanding contribution to news documentaries.

In Congress a contrary reaction was just as sharp. Edward Hebert, Chairman of the House Armed Services Committee, denounced the film as one of "the most unAmerican things I have ever seen on the tube" and announced he would review the CBS share of the annual $10 million spent on TV spot ads for military recruitment. Agnew assailed the film as "a propaganda attempt to discredit the defense establishment of the United States," and the Defense Department tried strenuously, but unsuccessfully, to prevent rebroadcast of the documentary.

The specific charges, however, were few: Congressman Hebert insisted that what seemed to be a six sentence passage from a speech by Colonel John MacNeill of the Pentagon was in fact a splicing together, in improper sequence, of six separate sentences; and that CBS deliberately attributed remarks of Premier Souvanna Phouma of Laos to Colonel MacNeill. CBS denied the latter charge, but admitted the former, asserting that this was normal technique in editing film (although CBS President Frank Stanton later laid down new guidelines which provide that notice should be given when such editing has taken place.)

On the basis of these alleged irregularities, the House Commerce Committee served on CBS and Stanton subpoenas requiring that all materials related to the production of "The Selling of the Pentagon" be submitted to the committee for examination. CBS refused the request, and set the stage for a confrontation between the television industry and the committee over how independent of broadcasting, despite licensing, television should be. Stanton maintained that the First Amendment, guaranteeing freedom of the press, applied to television as well as newspapers; he held that "this protection does not depend on whether the government believes we are right or wrong in our news judgments."

At this point the White House joined the fray—but on the side of the press. Herbert Klein criticized the Congressional investigation as an "infringement on the freedom of the press" and disassociated the White House from the inquiry. Harley O. Staggers, chairman of the Committee, nevertheless continued to press for citation for contempt and his Committee voted 25-13 to support him. Thereupon 21 House Democrats attacked the Committee's vote as "a serious threat" to the First Amendment; they were joined by the leadership of both parties. On July 13, 1971, the House voted, 226-181, to recommit—in effect, to kill—the Committee's proposed contempt citation. The vote was highly significant; for the first time in its history the House had denied a contempt citation that had been requested by a Committee and its chairman.

Managing the News

Another serious issue is management of the news. It is charged that the government is trying to influence the reporter and delude him into believing that gray or black is white. Obviously the reporter must depend on the policy makers for information; also obviously, there will always be official efforts to "manage" the news because officials are human and it is human nature to put the best foot well forward.

Administrations can manage newsmen by granting them exclusive interviews or briefings, by "leaking" stories to them or by doing social or political favors for them. Presidents traditionally have made themselves especially accessible to a few reporters whose influence, usefulness, or friendship gains them favored status (as indicated in Chapter 10.)

Allied to this issue of managed news is the question of off-the-record background conferences out of which come stories quoting a "well-informed (but unidentified) government official" or a "key policy-maker" or stating that "it can be said on the highest authority." Sometimes the correspondent is not allowed even this type of vague attribution and is told he must make his report on his own say-so, even though he may not have the time to check the official's "facts."

At such sessions trial balloons are floated and personal attacks made with impunity. Moreover, the motivation of the briefer may not be immediately apparent; then, if the story does not pan out, the official will deny its truth.

The defenders of the backgrounder say that, even though the practice has been abused, it has not been misused as much as some correspondents allege. Often these meetings provide important interpretative material; this is certainly true in foreign affairs and such complex domestic areas as economics. It was at a background briefing that the President launched his so-called "Nixon Doctrine" of self-help among the Asian nations. Mr. Nixon met with newsmen on Guam during a swing through the Pacific in July, 1969, after he greeted the Apollo 11 spacemen upon their return from the moon. He spoke for publication but he asked that his words not be directly quoted. At this backgrounder the President's first detailed definition of his Asian policy was spelled out—and it was on the front pages everywhere.

Mr. Nixon arranged another briefing a few days before the American campaign in Cambodia was due to end. He invited representatives of both newspapers and broadcasting networks to a five-and-a-half hour meeting with officials from the State and Defense Departments and the National Security Council. The briefing covered the operations in Vietnam and Cambodia. Officials denied that its purpose was to influence the media in advance of the President's final report to the nation on the move into Cambodia. Two of the country's leading newspapers, the *New York Times* and the *Washington Post,* however, both outspoken critics of the Vietnam war, were not invited.

Using the Johnson administration for illustration, the *Wall Street Journal* cited these examples of how a background briefing can be used to manipulate the news:

• In the midst of a world gold crisis, newspapers across the United States featured two stories bearing on the danger to the dollar. One, quoting "a realistic Administration source," reported that President Johnson had decided to order only a "moderate" troop increase in Vietnam, instead of the 100,000 or more men mentioned in early dispatches. The other story, quoting a "well-informed Administration official," announced that the President was "willing to go along" with Congressional leaders on $8 billion or $9 billion of appropriations cutbacks in return for action on the long-stalled income tax surcharge. A few days later it was revealed that the stories had come from President Johnson himself, who had informed a small group of newsmen about the decisions.

• Defense Secretary Clark Clifford went to the home of Philip Goulding, Pentagon information officer, to give several radio and TV broadcasters the Johnson administration's version of Robert Kennedy's proposal for a commission to reassess U. S. policy in Vietnam. Word of the proposal had begun to leak out and the administration thus achieved distribution for a statement without attribution of its side of the story.

• General William Westmoreland, then U. S. commander in Vietnam, told a group of correspondents at the home of *Baltimore Sun* reporter Charles Corddry that he was "deeply concerned" that the Cambodian port of Sihanoukville was about to become an important source of arms for Vietcong troops in South Vietnam and that the military was considering contingency plans to quarantine the port. The reporters agreed to hold their stories until the General had left Washington and then attribute them to "some U. S. officials." The purpose of the exercise, it was surmised, was to put extra heat on Prince Nordom Sihanouk, the Cambodian leader, to crack down on the arms shipments and to spur international action toward the same end.[7]

There is a certain amount of bridling in Congress because of the practice of putting out information without attribution. Senator Mike Mansfield, majority leader, has complained to his colleagues about "official but unnamed sources" who were reported to be re-defining policy in Vietnam. "As one Senator," he said, "I would like to know in order to estimate the significance of the story. Are these officials in the White House? Are they in the Defense Department? The State Department? The CIA? Or are they scattered throughout the Executive branch? Is it the head of a department who advances this new concept of Vietnamese policy? Or is it the chairwarmer at a Southeast Asia desk somewhere or a guard at the front door of the Pentagon or the State Department?" [8]

The issue is not quite as complicated as it might appear. Although at times it may be difficult to determine what is genuine background information and what is "dope" intended to drug the correspondent, a reporter who is sagacious and who has done his homework will seldom be misled. This might be a good rule: if, in a so-called "back-ground conference," an official attempts to provide news without allowing attribution, the correspondents should demand that it be put on the record; and if the official attempts to bind the reporters to secrecy about classified information which they feel should not be restricted, they should walk out.

There is a sharp difference between the "hand-out reporter," who takes unquestioningly what is thrust into his hand and the "hold-out reporter" who analyses the official communique and probes deeply to determine its validity. What is involved here is much less management of news than management and manipulation of newspapermen. There are correspondents who are ready to be managed if they can get a quid for their quo. To gain an exclusive story, they are willing to sacrifice their principles and play ball with officials for months before and for months after the piece is printed. (I have wondered at times whether the Pulitzer jurors should not ban prizes for exclusive stories obtained through this kind of deal.)

Incidentally, Presidents and their aides are not the only ones who manipulate the media as a means of spreading their views. Black militants like Stokley Carmichael and Rap Brown have been masters of the technique; they have used it to build their reputations and to distort the image of America's black community. During his campaigns for President and Governor of Alabama, George Wallace frequently told his audiences that the presence of newsmen at his rallies indicated how important his election was to the future of the nation.

Anti-war demonstrators used the press to create the impression that a huge throng of protesters would be bent on tearing Chicago down at the 1968 Democratic National Convention. Months before the convention, radical groups such as the Youth International Party (the Yippies) made public predictions that as many as half a million protesters would be converging on Chicago. They circulated reports that LSD would be put in the city's drinking water and that power stations would be threatened—reports which were published in some newspapers and surely contributed to the conflict that developed later between the police and the demonstrators.

At a Yale University rally in May, 1970, Jerry Rubin, a New Left leader, turned aside requests from students that a TV cameraman turn off the lights that were blinding them. "You don't understand," he said. "Let him shoot all he wants. I don't care what the commentators say about me. Just as long as they show our beautiful long hair and our beautiful free clothes. That's what your eight-year-old brothers and sisters will pick up. They'll become like us, part of the new revolution."

These various examples indicate how widely and how often efforts are made to manage the news. This is not surprising in view of the human desire to present the best visage to the world. Nevertheless the practice does add to the difficulty of presenting the news "without fear or favor."

Discrediting the Press

The third form of pressure is less subtle and more formidable; it is a simple unabashed effort to discredit the press. Back in October, 1969, Vice-President Agnew launched a crusade with that objective ostensibly in mind.

The skirmish (it was more like a battle) opened with a fusillade of speeches by the Vice President aimed at doves and other dissenters from the Nixon programs. Mr. Agnew referred to critics of the administration's Vietnam policy as "an effete corps of impudent snobs." [9]

The Agnew guns were first turned mainly on television. Among his charges were these: (1) comments on President Nixon's speech outlining Vietnam policy were "unfair and biased"—there was "instant" (and therefore "invalid") analysis; (2) there was an unusual and dangerous concentration of power in the hands of a "few networks," dominated by "a small group of men . . . a small and unelected elite" with a distinct bias; (3) this bias was a reflection of the viewpoint of an "Eastern intellectual establishment," whose ideas presented a "narrow and distorted" picture of America; (4) because of their monopoly, the networks could not claim, as they did, the protection of the First Amendment. Nor did Mr. Agnew spare the newspapers. He attacked "the concentration of more and more power in fewer and fewer hands," with the consequence that some papers had grown "fat and irresponsible," specifically the *New York Times* and the *Washington Post*.

Few of the many clashes between government and press produced a debate as extensive and as intensive as the one that grew out of the Agnew onslaught. The reaction in television circles was especially sharp; one TV official said, "I could not sleep all night, because of the Vice President's attack. I kept worrying that it might be another Wheeling." (The reference was to Wheeling, West Virginia, where in 1949 Senator Joseph McCarthy made his first speech charging that the State Department was riddled with Communists.)

Frank Stanton, President of CBS, described the Agnew speeches as an "unprecedented attempt by the Vice President of the United States to intimidate a news medium which depends for its existence upon government licenses. The American Civil Liberties Union called it a "clear and chilling threat" of censorship.

In response to Mr. Agnew's accusation that there was a "tiny closed fraternity of privileged men" responsible for network television news, the TV people insisted there was no such animal or aggregation. Television news, they said, is a form of group journalism; decisions are made continuously throughout the day and there is no built-in party line. As for "complicity" or "conspiracy," they reported that they hardly ever saw their counterparts, not even socially.

Newspaper publishers also responded sharply, Arthur Ochs Sulzberger, publisher of the *New York Times* said, "The *Times* has editorially discussed and opposed monopoly journalism. The separation of news and opinion is and will continue to be a basic credo of the *Times*." Katharine Graham of the *Washington Post* commented: "Our enterprises decidedly do not 'grind out the same editorial line.' The staff is given a maximum of freedom and they compete vigorously with one another."

Mr. Agnew had a variety of defenders—the most vociferous being politicians piqued at their treatment by the press and "Middle Americans" who resent the "Eastern Liberal Establishment." They charged that the press was guilty of stirring up antagonisms, of deepening the divisions in society, and, in the guise of presenting "atmosphere reporting," of providing "unattributed comment" in which one group denigrated others—police denigrating Negroes, Negroes belittling police; college students deriding their elders, elders the students; members of one race running down members of another.

Mr. Agnew said his statements were made entirely on his own, without consultation with Mr. Nixon, but there are strong suspicions that the President approved or certainly did not disapprove them.

So the debate has proceeded and these large issues continue to be discussed:

Question: *Is there a small group of men that attempt to brainwash the people—a dangerous concentration of power over the news flow?*

My answer is no. There is no discernibly uniform philosophy about TV news programming; the effort seems to be mainly to get news out first, to make it graphic — even to the point of sensation — and to fit in as many commercials as possible. The major decisions about news programs are made not by a few individuals but by a number of people, most of whom have their origins not in New York City but in the Middle West or the South. (I do not feel that this geographical fact is of any real significance; whatever their birth-and-early-career-places, correspondents or editors soon take on the patina of New York or Washington.)

Question: *Are these attacks evidence of a demand for censorship?*

I feel certain that neither the Congress nor the public generally would stand for any form of abridgement of the rights of free press and free speech. Nor do I see any possibility, presently or in the distant future, of a new wave of McCarthyism. Nevertheless, there are indications that the talk of censorship has made the press, or at least the weaker elements in it, pause and become less outspoken.

Question: *Is there a dangerous trend toward concentration?*

I suspect that there is such a trend, but I do not believe it is as ominous as has been alleged. Both government and public are alert, as they have never been before, to the dangers of an Orwellian press speaking with a single overpowering voice. In the case of one-newspaper cities, in which there has been consolidation, my observation is that the single publication does on the whole a better and fairer job than that done by any of the predecessor newspapers; the publishers of such newspapers seem to feel that it is now incumbent on them to present an improved news report and to give voice to a variety of opinion.

Question: *Are the media at fault, (a) in not labelling commentary clearly; (b) in attempting "instant analysis"?*

The answer here is a qualified yes. The labelling problem is greater for television than it is for newspapers or news magazines although all three are confronted with it. In the newspaper, of course, there is a sharp distinction between the editorial page and the news pages, even though opinion at times may intrude into the latter in the name of interpretation. On television the differentiation is more difficult because, by undue emphasis on a word or the lifting of an eyebrow, an "objective" commentator can convey his personal feeling. However the custom now is to label straight-out editorials on television.

As for "instant analysis," there is no objection to it, provided that the analyst has the required background and judgment. Certainly the more prompt the comment, the more will be its impact and pertinence.

Question: *Is there an "Eastern Liberal Establishment" whose viewpoint is not representative of the country's?*

My answer is an unhesitating "yes" and I have attempted to document it in Chapter 4.

Question: *Do the Nixon Administration and Dean Burch, chairman of the Federal Communications Commission, propose to use the licensing power to bring indirect influence to bear on television news and documentaries?*

Possibly, but I doubt it, for the same reason that I doubt that we are threatened with censorship. The outcry in Congress and the public prints would be so great that any such attempt would in all probability fail. If however the FCC refuses to grant a license or to renew one because it concludes after full inquiry that a station has not been objective in its news presentations or delinquent in providing access for viewpoints that differ from its own, this clearly is neither censorship nor manipulation but an effort to implement the formula prescribed by the Communications Act: that awards of licenses shall be made "in the public interest."

Question: *Are the critics of the news media genuinely concerned about "bias"?*

No, they are biased in favor of their kind of bias. In the long years of my editorship, I have been accused numberless times of bias; but almost invariably these complaints turn out to be accusations not that what has been published is slanted but that it is slanted in the wrong direction—that is, not in the direction of the critics. I suspect the Agnews would not be concerned about bias if the networks had presented the "Middle American" viewpoint and had attacked the Eastern liberals. I suspect further that the critics, in furtherance of the Nixon political strategy, have been chiefly interested in winning the applause of the resentful, the "antis" of assorted hues and loud cries. As James Reston wrote, "To be in the inner, inner circle of the Administration, you have to be an Agnewstic, which is defined as one who disbelieves anything printed or broadcast east of the Ohio River."[10]

On the whole, Mr. Agnew *et al* do have some solid points — the assertions about the existence of an "Eastern Liberal Establishment" and the fact that it does not represent the majority view in the nation—but they are inaccurate or illogical about others, and they swing their axes too broadly and too bluntly. Nevertheless, the debate they started has had a definite value in that it has raised fundamental issues about the role of the media in public opinion.

In concluding this discussion of the Agnew affair, an editorial that appeared in the *Washington Post* is especially pertinent. Commenting on a statement by the Vice President that he is entitled to the First Amendment right of free speech, the *Post* said:

"To our knowledge, there is no federal or state statute that prevents the Vice President from saying anything he pleases, but he must expect that its relationship to what the Administration is doing will be commented upon and judged. For even though he has an incontrovertible right to go around the country calling people and groups of people names, he should be aware that he has no related right to expect that he will be admired in consequence.

"That raises the second point: Mr. Agnew's powers and his perks. There is no 'right to respect' for government officials written into the Constitution of a country that got its start by spitting in King George's eye and which has done its best ever since to keep its public officials aware they are serving on public sufferance and often with a minimum of public tolerance. The glory and glamor and trappings of the office itself, in short, do not automatically compel either awe or respect—do not presuppose it. Mr. Agnew's failure to assimilate this idea is somehow akin to the spirit which temporarily foisted upon us the Ruritarian White House uniform.

"But if respect does not automatically come with the job or with its outward symbols, the Vice President should nonetheless be heartened to know that he does have certain powers which are wholly unshared with the critical press. For the press and the critics generally may howl their heads off at the Administration — its policies and its conceits — but the press has no power whatever to degrade or demean the highest offices in the land. Mr. Agnew can rest his fears on that account. The power to demean the Presidency or the Vice Presidency in this nation reposes solely with the men who hold the office." [11]

*   *   *

The questions raised in this chapter are not black or white affairs; they cannot be settled in the courts; they must be worked out in negotiation and free discussion between government and press. There is need of clarification to ensure that the press be free to maintain watch on government without hampering the proper operations of government or violating the rights of citizens. There is also need on the part of both government and press of a full sense of responsibility; government must provide accurate information and keep secrecy to a minimum; the press must present information without bias and without sensationalism.

These issues have a direct bearing on the problem of improving public opinion because they concern the nature of the information that flows from government to press and the freedom of that flow. Public opinion, if it is to be enlightened, clearly must have access to reliable information.

The relationship between the government and the press in general, between the President and the press in particular, and between the President and the people, plays a large part in the issue of Presidential credibility—the theme of the next chapter.

12: The Credibility Gap: A Widening Canyon

The phrase "credibility gap" first came into prominent usage during the Lyndon Johnson era and it persists today with regard to the Presidency of Richard Nixon.

In his relations with the people, the President must have, above all, belief. His words must ring true; otherwise he is certain to fail. Despite what has been said about the efficacy of "fireside chats" and press conferences, unless a President is believed no device can work in his favor.

The Johnson Gap

In the case of Lyndon Johnson (his is the classic example) the credibility gap developed because of his manner, his bad television presence, his proneness to operate indirectly rather than directly (a kind of game with him), because of episodes which were both dangerous and unbecoming for a Chief Executive; and, most of all, because of concealment of facts and failures to make good on promises.

The gap began to develop early in Mr. Johnson's administration, even at the time when he was gloating over his showing in the polls. He decided to act as Lyndon Johnson rather than as President— driving at high speeds, swimming nude in the White House pool, holding up his beagles by their ears. This was conduct that came naturally to him but he did not seem to realize that the Chief Executive is not an ordinary citizen and that the country expects of him a certain amount of dignity. These actions provoked widespread criticism and numerous wise-cracks.

In a way these were tangential matters; the big factor in the evolution of the mistrust was Vietnam. It began to take form in the 1964 campaign; the Republicans had provided for Mr. Johnson a large target in the person of Senator Goldwater, an outspoken, uncomplicated hawk. The President focused attention on the "nuclear scare" created by the Goldwater candidacy; he warned about the kind of hand that should control the "atomic trigger"; he promised that he would never send Americans to fight a war that Asians should be fighting. But within a few months after his election the escalation of the war began. The pre-election dove had turned out to be a post-election hawk; the incredibility fat was in the fire. The climax was reached with the enemy's Tet Offensive in January, 1968. Up to that time Mr. Johnson had been assuring the nation that we were winning the war, but Tet threw a dark cloud of doubt over his optimism and from then on suspicions grew steadily.

Another cause of distrust was Mr. Johnson's addiction to secrecy. If a correspondent reported that the President was about to take some action, he would cancel it or delay it until the prediction had been forgotten. When he decided to replace General William C. Westmoreland as commander in Vietnam, the General was not told of the decision until an hour after the President had announced it at a press conference; nor was Ellsworth Bunker, American Ambassador in Saigon, informed in advance.

James Deakin, White House correspondent of the *St. Louis Post-Dispatch,* reports that transcripts of Presidential talks were altered, newspaper stories denied and later confirmed. "The reporters, and through them the public, were misled." The disparity between Mr. Johnson's public and private postures was so profound, says Deakin, that "one can only be astonished at the task the man had set himself: to create a fictional human being for public consumption." Deakin describes the public pose: a man of "humility," conceding freely the right to disagree, welcoming criticism of any kind. And the private reality: Johnson slicing up a reporter for asking a "dumb" (the adjective was usually much stronger and quite unprintable) question; bludgeoning Senator Frank Church for his reservations about the Vietnam War ("Okay, Frank, next time you need a dam in Idaho, ask Walter Lippmann for one."), blasting a group of magazine writers ("Someone ought to do an article on you and your damn profession and your First Amendment.")[1]

It was a strange business in the light of Mr. Johnson's ability to spellbind in man-to-man talk. He used to say, with missionary zeal and an obvious sense of dedication, that his father was a teacher and that he looked upon himself, in a way, as a teacher too. But this impression did not get over to the nation. In his long Congressional career Mr. Johnson had achieved his ends by private consultation, arm-twisting and wheeling-dealing and it was difficult for him to shed the habit. There was in him an unending struggle between the man who wanted to be a statesman and the man who was basically the politician.

President Kennedy was guilty of concealment and of deluding the people on occasion, but he was able to get away with it because of his disarming charm. President Eisenhower also at times misled the public; but this too was forgiven because of the impression of sincerity and honesty he conveyed. In Mr. Johnson's case the image of the intriguer was never erased.

Yet Mr. Johnson was more effective with the Congress than Mr. Kennedy. A Texan, he introduced and steered through the Senate the first Civil Rights Law and he obtained from the Congress the enactment of much of the legislative program that Mr. Kennedy had been unable to push through. Mr. Johnson, I an convinced, was a much better President than he seemed to be. After he announced his retirement on the evening of March 31, 1968, the *New York Times* said editorially: "Lyndon Johnson has been subjected to as bitter criticism as any President in history—some of it deserved. Yet it is possible to observe today that he merits the respect, and, for many reasons, the gratitude of his fellow citizens. He labored mightily on behalf of this nation and always tried to serve the best interests of all the people. He had failures of understanding, but never of intent or effort. He has no reason to fear history's judgment."

And the Nixon Gap

When Mr. Nixon came into the White House the nation was ready, despite doubts in the past, to think the best of him and give him every possible break. The *New York Times* proclaimed his arrival with eight-column headlines: NIXON, SWORN, DEDICATES OFFICE TO PEACE: OFFERS A ROLE TO YOUNG AND DISAFFECTED AND A CHANCE TO BLACK AS WELL AS WHITE.

The nation did not question President Nixon's promises. A February, 1969, Gallup Poll indicated that, by a ratio of 12 to 1, people were sympathetic toward him and felt he could put an end to the Vietnam war and create unity at home. Throughout his first year in office he moved in low key and with the greatest caution. He was very conscious of the Johnson credibility gap and determined to prevent one of his own. He charged Herbert Klein, his Director of Communications, with the task of insuring believability; Klein said, "We are trying to keep an open house and make the facts known without trying in any way to manage the news."

During his first year, Mr. Nixon maintained his standing in the polls even though he did not make any real inroads into the large problems that confronted the nation. He initiated a program of withdrawal from Vietnam—a policy which the surveys indicated was welcomed by a large majority of Americans. When more than a quarter of a million people came to Washington on November 15, 1969, to demonstrate against the war, Mr. Nixon stayed inside the White House, insisting that he would not be affected by the massive show of opposition outside. Still the nation approved, because he was "calm," "firm," "seeking advice from others." (These were the adjectives used in the polls).

But the picture was soon to change. As Mr. Johnson had encountered a credibility gap over Vietnam, so a Nixon gap developed over Laos and Cambodia. In Laos, the administration maintained, only "armed reconnaissance flights" was authorized, yet correspondents reported that, in addition to bombing missions, U. S. troops were involved on the ground. The President issued a statement on March 6, 1969, which condemned the news reports as "grossly inaccurate," asserting emphatically that the United States had no ground combat troops in Laos. Then came other reports of greater U.S. involvement in Laos and these were not denied. A Harris poll in May, 1970, disclosed that, by a 56-26% majority, the American people felt that the President had been less than "frank and straightforward" about Laos.

The venture into Cambodia greatly increased public doubts. In a report to the nation on April 20, 1970, the President indicated that there had been substantial progress in his Vietnamization program and that "we have now reached a point where we can confidently move to a longer-range program for replacement of Americans by South Vietnamese troops." Then on April 30, the President told the country that the operation he had described only ten days before as proceeding successfully was in fact in grave danger from North

Vietnamese troops in Cambodia and that he had therefore ordered American combat forces into Cambodia to rout out the North Vietnamese; this action, he said, was "indispensable for the success of Vietnamization." The nation was shocked at the reversal of the optimistic reports.

Moreover, only four days before Secretary of State Rogers had told the Senate Foreign Relations Committee that the administration was still "considering" the Cambodian regime's request for weapons but he gave no inkling at all that action had already been taken. On May 16, it was revealed that the arms had been delivered two days *before* the Rogers testimony.

Despite the steady withdrawal of American troops from Vietnam and the emphasis on the Vietnam program, there was no perceptible rise in the Nixon credibility line as the war dragged on. Soon after the South Vietnamese troops, backed by American air power, attacked the Ho Chi Minh Trail in Laos in the spring of 1971, the Harris organization took a poll on this question: "Do you think that President Nixon has been straight-forward about the war in Vietnam, Cambodia, and Laos, or do you feel that he has not told the American people the real truth about the war?" Fifty-one percent of the respondents answered that they believed that the public had not been told the real truth; only 33% felt that the President had been frank with them.

In a Gallup poll taken in March, 1971, Mr. Nixon's credibility gap was compared with that of his predecessor. The survey revealed that seven in ten persons felt that his administration was not telling the American people all they should know about the Vietnam War; virtually the same percentage held this view of Mr. Johnson at a comparable point in his administration.

The Gallup organization released the results of a poll on May 23, 1971, headlined "President Nixon Facing Giant-Size 'Credibility Gap' on Vietnam War." It reported that "Only one person in five said that the Nixon Administration is telling the public all they should know about the Vietnam War. Chief complaints are that the public is not getting straight answers regarding casualty rates (both ours and the enemy's), and U. S. troop withdrawal figures."

Whether Mr. Nixon can solve the main problems involving his

credibility—notably inflation and Vietnam—before the summer of '72 remains uncertain.

Credibility, as Richard Neustadt has observed, is posing a crucial problem, not only for Mr. Nixon but also for the office of the Presidency. "Johnson suffered from this mistrust and now Nixon does. Ultimately, lack of trust in the king threatens the throne." [2]

"Enlightenment—Inspiration"

Potentially, then, the President is the most important of the "outside" influences that affect the formation of public opinion. His success depends on his ability to perform the three prime functions of the office: communication, enlightenment, inspiration; to establish an understanding with the people; to try, unremittingly, to inform and to lead them.

Keeping always in mind the disadvantages of overexposure, there should be more press conferences, more talks to the nation. But communication must be far more human and far more personal than speaking into a microphone or issuing press releases. The President must break through the barriers of isolation, resist the tendency to accept favorable information and reject the unfavorable, meet regularly with representatives of the various national groups—Democrats as well as Republicans, students as well as "hard hats," spokesmen for the suspicious East as well as the more favorable West, dissenters from the minorities as well as applauders from the majorities.

Lack of time is no alibi. If the nation is convinced that a President is fully dedicated to his work, it will surely be willing to have him reduce White House entertainment and other ruffled-and-trumpeted affairs; and even dispense with the throwing out of the first baseballs and the bussing of babies.

The insistent question asked from the time of Lord Bryce and still pressing today is: How is the President to learn what the country is thinking? No one has a definite answer, not even the pollsters. Yet one can suggest that out of the polls, out of increased contact with the "Non-Elite," as well as the "Elite," out of the responses to his talks to the nation, the President can get useful clues to public thinking and feeling.

Harry Truman, in a letter written to C. L. Sulzberger of the *New*

York Times, summed up, succinctly and convincingly, the problems and the opportunities of the White House: "Presidents from the time of George Washington have been subjected to attacks and abuse. It is the way that a free and open society keeps its government institutions on the alert. It is a small price to pay for an aroused and active public opinion . . . The Presidency, in large measure, depends on the occupant, his scope, his capacity to resist pressures from within and without and, most importantly, a sense of the times, as well as a sense of the future. Above all, the President must communicate with the people, to avoid the risk of a loss of public confidence." [3]

The ability to communicate, enlighten and inspire is vital to the President's relations with the people. It is also all-important in his dealings with Congress. The relationships between White House and Capitol are described in the following chapter.

13: President and Congress: A Classic Duel

There is the President and there is the Congress, each making its play for public opinion. The issue is the accretion of the executive's power and the diminution of the legislature's influence in foreign affairs — an issue which began to take shape at the turn of the century and has been growing in intensity ever since. The significance for public opinion is clear: assuming that the Congress represents the people, then, as the Presidential voice becomes stronger, the voice of the voter becomes steadily weaker.

This situation has come about even though the Constitution is quite explicit: Congress shall have the power "to declare war" (Article I, Section 8); the President shall be "Commander-in-Chief of the Army and Navy of the United States." (Article II, Section 2). *The Federalist* defines "Commander-in-Chief" as meaning that "the President shall direct the operations after Congress has decided to make war."

James Madison defended the partition of governmental power in *Federalist 51*: "In order to lay a due foundation for that separate and distinct exercise of the different powers of government which to a certain extent is admitted on all hands to be essential to the preservation of liberty, it is evident that each department should have a will of its own. . . . The great security against a gradual concentration of the several powers in the same department, consists in giving those who administer each department the necessary constitutional means and personal motives to resist encroachments of the others. . . . Ambition must be made to counteract ambition." [1]

The Political Realities

Historically and traditionally, as a result of this system of checks and balances, the relationship between President and the Congress has been one of conflict. Certain political realities contribute to the struggle:

109

• The President and the members of Congress, though both popularly elected, represent very different constituencies. The President presumably speaks for the nation as a whole; members of Congress speak for segments of the electorate.

• There is a difference in time perspectives. Whereas many members of Congress are, or hope to be, career legislators, the President has only four or at most eight years in which to shape American society to his concepts. Moreover, as Nelson Polsby, political scientist, points out, to speak of an "eight-year span" is deceptive: "Discount the period just before and just after elections or especially the critical period just prior to the decision whether there is to be a second term or not. How much time remains? Not very much." [2]

• The President and the Congress have differing attitudes toward legislation. While it is to the legislator's advantage to remain uncommitted in order to bargain with the Chief Executive or interest groups, or to avoid controversy, the President usually must speak up unequivocally in advocating legislation.

In the conflict between White House and Capitol Hill each side has its weapons. The President possesses the threat of veto over legislation, the power to make innumerable patronage appointments, the right to designate the location of government-financed projects, and, far from least, considerable say over the allotment of Congressional campaign funds. All of these are potent factors that tend to induce legislators to follow the Presidential line.

The office of the Presidency itself is a powerful influence in mustering Congressional support or weakening Congressional opposition. "Only the crustiest and most independent Congresmen and Senators," says Polsby, "fail to warm to considerate personal treatment by a President of the United States. A private breakfast, a walk in the Rose Garden, an intimate conference, all duly and widely reported in the press, give a man a sense of importance which may not only flatter his ego but may also remind him of his responsibilities as a legislator, as a trustee of the common weal." [3] A dissenter who may be quite vocal in the Senate cloakrooms will usually find it difficult to say no to the President in the White House. As Walter Bagehot has observed: "No man can argue from his knees."

Yet the Constitution, tradition and precedents have not left the Congress defenseless. On the contrary. As a matter of practice, the

Congress can block Presidential legislation more easily than the President can achieve its enactment. It has devices such as the filibuster—a cherished tool of the Senate; the committee quagmire—a swamp in which a bill can be sunk with hardly a trace; the authority to investigate departments in the Executive branch; and the right of post-audit over federal expenditures.

The Senate has special resources, such as the power of impeachment (even though exercise of that power was attempted only once, against President Andrew Johnson, and then unsuccessfully) and the right to approve Presidential appointments, including those on the Cabinet level. (Presidential choices are customarily approved; only occasionally is this tradition breached and then usually because some members of the President's own party have found the candidate particularly unsuited for the job, as notably in the cases of Judges Clement F. Haynesworth, Jr., and G. Harold Carswell, whom Nixon had nominated for the Supreme Court.)

If a President is to achieve a program, he must possess a large talent for persuasion. In the honeymoon period, Presidential legislation is likely to have a favorable reception, but the sweetness and light usually are short-lived. In approaching members of his own party, the President must convince them that what he wants is in their own and the party's interest. In approaching members of the opposition, he must persuade them that what he wants is in the nation's interest.

All other things being equal, members of Congress try to please the President, those of his party eagerly, those of the opposition when there is a tit for tat exchange. Seldom does he have to make deals with legislators of his own party or give a dam or a post office for a vote; a promise of goodwill usually does the trick.

A well-documented example of Executive pressure on Congress was Mr. Nixon's effort to bring about the confirmation of Judge Haynesworth. A month before the Senate vote it became apparent that the nomination was in deep trouble; a surprisingly large number of Republican Senators were ready to vote against confirmation. The White House then began a three-pronged campaign to influence public opinion and the Senators themselves.

One technique was a verbal appeal to the "grass roots" by the President and his top aides, asking support for the nominee and asserting that his conduct as a member of the bench had been wholly proper. (The main charge against Judge Haynesworth was a lack of ethical sensitivity in that he had ruled on cases in which he had a personal financial interest.)

A second technique was directed at the press in the effort to influence opinion—and thus the Congress. A stream of documents making the White House case for Haynesworth flowed out of the Executive offices (usually from Presidential aides Herbert Klein and Clark Mollenhoff) to reporters and editors; in addition, there were telephone calls from the White House to publishers.

The third technique was aimed at Republican Senators. Officials in the White House and the Justice Department called state, county and regional party chairmen and big business contributors and urged them to put pressure on undecided Senators from their states. Senator Len B. Jordan, Republican of Idaho, publicly protested that, after he had written a private letter to Attorney General Mitchell informing him that he would vote against Haynesworth, he received calls from his state leaders urging him to support the nomination. Senator Mark Hatfield, an Oregon Republican of liberal persuasion, reported that the day before the vote he had been warned by a friend at home that should he oppose Haynesworth, he might face a concerted challenge to his re-election in the 1972 primary from a conservative Republican. Senator William B. Saxbe, Republican of Ohio, received a slew of letters from contributors in his state threatening him with the loss of financial support for a re-election campaign if he opposed the confirmation. Some Senators yielded to the pressure but Jordan, Saxbe, and Hatfield voted against Haynesworth; the nomination was rejected, the intensive Presidential drive defeated.

White House and Hill

Obviously a President has neither the time nor the inclination to do all the negotiating with the Congress; he leaves the task to deputies. He must select such agents most carefully. During the Kennedy administration, the White House staff exacerbated the latent conflict between Executive and legislature; the young Ivy League New Frontiersmen were too brisk and too impersonal for the taste of the older, more folksy members of Congress. Moreover, the veterans on

Capitol Hill felt that the President held them in haughty contempt; as a matter of fact he was quite remote in his dealings with them.

"The most widely shared and loudly voiced grievance that Congress has against administration practices," as Meg Greenfield pointed out in 1961, "concerns the unremitting attention it receives from those it describes simply and without affection as 'the young men.' They badger, to hear the members tell it, they hector, they even chase. . . . To the White House counterclaim that pushing and prodding sometimes help and never hurt, one Congressman replies by citing the case of a young liaison man, the very sight of whom at the cloak-room door, he claims, is enough to cost the administration twenty-five votes." [4]

Mr. Kennedy was a firm believer in the force of public opinion as a counter to Congressional power. He often remarked privately that even though the Congress might be against him, he had the people with him and therefore in the long run he would prevail. Yet at times he expressed irritation at the apathy of the public; he believed that when the voters were genuinely concerned they could surely get what they wanted from the Congress and from the White House.

Mr. Kennedy's relationship with the Congress was in sharp contrast with that of President Johnson, who had grown up on the Hill and knew how to deal with the Hillsmen. ("Hill-billies," the Camelot Crusaders might have called them.) He kept a virtually open White House for members of Congress and sat down frequently with them to find out what they were thinking and, by "reasoning together," to win them to his views. He gave high priority to his administration's Congressional liaison men; Lawrence O'Brien, his head coordinator, reported that "the President has told his Cabinet members many times that no persons in their respective departments can be more important than the heads of their Congressional relations activity." All of which tends to explain why Mr. Johnson got most of his legislative programs through Congress and Mr. Kennedy did not.

Mr. Johnson looked upon Congress as an excellent barometer of the national viewpoint. In a broad way, undoubtedly, it registers the basic desires of the country on such questions as Vietnam, national defense and economic policy. But on the whole, members of Congress are rated by the voters according to their performances in local rather than in national or international affairs.

But whether or not the Congress is truly representative of the national viewpoint, Mr. Johnson assumed that it was. And in the White House he was still applying the methods he used on Capitol Hill.

President Nixon's relations with the Congress have remained strained because, among other reasons—

• He lashed out at the Senate for refusing to support his appointments to the Supreme Court — a kind of emotional outburst that is not easily forgotten by the Congress.

• He campaigned vigorously against the Democratic candidates during the Congressional elections in 1970—which is not the way to handle a Congress controlled by the opposition. He also campaigned against members of his own party who disagreed with his philosophy.

• He allowed Vice President Agnew to attack "radic-liberals" and "permissivists" in the Congress. Even though Mr. Agnew was the voice, it was clear that he spoke for the President.

• He repeatedly has made some harsh statements about Congress. Examples: "The problem with most politicians is that they talk so much they think too little." "More members of the Congress should go home and contemplate a bit more often." "The 91st Congress was one that would be remembered in history not for what it did, but for what it failed to do."

• He has done little to smooth the icy slides, even though his program has had hard sledding in Congress.

The Executive Privilege Issue

A major issue has arisen between the President and the Congress over "executive privilege"—a prerogative which the Chief Executive invokes when he decides to deny information to the legislature.

The phrase is not mentioned in the Constitution nor can any clause in that document be cited as direct authorization for the practice. Yet its use dates back to the very beginnings of American government, from the time of George Washington to the present. In 1790 Thomas Jefferson, then Secretary of the Treasury, refused to provide Chief Justice John Marshall with the Burr papers, arguing that "All nations have found it necessary, that for the advantageous conduct of their affairs, some of these proceedings at least, should remain known to their executive functionary only. He, of course, from the nature of the case, must be the sole judge of which of them the public interest will permit publication. Hence, under our Constitution, in requests of papers, from the legislative to the executive branch, any exception is carefully expressed, as to those which he may deem the public welfare may require not to be disclosed . . ."

Executive privilege is supposed to be the "right" of the President and members of his Cabinet to withhold from Congress information of an internal or sensitive nature. But Congress contends the Chief Executive has extended the privilege to include a "right" to formulate policy in secret without the advice, consent or even knowledge of Congress.

A sharp dispute over the executive privilege issue arose when Elmer Staats, the U. S. Controller General ruled on August 18, 1971, that the funding of foreign military aid would cease within a few weeks unless the Nixon Administration released a document for which the Congress had asked.

While testifying before a subcommittee of the Senate Foreign Relations Committee, Lieutenant General Robert H. Warren, Deputy Assistant Secretary of Defense, had acknowledged the existence of the document requested by the Congress—a five-year projection of the military assistance program—but said that he was not authorized to release the paper. Mr. Staats held that under the 1961 Foreign Aid Act the administration was in violation of the law unless the President furnished the document or formally claimed executive privilege and gave his reasons for withholding the information requested by Congress.

Senator Fulbright has proposed legislation that would compel government officials to appear before Congressional committees and would include a provision stating that information can be withheld from Congress only on the basis of a formal invocation of executive privilege.

The debate over executive privilege has been extended by the Congress so that it now includes the issue of Congressional exclusion from the making of foreign policy, particularly with reference to presidential war-making powers. Various attempts have been made to curb Mr. Nixon's power—measures designed to prohibit the President from involving the country in war without Congressional approval, to limit the use of ground troops in Vietnam, and to set a deadline for withdrawal. The *New York Times* commented editorially on January 3, 1971: "Since confidence between Senate and President has almost vanished, the Senate by restrictive language tries to prevent Mr. Nixon from doing what it fears he might do. He seeks to retain the freedom to act while disavowing the intention."

The Case Pro and Con

Various reasons are advanced to justify the increase in Presidential power in foreign affairs. There is the argument of technology: the world has moved into the space age with weapons of destruction so swift and so deadly that decisions involving national defense must be virtually immediate; thus there is no time for the slow processes of democratic assemblies. Accordingly, it is contended, the Congress should recognize that the United States could be attacked, possibly destroyed before it could even begin to debate a declaration of war and therefore should give over the power to act to the Chief Executive.

A second argument is that many more sources of information about foreign affairs are available to the President than to the Congress and that consequently he is more knowledgeable than the Congress about the requirements of the national interest; and, in any event, foreign relations are so intricate that they call for a kind of expertise the Congress does not have. Moreover, it is contended, much of this information is so "inside" that it cannot be entrusted to the Congress—and obviously not to the people.

In a statement before the Senate Foreign Relations Committee on August 16, 1967, Professor Ruhl J. Bartlett attempted to answer those who defend the extension of Presidential power.

On the argument that the advent of the nuclear age has made a vast difference: "The President has and has always had the duty to use the armed forces at his disposal to repel sudden armed attacks on the United States, and there has never been a case in all history of the United States when the imminence of danger to the nation was so great that decisions to do more than repel attacks could not be entrusted to Congress." (I think Professor Bartlett underestimates the potential speed of attack in the nuclear era; in this regard history seems to offer no guidance for the future.)

On the argument that expertise is needed: "In addition to being insulting, this argument is utterly fallacious. Experts are needed in the mechanics of many things . . . but there are no experts in wisdom concerning human affairs, or in determining the national interest; and there is nothing in the realm of foreign policy that cannot be understood by the average American citizen." (The question here is again the question raised repeatedly in these pages as to whether the average American citizen has the information with which to reach enlightened judgment in such matters. The evidence is that he does not.)

On the argument that secrecy is urgently required: "It is true that diplomatic negotiations, in many instances, may require secrecy, but the results of negotiations and the factors that influence them should be opened to all. Nothing is more destructive to democratic institutions than the concealment of information essential to them." (True, but as Professor Barlett concedes, the slogan should be "open covenants, privately arrived at." And surely military strategy should not be telegraphed to potential enemies.)

Summing up his position, Professor Bartlett says:

"Perhaps in conclusion I may be allowed a judgment on the basis of my study of human affairs and American history. It is that the greatest danger to democracy in the United States and to the freedom of its people and to their welfare is the erosion of legislative authority and oversight and the growth of a vast pyramid of centralized power in the Executive branch of the government.

"The framers of the Constitution bequeathed to the American people a great heritage, that of a Constitutional, federal, representative government, with its powers limited in scope and divided among its three separate branches; and this system was devised, not because it would produce efficiency or world dominion, but because it offered the greatest hope of preventing tyranny."

All this is also true, but the question still is whether we have not entered a new period in which the old theories and philosophy require modification.

Two recent case histories—the war in Southeast Asia and Mr. Nixon's Supreme Court nominations—throw some light on the issue of Presidential versus Congressional power.

The Cambodian Controversy

There has been the sharpest kind of clash between the Chief Executive and the Congress over our operations in Southeast Asia. The story begins in August, 1964, with the adoption of the Gulf of Tonkin Resolution, which authorized the President to "take all necessary measures to repel any armed attack against the forces of the United States and to prevent further aggression." President Johnson gave this reason for requesting adoption of the resolution: "I have concluded that I should now ask the Congress, *on its part,* to join in affirming the national determination that all such attacks will be met and that the United States will continue in its basic policy of assisting the free nations of the area to defend their freedom. I urge Congress to enact such a resolution promptly and thus to give convincing evidence to the aggressive Communist nations that our policy in Southeast Asia will be carried forward."

At intervals, in the course of the Vietnam war, questions have been raised in the Congress about the application of the resolution and assertions made that the President was far exceeding the intended grant of power. Mr. Nixon's widening of the war into Cambodia in the spring of 1970 brought the issue to a head. As Tom Wicker of the *New York Times* wrote, the move revealed "Congressional impotence" and was evidence that "one man alone holds in the world's oldest democracy the absolute power of war and peace, life and death. If that is indeed the pragmatic fact, it is repugnant to the Constitution, to democratic theory and to American ideals; and if that is indeed what the system is come to, it ought to be changed." [5]

In the Congress itself the fight for greater Congressional participation in such prime decisions was led by Senators John Sherman Cooper, Republican of Kentucky, and Frank Church, Democrat of Idaho, who introduced an amendment to a military sales bill intended to prohibit the President from sending any American ground troops into Laos, Thailand, or Cambodia. The purpose of their amendment, the Senators said, was to "prevent the United States from backing into another war in Asia."

The amendment was immediately attacked by President Nixon's supporters as an assault on his powers. Senator Robert Griffin, Republican of Michigan, called the amendment "a slap in the face of

the President that undercuts and undermines him," and Ronald
Ziegler, White House Press Secretary, said that there could be "no
restraint on the powers of the President as Commander-in-Chief as
stated in the Constitution."

The anti-war forces eventually prevailed, and the Senate adopted,
58-37, the Cooper-Church amendment. But when the bill reached
the House, the administration's supporters engaged in a series of
parliamentary maneuvers which succeeded in cutting off debate.
The bill was then passed without the amendment and sent to conference to reconcile the House and Senate versions.

At this point the administration launched its final and strongest
attack on the Cooper-Church amendment. A memorandum from the
State and Defense Departments went to the members of the conference committee, saying: "The Administration opposes this amendment and urges that it be stricken. The restraint imposed by this
section appears to affect the President's exercise of his lawful responsibilities as Commander-in-Chief of the armed forces."

The administration did not succeed in eliminating the amendment
in the conference committee; however, the conference agreed that the
Senate amendment prohibiting the use of ground troops in Laos, Thailand and Cambodia should not prevent the President from taking
any actions he deemed necessary to insure the safe withdrawal of
American troops from South Vietnam or to obtain the release of
American prisoners.

This compromise amendment (approved 234-185 by the House and
70-2 by the Senate) fell far short of what Senators Cooper and Church
had hoped to accomplish.

Despite the administration's success in considerably watering down
the language and force of the amendment, this fact remains: the
approval of the Cooper-Church amendment constituted the first
successful Senate challenge to the President as Commander-in-Chief
voted during a shooting war. It opened the way toward greater Congressional participation in the war-making decisions of the government.

The Court Conflict

The contest over the nomination of Judge Carswell to the Supreme
Court added fuel to the controversy over Presidential power. When

Mr. Nixon sent the nomination to the Senate he set out his concept of Presidential powers in a letter to Senator Saxbe. "What is centrally at issue in this nomination," he wrote, "is the constitutional responsibility of the President to appoint members of the Court — and whether this responsibility can be frustrated by those who wish to substitute their own philosophy or their own subjective judgment for that of the one person entrusted by the Constitution with the power of appointment." The Senate's true role, Mr. Nixon said, was "to advise and consent"; any other role threatened to undermine "the institutional powers of the President."

This view of the Presidency was immediately challenged by Senator Birch Bayh of Indiana, who contested Mr. Nixon's right to "appoint." He quoted Article II, Section 2 of the Constitution, which provides that the President "shall nominate, and by and with the consent of the Senate, shall appoint" Supreme Court members. Mr. Nixon's views were attacked also by Senators McGovern, Mansfield and Javits, who contended that the Senate had the responsibility of judging the merits of the President's nominees to the Court.

There is no doubt, it seems to me, that a good case can be made for the President's right to choose his own men for the Executive branch, but surely the Constitution gives the Senate the right—more than that, the duty—to pass upon the President's nominees to the Court. There is a vast difference between the two categories: the persons the President selects for his Executive departments will be working for him, whereas the members of the Supreme Court should be as independent of him as they are of the third branch of government, the Congress.

A Middle Course

On the one hand, then, you have the President who in using the phrase "advise and consent" accents the "advise" and tends to overlook the "consent" and on the other Congress, which emphasizes the "consent."

There is, in my belief, a feasible middle course. I agree with Senator Javits that the basic issue lies beyond the strictly Constitutional question. It arises out of the fact that President Nixon has overlooked the prescribed role of the Congress in foreign policy. The

President, according to Mr. Javits, rarely takes the Senate into confidence in reaching a decision, whether it be Vietnam or the anti-ballistic missile; "such secrecy is repugnant to the democratic process."

The argument is not so much the Presidential right to declare war as the tradition that the President shall consult with the Congress before important decisions are reached. A group of distinguished lawyers opposed to the invasion of Cambodia observed, in a brief inserted into the *Congressional Record*, that the President's move into Cambodia was "not without historical precedent, and not without justification under a broad interpretation of the collective security theory. However, the real question is whether the balance has shifted too far in favor of the Executive." [6]

As Commander-in-Chief, the President can direct the armed forces of the nation and the Congress can act only after the event when it is usually too late. It can use, as has been suggested, its still unchallenged power over the purse; but even this power cannot alter the reality of the deployment of American troops across a national border. The answer, then, seems to be this: when there is time for consultation — as, for example in the Cambodian invasion—the President shall consult with the Congress; when there is not time—as there was not when the Japanese attacked Pearl Harbor—then the President shall fully brief the Congress on the action he has taken and consult with the Congress on the next steps. Thus can the intent of the Constitution be adapted to the exigencies of the nuclear age.

Presidential Use of Television

Another clash between the Executive and the legislature—and, more broadly, between the President and the opposition, both loyal and disloyal—has arisen over Mr. Nixon's use of television to appeal to the country over the heads of the Congress. In the first eighteen months of his administration, he pre-empted prime television time (the evening hours between 7:30 and 11) more often than the three previous Presidents combined in the 18 years of their administrations. As James Reston put it: "Thoughtful observers have wondered what would happen if a determined president who had both the will and the ability to use the networks effectively really set out to exploit television for his political advantage. President Eisenhower had the personality and the popularity to use television in this way, but not the will. President Kennedy had the ability and the will to use it, but for some unexplained reason was afraid of what he called 'overexposure.' President Johnson had the will but neither the personality nor the ability to use it effectively. But President Nixon has indicated determination and an ability to use televesion to achieve his political objectives." [7]

In an effort to counter the Nixon television campaign, Congressional and other critics asked the networks for free time to present their views, basing their request on the FCC's "fairness doctrine," which stipulates that both sides of an important issue shall be presented over the airwaves. Mr. Fulbright introduced in the Senate a resolution which calls upon television stations to provide at least four opportunities a year for members of the House and Senate to respond to a President on public policies, contending that the House and Senate, as coordinate branches of the government, have the same right to present their views as does the President.

The Columbia Broadcasting System made the first move in response to these various demands; it announced that it would provide prime broadcast time four times a year for the opposition to reply to a Presidential broadcast. Then the FCC, on August 14, 1970, issued a wholly surprising decree—surprising because the chairman of the commission, Dean Burch, is not only a Nixon appointee but also a close associate of the President—asserting that Mr. Nixon had made such extensive use of television to explain and defend his conduct of the Indochina war that "it would be clearly contrary to the public interest if the opponents of that policy could not present their views." Curiously the statement did not refer directly to the President, either as Chief Executive or as Commander-in-Chief; it said the obligation "arises not from a single speech, but from the unusual facts of this case—five addresses by the outstanding spokesman of one side."

Assuming that the opposition should have its days in the TV courts, it is not easy either to write or to apply an exact formula. The FCC discovered this; apparently unable to reach a solution, it left it to the networks to propose one. There are many questions that must be answered before such a formula can be made effective, among them: Who shall speak for the opposition? Members of Congress? If so, what representatives of what group in Congress? Critics outside of government? How is it possible to make a choice among the large number of diversified groups? And who in any group? And how soon after the Presidential statements shall the other side or sides be presented? How much impact can the counter-argument have if a considerable time elapses between the Presidential and the opposing arguments? Shall the President or a Presidential spokesman have the chance to reply to the reply? And how long does this process go on?

These are apparently unanswerable questions and a different approach toward solution of the problem is indicated. One obvious suggestion is that the networks ration the Presidential prime time, giving him such access when he speaks as President and restricting access when he speaks as a propagandist. But even if such a distinction can be made (which is highly doubtful), it seems inconceivable that any network could turn down a Presidential request for time.

As I see it, these fundamentals must be taken into consideration: what the President says is news, no matter how propagandistic or illogical or prejudiced his statements may be; he is the President, he has the power and his words, even though they may be insignificant, have significant impact because of the prestige of his office. Senator Fulbright contends that the President should be treated as an ordinary mortal and not a superman. This may be true, but it is irrelevant. The overriding fact is that the office, if not the man, is uniquely powerful in contrast with that of any other citizen, in the Congress or out.

Assuming, then, that Presidential statements are *per se* news, provision should be made for presentation, immediately after a Presidential utterance or as soon as possible thereafter, of a debate between those who support the President and those who oppose him. In this way the dilemma could be resolved and useful discussion achieved.

Another step by way of restoring the balance between executive and legislature is suggested. While Mr. Nixon has been using television as no President before him has used it, the members of Congress have been making their rebuttals either in the often-deserted legislative chambers or on television programs, many of which are presented during off-hours. Moreover, even if such programs are aired during on-hours, they face competition with the "Gunsmokes" and "Laugh-ins" whereas the President, when he speaks, has all three networks as his outlets. Except for the occasions when a Congressional committee permits its presence at a hearing, television is now barred from the Congressional chambers. The proposal is that all the proceedings in the Congress be televised as a means of offsetting the Executive's advantage.

Objection has been voiced to a television presence in the Congress on the ground that members would become actors, playing up to the cameras. But in the televising of the proceedings of many state legislatures this has not proved to be the case. Nor is it true of sessions at the United Nations, where the delegates carry on the business at hand seemingly without regard to the cameras. As for the Congress, if a member is too frequently absent or nods, un-Homer-like, during an important debate, the reaction back home would surely alert or even waken him.

*   *   *

There is no doubt that, whatever the solution, the President will have the advantage; the voters gave him that advantage by electing him to office. This is the way of democracy, which basically is a system that provides freedom to elect and freedom to turn the rascals out. If this issue of executive versus legislative power indicates a fault in the democratic system, so be it; it should not be greatly deplored because that same system bestows so much more in the way of benefit.

So much for the President—his problems, his performance, his political acumen. And now, in the next chapter, a profile of the second of the large government forces that reflect and mold public opinion: the Congress of the United States.

14: The Role of Congress: Mirror and Molder

In the public opinion process the Congress plays a double and often decisive role: it reflects (or tries to reflect) the popular viewpoint and to some extent helps to mold it. It is through his Congressman that the voter can make his opinion heard in Washington — by personal contact, by letter, ultimately by his vote. These are the people's delegates, the House of Representatives and the Senate too.

Congressmen Are People

What manner of people are the members of these august bodies? Here are the vital statistics for the 92nd Congress: the average age of Senators is 56.4 years, of members of the House, 51.9; of the 534 members of the House and Senate, 301 are lawyers by profession; there is one black in the Senate and 12 in the House, one woman in the Senate, 12 in the House.

There is indubitably a generation gap. Power is based on longevity, not on competence or even on the vote of their colleagues. Of 21 chairmen in the House, three are in their 80's, six in their 70's, nine in their 60's, two in their 50's and only one in his 40's. Of the 17 chairmen in the Senate, one is in his 80's, five in their 70's, four in their 60's, six in their 50's, and again only one in his 40's. These older men wield enormous power; they determine in large part what bills shall reach the floor for discussion and vote. Although they generally have the advantage of experience over their younger colleagues, in many if not most instances their creative powers have waned and they are stubbornly set against change.

The younger members in both parties are calling for reform of the seniority system used in assigning committee chairmanships. Up to now, however, the reformers' only alternative has been a proposal that the party caucus review all seniority candidates, but this change would not affect most of the present chairmen. In his annual report as minority leader in January, 1970 Senator Hugh Scott concluded with a quotation from the Latin: "All things are changing, and we are changing with them." Apparently, though, Congress is not changing fast enough for him, because he added: "Clearly the temper of this age of Aquarius calls for less bureaucratic omphaloskepsis"— meaning "contemplation of one's navel as part of a mystical exercise." (As for the Age of Aquarius, it is astrologically speaking, the "age of enlightenment"—an era when the young rise up, disavow the old beliefs and renounce the old believers.)

Robert Bendiner, a *New York Times* editorial writer, says that, "Congress as an institution has failed over a long span of years to change in the least degree with the times. In its organization, its division into feudal baronies, its veneration of procedures which are neither democratic nor efficient, it is in fact running a grave risk of becoming no more than a negative check on the Executive Branch or perhaps a captious subordinate of the judiciary." [1]

Critics of Congressional procedures have suggested, among others, these reforms: that the chairmanships be rotated among the members of each committee; that the Speaker of the House appoint chairmen, subject to the approval of the party caucus; and that the term of office be four years with a three-term limit on any one occupant. To further democratize committee proceedings, the critics suggest that whenever a majority of a committee desires to hold a meeting it be able to do so (under present rules, only the chairman is so empowered).

The Tough Job of Law-Making

The process of legislation is a complex and extensive one. The number of decisions a Congressman must make is staggering—and constantly increasing; ten years ago there were fewer than 100 roll call votes in a single session of the House; today the number approaches 250.

The scope of issues in fantastically wide. In a single day the House recently discussed "the financing of airport facilities, the disposal of surplus lead, the sale and advertising of cigarettes, Congressional ethics, the use of Defense Department facilities for the production of movies, aid to the arts, the treatment of laboratory animals, the creation of a national wildlife refuge, textile imports, the payment of postal employees, chemical and biological warfare research, patents and copyrights, and more." [2]

How well equipped are the members of the Congress to deal effectively with legislation so wide in range and so complex in character? How knowledgeable and perceptive are they? They are, I am convinced, more informed, more thoughtful and more conscientious than critics generally rate them. By and large, most of them at least try to make an earnest effort to understand issues so that they can vote intelligently.

On the whole the members of Congress are somewhat better informed and more sensitive to public opinion than many of the "Elite" —including editors. Inexact as Congressional methods of measuring opinion may be, the members make periodic attempts to gauge it. Because of the complexity of current affairs it is almost impossible for a member to have complete knowledge about matters that range from the ABM to post offices; but they study reports, they hold committee hearings, they have staffs that provide help by way of summation and information.

The views of colleagues have a substantial impact on a member of Congress. A legislator must make many decisions on issues about which he has insufficient knowledge and for which there is no consensus of constituent opinion; in these cases he will often rely on the judgment of an associate. Or he may turn to a member whose district is similar to his own rather than undertake the sometimes difficult task of polling his own voters.

In any analysis of the Congress a fundamental distinction between Senate and House must be made: a Senator must answer to the public only once every six years, a Representative three times as often. Fletcher Thompson, a Representative from Georgia, says: "A Congressman cannot afford the luxury of being a statesman, as a Senator can. A Congressman runs every two years. He can't run very far from basic public opinion in his district or he won't get re-elected. A Senator can do this; only in the last two or three years must he be really concerned about his appeal to the public."

Three Basic Questions

These are the three fundamental questions that confront every member of Congress in making decisions as to how he shall vote:

How shall he determine, inasmuch as he is presumed to be their spokesman, what are the wishes of his constituents?

Having, if possible, appraised this "public opinion," shall he look upon it as a mandate to be followed without questioning or shall he act according to his own best judgment?

If the mandate and his own judgment are in conflict, how should he then educate his constituents to what he considers the "right" opinion?

In an effort to obtain light on these issues, I sent a questionnaire to the members of Congress. Replies were received from 15 Senators and 94 Representatives; in addition, 17 Senators and 11 Representatives were interviewed personally. The sample that resulted is a representative one, both geographically and politically, and it provides the basis for the observations and conclusions that follow.

Survey of the Influences

Asked what influences determine their voting decisions, 101 of the 137 members of Congress who responded in the survey said that the most important factor was their own viewpoint; only 36 placed constituency opinion first. But these figures should be taken with large grains of salt. Most members are influenced by "grass roots" sentiment; almost all strive constantly to discover it. In any case, all members should try to fathom it because even if their votes, as many of them contend, are influenced by their consciences rather than their soundings, they should be aware of public opinion so that they can educate it even if they do not bow to it.

Communication between legislator and voter is, of course, vital to the democratic process. Significantly, 62 of the 137 members listed "personal contacts" as the single most important method of determining opinion trends in their districts; 52 listed it as second or third.

Members of Congress generally consider the mail from constituents an invaluable clue to public opinion even though there are studies showing that fewer than a quarter of the voters have ever written to their representatives in Washington. Twenty members in the Congressional survey listed the mail as the most important factor in influencing their decisions; 75 others rated it second or third.

An enormous volume of mail pours into the Congressional post-offices; deliveries take place five times a day in the House, some members receiving several hundred letters daily. Representative Jim Wright of Texas says: "When Congress is in session and the Senator or Representative is work-chained to his desk often for weeks on end without the opportunity of a trip home and touching base personally with the voters, he becomes increasingly sensitive to the opinions expressed in the letters, telegrams and petitions sent by his constituents." [3]

Senator Harry Byrd, Jr., of Virginia says: "I try to see as many letters as I can, especially those that affect legislation, or give viewpoints on matters before Congress. Most Senators don't do this. I spend four hours a day reading mail. They say I'm a damn fool to spend so much time on it. But I say it's damn foolish to get out of touch with your constituents."

Other Senators pay much less attention to mail. William Spong, Jr., of Virginia says, "There are five million people in Virginia. Even at peak periods, the mail we get represents a very small percentage of them. We must assume that some of the people we don't hear from will be on the other side of the issue." There are two facts that support the Spong view: those who disagree with their representatives are much more likely to write letters than those who agree; and mail is often generated by organizations which persuade people to sign form letters endorsing their causes.

Augustus Hawkins, who represents a low-education constituency in California, says: "Mail is not a good indication. My district is not too sophisticated in terms of writing. And the few who do write don't reflect the true sentiments of the area. Those persons involved in a situation may be a poor indication of public sentiment in general."

Polls — And Non-Polls

Another guide to public opinion considered important by members of Congress is the personal poll. Of the 137 members questioned 89 take some sort of survey, usually as part of their newsletters. Twenty-four listed such polls as their chief sources of information about their constituents' views, and 40 more placed them second or third.

Polls by members of Congress, usually done by mail, follow few sound   sampling procedures; often they go not to a representative group but to whoever happens to be on the legislator's mailing list. Moreover, there is no way to ensure that they will be returned; the suspicion is that the completion rate is no higher than 20%. Frequently the questions asked are biased, reflecting the leanings of the legislator who often uses the results as justification for maintaining a position. For instance, the first page of a newsletter sent out by Congressman Fletcher Thompson of Georgia was devoted almost entirely to arguments in favor of the Safeguard Missile System; it reported that "one of the strongest foes of the Safeguard System was the *Daily World*, a Communist paper," and it put this question: "Do you favor installing Safeguard missiles to protect America from foreign nuclear missile attack?" The response was 80% in the affirmative.

In response to a request for an appraisal of Congressional polls, Dr. George Gallup said: "The results [of these polls] pertain to some select, often unspecified group of respondents—and not to the opinions and attitudes of all the voters of a particular district. This is disastrous, because the results are usually falsely interpreted by the Congressman and presumably by the general public as representing the opinions of the leaders of a particular district." He added: "The only bad polling done in America is done by Congressmen. They are still doing a stupid and primitive job."

Most Congressmen do not pay much attention to polls of the type taken by Gallup and Louis Harris, primarily because they are national, whereas the members' major concerns are local or regional. Some express distrust of such polls; Representative Martha Griffiths of Michigan says: "That's their own theory of what the American people think. It's not my theory." And Representative John Conyers of Michigan says: "My judgments can't turn on how they feel. The problem is, how can I affect their opinions?" Representative Richard Fulton of Tennessee agrees: "I don't pay any attention to polls. I think we are elected on the basis that the people we represent will expect us to be well-informed on issues. I don't think the people in my district would want me to vote for or against legislation just because Harris or Gallup polls indicated public opinion one way or the other."

The determination of constituent feeling is often the most difficult task faced by a member of Congress. Obviously it is easier for a Representative to assess opinion in a small district than for a Senator to gauge statewide sentiment, and simpler for Senators from the smaller states than for those from the more populous ones. For a Representative from a homogeneous district the task is, of course, easier than for one with a mixed constituency where there is rarely a consensus.

Donald R. Matthews and James A. Stimson, in a paper read at the 1969 meeting of the American Political Science Association, made this statement: "In order to test the wind, there has to be some wind blowing; constituents must have opinions and somehow communicate them to their representatives. Members agree that their constituents seldom tell them what they want to hear. Their communication, generally, is concerned with matters of small significance but large feeling. 'I think the only time they become really concerned,' one member said, 'is when we have emotional issues . . . . but in maybe 90 per cent of the bills, they take no interest at all.' Other members say that sometimes their constituents are vocal on important matters, but only if they are personally affected."

Most legislators say that they get their best feel of public sentiment on their visits home. For example, Senator John Pastore of Rhode Island puts his confidence in what he calls a "grass roots poll:"

"Take Vietnam as an example. Well, I go back home and I go to the political club and there are fifteen guys there I have known for a long time and they tell me what they think and what they feel the people around them think. I believe they are better sounders of public opinion than the pollsters, so I get a fill-in from them. They tell me that something has to be done about Vietnam because people are fed up with it.

"Then I go to church and after the services women come to me and talk as we have talked for years about their thoughts and they say that what is going on in Vietnam is the slaughter of the best of American youth and somehow it has to end. Then I go to the Rotary Club and they tell me how they feel about things and it all adds up. So this is my idea of what the voice of the people is and I suspect it is as good as any so-called scientific survey—in fact, much better, because people talk freely to me, whom they have known for years, whereas they are very suspicious of any outside interviewer."

"A Ball of Wax"

What complicates the task of determining constituent opinion is a lack of basic information among the voters. On the question of knowledgeability most respondents in the survey asserted that their constituents are better informed today than ten or fifteen years ago, attributing this progress to improvement in the news media and to an increase in educational opportunities. (A note of caution: there is a tendency among members of Congress to contend that their districts or states are better informed that the rest of the country; it certainly ups their egos if they convince themselves that they are the chosen of the chosen people. Representatives from Iowa, California, Vermont and Wyoming, for example, rated their constituents as being above the national level in public information—surely dubious claims.)

On the other hand, Representative Richard Bolling of Missouri reports that he has come to the conclusion that the public generally has scant interest in many legislative issues: "Seventy-five per cent of my constituents don't have strong, detailed, views on Vietnam. Yet 90 per cent have views on flood control. That is a narrow, district-oriented issue. The nearer to them an issue is, the more likely there will be a consensus."

Warren Miller and Donald Stokes of Michigan University's Survey Research Center report: "Far from looking over the shoulder of their Congressman at the legislative game, most Americans are almost totally uninformed about legislative issues in Washington. The representative has very imperfect information about the issue preferences of his constituency, and the constituents' awareness of the policy stands of the representative ordinarily is slight." [4]

It is clearly not easy to pin down with any assurance the influences that operate on members of Congress. Messrs. Miller and Stokes report that no single factor influences a legislator's decisions; sometimes he follows his conscience, sometimes he looks to his district, sometimes to his party, sometimes to other factors; the choice of a course depends primarily on the type of issue involved.

Senator Jack Miller of Iowa offers this summation: "It's quite a ball of wax. You end up with a feeling. There's nothing particularly scientific about it."

Mandate or Conscience?

Whatever methods are used to appraise opinion, there remain two other questions that confront the member of the Congress: Shall he merely ascertain the majority view in his district or state and unquestioningly vote its desires, or shall he exercise independent judgment? And if he moves on his own, how does he deal with the dissent of a large group, possibly a majority among his constituents?

Senator Franch Church of Idaho describes the dilemma: "Some things come along on which, for one reason or another, opinion is absolutely and wholly formed. To oppose that opinion is to invite political defeat—immediate death. Then you must weigh its importance. Is this an issue of such importance to the country that I should take a stand and take defeat, or should I reflect the viewpoint of my constituents—recognizing the facts of life?"

Some members of the Congress adhere to the mandate theory. Senator Warren Magnuson of Washington, for instance, states bluntly that "the representative should try to ascertain what is the will of the people and carry out that will." Others advocate the opposite course—the course of conscience. Representative Philip Burton of California says: "I have long since established in the eyes of my constituents that I am my own man, that I weigh the facts, not the mail, and that I do not respond to political pressures, either from home or subtle political pressures in Congress."

Most legislators strike a balance between the two philosophies and follow a kind of formula evolved by Senator Alan Cranston: "Where there's a fundamental principle involved, I must vote my conscience. When it's not that important, I consider public opinion." Senator Byrd feels he has a two-fold obligation: "One is to represent the people. But you owe them more than that; they pay you $42,000 a year and they expect you to analyze and study the issues and to reach conscientious conclusions. They don't have the access to information or the time or the interest to do such study and analysis on their own."

On domestic issues, such as taxation or civil rights, a member of the Congress is likely to follow his constituency's wishes; in foreign affairs, largely because his constituents are so unknowledgeable in this area, he usually feels free to exercise his own judgment—except, of course, on such emotional issues as Vietnam. Or if he is inclined not to trust his own conclusions in world concerns he looks to the party leaders for guidance.

Often a member of the Congress, in appraising public opinion, comes to the conclusion that a majority of his constituents disagree with him on a particular issue. (In our survey only two respondents reported that they *never* disagreed with the opinion in their districts; 76 others said they were *often* in disagreement.) If a member of Congress decides to follow his own judgment rather than the popular viewpoint, most legislators agree that he must try to educate his constituents to his own thinking through television and newspaper interviews, newsletters, speeches and personal contacts. Senator Griffin of Michigan says that public opinion operates on a "two-way street": "If a Congressman votes the way he thinks is right and is defeated, he has made a real error in failing to inform his constituents. He is a molder of opinion and defeat means that he has not done a good job of education."

Representative Bolling of Missouri feels the same way: "I believe I am skillful in the methods of communication. I use all of these very energetically when I am aware there is a difference of opinion. I have a major responsibility to lead, not to be merely the recipient of polls. One must be a skillful communicator."

Other members of Congress—they constitute a minority—do not try to educate their constituents to their own views when there is disagreement. Former Senator Ralph Yarborough of Texas says that he does not believe there is much that can be done by way of such education: "I usually vote and don't explain. If the media are against you on an issue, it is not necessary to explain; it means the public is going to be against you."

If, as often happens, a member of Congress differs vigorously with his constituency on important issues, how does he manage to get elected? Senator J. William Fulbright of Arkansas is an obvious example. His foreign policy position is certainly contrary to that of most of his constituents, yet he has been repeatedly re-elected. One part of the answer is his willingness to carry out his voters' desires on civil rights issues; so long as he does not oppose segregation they will forgive him any possible "mistakes" in foreign affairs. The other part of the anwer is the excellent job Senator Fulbright performs in taking care of Arkansas' special needs.

Mr. Fulbright's system provides an almost textbook pattern. He has addressed himself to the task of raising the standard of living in Arkansas as a whole and he has used what he calls his "surplus approval" gained thereby to freely take foreign policy positions which he feels are in the national interest. Not long ago Mr. Fulbright was seen in the lobby of a Washington hotel on his way to a reception of the National Feed Grain Association; he carried two bulging briefcases—one with foreign policy material and the other with Arkansas homework. He explained: "The connection is by way of Arkansas. The state is a large producer of feed grain. And if I don't feed on Arkansas' problems of feed grain, I won't get a chance to feed on the nation's problems of foreign policy."

All members of Congress perform a type of local service in some degree or other. Representative Bolling, a liberal from a conservative Missouri district, openly attributes his success at the polls to this factor. "I get elected because I do an absolutely great job of constituency service," he says. "That's an essential part of a Congressman's function. Every legislative contact that I can make with my constituents I make . . . I get the bacon—their share and a little more . . . I campaign on the fact that I get things done for Kansas City." If a Congressman brings home the bacon his constituents are likely to reward him with a well-cooked vote.

Previous chapters have described the pressures on members of Congress: from the White House, from their constituents, from their home "establishments," from their party leaders. One pressure, far from being the least important, is that exerted by the lobbies. This is the theme of the next chapter.

15: The Lobbies: Some Good, More Bad

The British had the word for it: "lobby," meaning corridor or passage. When the House of Commons voted, members walked into two "division lobbies," the "ayes" into one, the "nays" into the other. There was also the "entrance lobby" where members met the public, to be button-holed or otherwise influenced. Thus the pressures applied to the legislators became known as "lobbying." The British invented the word; we perfected the practice.

Of the forces playing on the Congress, the lobby is among the most mysterious and the most debated. Some say it serves a useful purpose; others indict it as wholly pernicious; neutral opinions are few. But, whatever the evaluation, lobbying is big business in the Congressional halls, in the clubs, on the golf courses and in other "Elite" places in which Senators and Representatives gather with their peers and former peers.

The Uncertain Statistics

Trustworthy statistics about the extent and accurate information about the methods of lobbying are hard to come by. The Regulation of Lobbying Act, a measure passed in 1946, calls for little more than the reporting of limited types of information; moreover, it does not really control or "regulate" lobbying. However, it is estimated that there are probably 6,000 to 7,000 lobbyists operating on the Congress (which would make it a baker's dozen of lobbyists for each Congressman) and a like number focusing their efforts on the Executive Branch. Even though lobbyists report expenditures of only four or five million dollars a year, the amount they spend to persuade or pressure the law-framers and the law-makers in Washington and to water the "grass roots" at the lower levels is probably close to a billion dollars annually.

A lobbyist, according to the Regulation of Lobbying Act, is one who exerts "direct pressure" on the Congress, but this does not take into account all the lobbying that is done to influence the public directly and thus the Congress indirectly.

The vagueness about lobby operations directed at Congress is compounded because no federal agency has the clear responsibility for checking reports and making certain that all lobbyists are registered. The House clerk and the secretary of the Senate merely receive and collate the reports; and the long-standing policy of the Justice Department has been not to seek out violations on its own but to act only if a very serious complaint is brought from outside. As a result, there have been fewer than a half-dozen prosecutions since 1946.

The Variety of Lobbies

There are two basic types of lobbies: groups with a single interest and groups which function in areas covering broad spectrums. The list of single interest lobbies is almost endless, but few of them have the influence of the broad-range groups. Of the latter, the AFL-CIO is among the most active, with a half dozen lobbyists, a research staff, many publications and multiple allies among labor and other organizations; it covers a wide range of issues, from civil rights and welfare to product safety. However, the influence of labor has declined in recent years because the unions are no longer growing as rapidly as they did in the period after World War II and because in recent elections labor leaders have been unable to deliver the votes as they once did.

The Chamber of Commerce of the U. S., with about 35 professional employees, a half dozen registered lobbyists and channels to business groups all over the country, plays much the same role on the political right as labor does on the political left. Like labor, it is concerned with many issues; it was active in the fight against the one-man, one-vote philosophy, in the defeat of the oil pollution bill in 1968 and in developing backing for Judges Haynesworth and Carswell. Other important broad-spectrum groups include the National Association of Manufacturers and the American Medical Association.

There has been a decline in the influence of the once powerful farm bloc. Only about thirty or forty members of Congress now come from districts with any substantial rural populations; the farm bloc cannot win a House vote on its own and needs urban support. Nevertheless agriculture still maintains a large lobby; the big three of its pressure groups are the American Farm Federation, the National Farmers' Union and the National Grange.

Representing private electric power is the National Association of Electric Companies, the top spokesman for an enormously powerful segment of industry. Also in the public power sector are the United Mine Workers, who fear coal will lose out to other fuels; and the oil and natural gas industries which compete with coal in the power fuel market. The effectiveness of the oil lobby was demonstrated when it won three major legislative victories in the 1969-70 session of Congress involving liability for oil tankers, pollution depletion allowances and import quotas.

The housing and urban affairs interests maintain a massive contingent of lobbyists. The most prominent are the representatives of the National Association of Real Estate Boards, which led the fight against open housing legislation a few years ago, and the National Housing Conference, a liberal group linked to the labor movement.

Taken together, the defense and aerospace industries probably form the largest and most powerful lobby bloc in the capital. The group includes all the big automobile makers, technology firms and airplane companies. The Aerospace Industries Association reported lobbying expenditures of $23,783 in 1968 but this probably represents only the amount spent for postage stamps.

The defense-aerospace complex has enormous influence in the Congress because of its size, the large number of persons it employs, and the importance of defense contracts. Its lobbyists persistently press for bigger government spending on weapons and maximum military "preparedness" in general. Not surprisingly, they find considerable sympathy and support in the Pentagon.

Most of the Defense Departments technical data about weapons and their potential role are compiled by defense aerospace companies. With rare exceptions, the Congress is not equipped to challenge such information or the conclusions based upon it. (The anti-ballistic missile debate provided such an exception; Senators were able to question the workability of the proposed system only because those leading the fight against the ABM, had the advice of their own experts and scientists.)

The National Association of Broadcasters, a potent outfit with a permanent staff in the capital, represents the radio and television industries. In times of "crisis" officers of the networks fly down from New York and spokesmen for the state associations of broadcasters join the procession.

The expansion of federal activities in various areas has brought about the formation of new groups of lobbyists such as those speaking for the civil rights movement (still represented primarily by the National Association for the Advancement of Colored People), welfare and health services, teachers, urban and suburban interests, and small business.

The Lobby Gambits

Methods of lobbying as well as the nature of lobbyists have changed. "Grass-roots" lobbying plays a more important role than it once did; this is particularly true since the advent of television. And with the growing complexity of government and the increase in decision making by the executive branch, lobbying of the executive departments by private groups has greatly increased. This typically is the way a lobbyist functions:

Step 1: An effective operator ferrets out "inside information," through personal contact with members of the Congress and with government officials. In this respect, former Congressmen and former federal employees have great advantages; they have easy access to ex-colleagues; they know where to find information which is not generally available; they have entry to high officials who do not bother with the ordinary run of visitors; and, in soliciting legislators' support, they promise political backing and campaign contributors.

Step 2: The lobbyist prepares a brief setting out his client's cause and rebutting the opposing case. This requires the services of research specialists, of attorneys who develop legal points and writers who prepare statements for submission to Congressional committees and distribution to the press.

Step 3: The lobbyist is then ready to go into action. He may appear at a Congressional committee meeting or he may have personal discussions with members, often over cocktails or at dinner. Meanwhile, a public relations campaign has been launched, designed to apply the "grass-roots" pressure—advertising, speeches, and appeals to the public to write to members of the Congress in behalf of the cause the lobbyist espouses.

The amount of time, manpower and money expended on these efforts would seem to indicate that the lobbyist is highly effective. Yet if the responses to our Congressional questionnaire are to be believed, lobbying has only a negligible influence on a Congressman's voting decisions; only six members listed lobbying as among the top three determinants of their votes. This may be because there are so many different groups exerting pressure that a Congressman does not feel the need of responding to any single group and this kind of balancing off allows him far more freedom of action than he would otherwise have. Or it may be that legislators are reluctant to admit they are susceptible to lobbying efforts.

The Case Con and Pro

The basic argument against lobbying is that the lobbyist exerts unusual pressure to gain benefits for his client, regardless of the basic rightness of his cause or the potential ill-effects on the community. An industry with the money to hire an expert public relations firm, a battery of researchers and knowledgeable, well-connected lobbyists can get a hearing in the Congress, particularly if it has political muscle. A skillful lobbyist can distort or blanket out the needs of a group with a far more worthy case but without the financial resources to carry on a propaganda campaign.

The basic argument for lobbying is that it is an indispensable mechanism for supplying to the Congress information required for legislating that is not otherwise available, for facilitating an exchange of ideas and for furnishing clues as to how public opinion is running. For example, when the Congress is drafting civil rights legislation, the judiciary committees attempt to find out what the Negro community wants and needs by talking, in private and at length, with spokesmen for the NAACP and other black groups.

The facts about hunger in the United States—while well known to a handful of government experts and advisers to minority organizations—received scant public attention for many years. Then, at a little publicized meeting late in 1966, some black leaders, a few welfare officials and former spokesmen of the anti-poverty crusade met and decided to make hunger a major issue to take the place of the anti-poverty crusade. Money was supplied by foundations and union groups; women's organizations provided articulate support. What emerged was the widely publicized report of the Citizens Crusade Against Hunger. With the aid of Senators McGovern, Kennedy, Clark, and Javits, and some members of the House of Representatives, this citizens' lobby began to pound home the fact that ten to fifteen million Americans were hungry amid the greatest agricultural abundance in the world's history. And slowly the crusade began to have an impact on opinion.

The value of lobbying has been demonstrated also on the many occasions when the Congress has prepared legislation to implement agricultural programs. At hearings before the agriculture committee of both houses, representatives of the farm lobbying groups have revealed potential inequities. For example, in an effort to hold down surpluses the Congress proposed to compute a farmer's harvested acreage for certain specific years to determine what he might plant in the future; at the hearing on the bill, a lobbyist for Kansas wheat growers reported that in three of the five years to be covered by the computation there were terrible blights in his part of the country and the harvested acreage was therefore far below the norm.

Medicare was promoted through a lobbying effort started by the AFL-CIO. A key factor in obtaining the legislation was the labor movement's crusade to bring to the attention of the Congress and the public the facts about the appalling plight of the elderly. Urban problems constitute another area where the informational aspect of lobbying has been useful. A score of cities and states have in recent years established offices and hired representatives in Washington in an effort to show why more federal funds are needed and to keep up with the proliferation of federal programs (there are now at least 400) that affect states and localities.

The Congress, in its attempt to curb the abuses of lobbying, has found itself involved in Constitutional questions. To say a man cannot run an advertisement opposing some policy would almost certainly breach the First Amendment; to say he cannot approach the Congress with some request would impinge on the people's right to petition their elected representatives.

But some legislative changes are essential: the creation of an enforcement unit to check reports and prosecute those who lobby but do not register or file accountings; the setting of unequivocal standards for reporting expenditures, including the amounts expended on "grassroots" lobbying; provision for government disclosure of meaningful reports; the closing of loopholes that exempt such organizations as the Chamber of Commerce and the National Association of Manufacturers from filing spending reports.

All in all, however, lobbies constitute an important and probably necessary component of the Congressional process; reform of the lobby system, not its abolition, seems to be the right course.

So much then for the first of the great forces that tend to mold opinion — the government, predominantly the Executive and the Congress. The second important influence is that exerted by the news media. The discussion of these begins in the following chapter.

Part III

THE MEDIA

In these chapters the role of the media in the opinion process is described—the electronic media: television and radio; and the print media: mainly newspapers.

These questions, among others, are discussed: What makes—and what should make—news? What sort of job is the press doing? Where is television headed, if any place? Has the newspaper a future? Can the press overcome its credibility and responsibility gaps?

16: The Press: Contrasts and Contradictions

Nowhere in the world and at no time in history has communication been as extensive and the instruments of communication as potentially powerful as they are today in the United States. Of the "outside" forces that mold public opinion, the media of mass communication are surely among the foremost: the electronic forms — television and radio; and the printed forms—the newspaper and the magazine. "The power of the press" is a phrase universally accepted. (The term "press" is used in these pages as including all the instruments designed to provide information to the public.)

The Basic Statistics

In recent years television has added new dimensions and new "ghosts" (those disconcerting shadows that inadvertently appear on the screen and are symbolic of TV's miscues) to the communications picture. There are approximately 881 TV stations in the country, 682 commercial and 199 educational. Of the nation's households, 94% have at least one TV set; the average set, it is reported, is tuned in six and a half hours a day; between his second and sixty-fifth birthday, a member of the so-called "television generation" will spend the equivalent of all his waking hours for 3,000 days—more than eight years of his life—before a TV set. By the time a five-year old child enters kindergarten, he will have spent more time in front of the TV set than is expended by a B.A. student in a classroom during his four years in college.[1]

Even though television has grown to giant proportions and even though it attracts twice as many advertising dollars as any other medium, it has not eliminated radio. Far from it. Radio beams its programs daily from more than 6,224 commercial stations; radio sets outsell TV sets two to one: there are now almost 300 million of them in use, 80 million of them in automobiles.

The newspaper statistics are likewise impressive—1,752 daily and

8,855 weekly newspapers, with a total circulation of 62½ million copies a day. The increase in recent years has been nearly a million copies annually, but this growth has not kept pace with the population increase. The newspaper percentage of the press advertising dollar has decreased, from 31.8% in 1959 to 29.5% in 1970. (The annual advertising pie in 1970 was valued at $19.6 billion, of which $5.745 billions went to newspapers.)

The category of print media includes 1,800 magazines if numerous trade publications are counted. But no more than 100 of these are entitled to claim either wide circulation or significant impact on opinion. The variety is almost infinite: magazines appealing to men in the street, women in the kitchens, playboys, doctors, lawyers, et al. They range in circulation from the *Readers Digest*, with a sale of more than 17 million copies, to certain avant garde publications which appear almost at the whim of the publishers or when there happens to be cash in the bank.

In this book the concentration in the print category is on newspapers because these are the important media in the formation of opinion. The newsweeklies certainly have a news readership but they are in the main secondary rather than primary productions. Books obviously also influence opinions but we are dealing here with publications and instruments that have more immediate news impact.

The Large Impacts

The great impact of the mass media on public emotion and the considerable, though lesser, impact on public thought are constantly demonstrated.

Consider these episodes in the annals of electronic communication: *in the early days*—the hysteria produced by the Orson Welles broadcast of the "invasion from Mars" (1938); the revulsion that came with television's unmasking of Senator McCarthy in the '50's; *later*—the shock of actually viewing, on the screen, the killing of Lee Harvey Oswald; the long ordeal of the Bobby Kennedy funeral; the fascination in watching, from the living room, the landings on the moon; *today*—the conflicting emotions aroused by the portrayal of the horrors and the bravery, the hopes and the futilities of the Vietnam conflict.

Consider also the potency of the printed word: *in the past*—the stir created by the newspaper disclosures of the Tweed Ring's hold on New York City and of the Teapot Dome Scandal involving links between industry and the government; the large hopes for the League of Nations and the United Nations inspired in the beginning by the press—and the later disappointments; the response to the words of a Woodrow Wilson or a Franklin Roosevelt or a John Kennedy; *more recently*—the shock over the My Lai incident in Vietnam; the frustrations induced by the portrayal of the campus rebellions; the puzzlement over the contradictory reports about inflation; the demand for prison reform that came after Attica.

Television and radio have tremendous mass appeal; the newspapers generally, with the exception of the tabloids (the term is used here to indicate a type of newspaper rather than a format), are most likely to attract the "Elite" and those who look to the "Elite" for guidance. The newspaper is an institution with a long tradition and potentially the medium best qualified for the task of presenting information. Television unabashedly sets entertainment as its first priority; radio, even though it devotes more time to public affairs than does television, still puts its emphasis and its chips on entertainment.

Each of the media has advantages and disadvantages. Television and radio have the assets of speed and immediacy; TV's pictorial impact is obviously a plus, yet its liabilities arise in a way out of this same plus (if a news program is based largely on film, there is little time for explanation). The newspaper has advantages in range of coverage, in space, and of course, in convenience. In addition to these general differences, there are three specific and salient ones—in controls, in techniques, and in advertising.

Basic Fact: TV Is Licensed

The fundamental difference between the electronic and the print media is that one is regulated and the other is not. This is a decisive factor in the viewpoints of the media and in the public's attitudes toward them. Anyone is free to start a newspaper and to pronounce in it what he damn well or badly pleases, theoretically at least. "Theoretically" because to launch a newspaper these days involves a

large investment; in a medium-sized city the cost is $5 million or
more; the purchase of a newspaper in a metropolitan area requires
even larger sums. Samuel I. Newhouse paid $51 million to add the
Cleveland Plain Dealer to his chain, and the Knight Newspapers, Inc.,
paid $55 million for the *Philadelphia Inquirer* and the *Philadelphia
Daily News.*

There is no requirement of government license, no official prescrip-
tion of standards to which a newspaper must conform, no limit on the
number of newspapers, no government controls, so long as the laws
governing monopolistic practices are not violated.

Television and radio, on the other hand, are licensed by the government. It cannot be otherwise; the airwaves and frequencies are held
to be in the public domain and therefor subject to regulation for
"the good of all the people." The problem is that there are too few
channels—or at least too few desirable ones—to meet the calls for
their use, not only from commercial and public television and radio,
but also from the military, the police, the transcontinental telephone
and teletype services, the forestry and the rural electric service and
many others.

Because of technological limitations (a channel has room for only
one broadcast signal at a given time) there cannot be unregulated
competition on the airwaves. If broadcasters were free to select their
own channels, there would be chaos; the more than 7,000 television
and radio stations would be jumping frequencies and interfering with
one another's programs—which happened in the 1920's at a time
when there were far fewer stations.

The broadcasters argue insistently that the First Amendment
guaranteeing freedom of the press applies to them in the same sense
and with the same emphasis as it does to the newspaper. But for the
very reason that the electronic media are regulated and the print
media are not, this reasoning is false. In the case of the electronic
press, because of the limitation of channels, there must be selection and
regulation—tasks performed by the Federal Communications Commission. So the electronic press is not free in the sense that the print
press is.

On what basis, one asks, can the Federal Communications Commission decide to grant or renew licenses except on the basis of performance?

The Communications Act of 1934 prescribed that the FCC require that the nature of service rendered be "as public convenience, interest or necessity requires." Licenses are granted for periods of no longer than three years; at the end of each period, the stations must apply for renewal. The Commission consists of seven members appointed by the President for seven-year terms; no more than four Commissioners can belong to the same political party and Senate confirmation is required for their appointments. Thus the system of executive-legislative checks and balances is in effect, but the nature of a Commissioner's role makes him judge, legislator and administrator.

The mathematics of licensing are startling. A TV station pays an amount 12 times that of a high-cost 30-second spot commercial for its yearly license; a radio station, 24 times the cost of a single one-minute spot announcement. This amounts, in the case of CBS's television station in New York City to about $80,000 and for the two CBS radio stations in New York to an approximate total of $10,000 per year.

Because of substantial advertising revenue, a television station is highly valuable property; in 1969 sponsors spent $3 billion on TV advertising; a one-minute network commercial during a professional football game can cost $75,000. It is estimated that the average TV station recovers the amount of its investment (in plant, services etc.) in a three-year period. This is indeed big private business, even though basically it is public not private enterprise.

The FCC presumably awards a license or grants a renewal because it adjudges the assignee to be the best qualified among the applicants "to promote the general good"; in making this judgment the Commission considers the past performance of a station and its potential. What are the criteria? It is difficult to discover any precise interpretation of the Commission's mandate. The presumption is that the standards used are: the need of a community for an outlet, the broadcasting experience of the applicant, his financial qualifications, his programming and operating plans and his sense of public service. As for the obligations with regard to performance, the FCC expects licensees to take the necessary steps "to inform themselves of the real needs and interests of the areas they serve and to provide programming which in fact constitutes a diligent effort, in good faith, to provide for those needs and interests." [2]

The Commission has set out eleven major elements it holds necessary to meet the requirement of public interest: opportunity for local self-expression, programs for children, religious programs, educational programs, public affairs programs, editorialization, political broadcasts, news programs, sports programs, services to minority groups, entertainment programming. It is fascinating that of the eleven elements outlined by the Commission, entertainment is listed last, whereas in practice it is first. The FCC does not specifically prescribe what programs shall be shown or what time shall be allotted to them. In setting up the Commission, Congress made it clear that the agency was not to make "arbitrary or capricious" decisions and it was prohibited from any actions that could be construed as censorship or interference with the right of free speech.

The broadcasters are likely to cry "censorship" when the FCC examines programming. Yet the history of regulation strongly suggests that the Commission has been too lenient rather than too stern in its grants and renewals of licenses and that it has been delinquent in failing to ensure that licensees live up to their original promises. Public hearings have been rare; station owners seldom have had to prove that they have been serving the best interests of their communities; they have not been called to account for imbalance in their programming. Newton Minow, once chairman of the FCC, has said that far too many licensees regard the frequencies as theirs, not the public's and that "the license is operated not in the public interest but to get the greatest financial return possible out of their investment."[3] Fred Friendly, the Ford TV commissar, has called the Commission at best a "referee" and at worst "blind, deaf and unimaginative."[4]

The Commission is one of the most undermanned and under-budgeted of the regulatory agencies; in the two decades from 1950 to 1970, it has been able to do little more than struggle to keep up with the mushrooming broadcast industry. In the course of these 20 years, commercial TV stations increased from 104 to 680 and radio stations from 2,835 to well over 6,000. Yet the increase in the FCC staff was only from 1,205 to 1,456; and of this total less than 300 employees are in the Broadcast Bureau.

As an example of the need for a sterner FCC policy, there is the case of Station WLBT in Jackson, Miss. A group consisting of members of the Church of Christ and spokesmen for the black community appealed to the FCC to refuse renewal of the station's license on the ground of discrimination against the black population— inadequate coverage of civil rights news, lack of attention to the black community in general, frequent unpleasant references to Negroes. The FCC dismissed the complaint, holding that the complaints had no standing before the Commission.

The plaintiffs then went to the U. S. Court of Appeals and in 1966 won a ruling which asserted the public's right to make formal challenges of licenses. Judge Warren Burger, later to become Chief Justice of the U. S., wrote the decision, holding that "the broadcast license is a public trust, subject to termination for breach of duty."

This was hailed as a landmark judgment. The challengers again petitioned the FCC and again the Commission ruled against them. In 1969 the complainants went to the Court of Appeals once more and Judge Burger handed down a second decision in which he praised the challengers, rebuked the FCC, withdrew the station's license and invited new applications for the franchise. Speaking for a unanimous court, Judge Burger said: "Broadcasters are temporary permittees—fiduciaries of a great public resource—and they must meet the highest standards which are embraced in the public interest concept."

The FCC is reluctant to exercise its potential powers, largely, one suspects, because of the pressures put on the Congress by the broadcast industry. In this connection it must be kept in mind that the FCC must have the approval of the Commerce Committees of both Senate and House for any strengthening of its rules.

Television has become all-important in politics. Politicians cultivate the friendships of station owners and are most reluctant to oppose them. Nicholas Johnson, an FCC member, says, "The FCC suffers from the virtual domination of its day-to-day activities by the very industries that it is supposed to regulate. The political power of the broadcasting industry is, in my judgment, unsurpassed by that of any other industry in America today. It is the broadcaster who controls what information the American people will receive, what candidates they will be permitted to view and to hear from . . . and every elected candidate is very mindful of this power." [5]

The broadcasters suffered a setback in 1969 when the Supreme

Court upheld the FCC's "Fairness Doctrine," which requires that both sides in public issues be given coverage. The decision applied to personal attacks in the course of discussion of controversial issues and in political editorializing. The broadcasters contended not only that the doctrine was an abridgement of their rights under the First Amendment, but also that it inhibited coverage of controversial events. The FCC argued that the doctrine was the only way the public could be protected against misuse of the air waves; the court agreed, ruling that the public's rights to the broadcast channels took precedence over the rights of broadcasters.

Yet for each step forward by the FCC, there seem to be one or more steps backward. For example, on January 15, 1970, the Commission announced that it would not entertain license challenges against radio and television stations that "substantially" meet the programming needs of their communities and that a license challenger could not win his case on evidence that a broadcaster held a local media monopoly through the joint ownership of newspaper, television and radio facilities. (In 44 major markets the only local newspaper owns the only local television station. Overall, newspaper and magazines own 381 FM radio stations and 183 TV stations.)

The policy was announced after broadcasters had charged that the Commission intended to restructure the industry through the wholesale denial of license renewals and after Senator Pastore had introduced a bill that was attacked on the ground that it gave undue protection to the existing licensees. The pressures apparently had worked.

Out of the study of the operations of the FCC come these conclusions: that television is not operating adequately "in the public interest;" that the FCC should exercise more continuous and effective control over the industry; and that until this control is established, television will not perform as it should perform for the public good.

Basic Fact: Newspapers Are *Not* Licensed

The newspapers' controls, such as they are, are private rather than public and they operate inside rather than outside the industry. Editors like to think they are completely free to print or not to print, according to their own judgments; publishers talk constantly of the "sanctity" of the editorial office. In reality, however, editors generally are subject to the directions and whims of their publishers.

This kind of control arises frequently out of political orientation. A staunchly Republican publisher — for example, the late Col. Robert McCormick of the Chicago *Tribune* — made sure his editors stressed the Republican point of view. Similarly, a liberal Democratic paper like the *New York Post* reflects the political leanings of its publisher, Dorothy Schiff. Or a publisher may have a pet crusade and the editors become his crusaders in his search for holy grails.

Another form of internal control is economic. The publisher in most instances is a business animal. His eye is still likely to be on the "hard-ware" — the machinery and the materials — rather than on misnamed "soft-ware"—the editorial content. He determines the size of the editorial budget. And if he decides to cut payrolls he is likely to make the first slices in the editorial departments; if the editorial budget is reduced, then obviously the amount and quality of news coverage will suffer. Thus, even though newspapers are not licensed, they are subject to a diversity of controls.

Two Other Differences

There are two other important differences between the electronic and print media. The first is in techniques, which is especially important because it largely determines the range and the nature of coverage. (This is discussed fully in Chapter 18 which deals with the performance of television.)

The other factor is advertising — the one element common to both the electronic and the print media. In the case of TV and radio, there is, of course, no return from circulation; total revenue comes from advertising. In the case of newspapers, circulation brings a considerable return — approximately 30% of the total revenue.

The advertising pattern has been changing since the advent of television and this could be significant to the future welfare of the newspaper business. While newspapers in 1970 carried more advertising than any other medium, most of this was in retail and classified copy; their share of national advertising, a source of large revenues, has been steadily declining; in 1950 it was 16% of the total, for 1970 it is estimated at 9%.

Television and radio have been structured to serve as advertising vehicles. The dominant objective is mass appeal, designed to sell goods, to implant the image of a product in the viewer's mind or to improve a sponsor's "profile." The advertiser feels the need of some sort of audience-measuring device as a marketing guide and this has led to the rating system, almost the key element in the programming structure.

The king-pin in the ratings field is the Nielsen survey, which is sold to advertisers on the three big networks for $1 million a year and also to advertising agencies and television stations. This is the method of Nielsen operation: 1,200 households are selected by computer to represent a cross-section of the 60 million homes in the nation. (The record of one Nielsen family is presumed to reflect the viewing habits of some 52,000 families.) In each of these homes the TV set is equipped with an audimeter, an electric device that records minute by minute, what channel is tuned in and at which time. Analysts in Chicago then feed the records into computers and these churn out the ratings. A rating is an estimate of the number of homes viewing a certain program; for example, a rating of 20 indicates that 20% of all American homes with TV sets are tuned to a program at a given minute.

Advertising agencies, basing their decisions to a considerable extent on the ratings, play a major role in determining what programs can most effectively reach the consumers they seek. In this way the advertiser, through his agency, exercises editorial power—including some censorship—over programs. Only rarely does the sponsor aim for quality rather than quantity; his approach is likely to be timid and cliche; he is deeply concerned about offending any segment in the political audience and even a small amount of critical mail can produce goose pimples all over his corporate body. He is neurotically fearful; a manufacturer of non-filter cigarettes, for instance, wanted the villains in a drama to be shown smoking filter cigarettes.

Public affairs coverage generally has been gravely affected by this demand for large audiences. Because they do not attract advertising support, such programs are becoming rarer and rarer. News documentaries bring in only a quarter to a third as much money as a motion picture in the same time period; in the 1969 season not one of the top thirty television advertisers chose to sponsor a news documentary. Network news programs fall far short of making a profit, according to Richard S. Salant, President of CBS News.

And yet the number of commercial interruptions in television news has become appalling. Four years ago the half-hour evening news program usually contained a single commercial; now, with the same amount of advertising divided into smaller segments, there are often ten commercial interruptions. Pictures of deodorants, shampoos, girdles both female and male, mouthwash and eyewash, generally are placed between headline and story. (Ironically the commercials often are presented more expertly than the news.)

There are some signs of change. A growing number of sponsors and network advertising people are looking into the composition of the audience — by age, sex, income, education, and residence—rather than settling for simple over-all totals as guides to the selection of programs; they rightfully contend that, in making program decisions, ratings must be combined with imaginative judgment and program experience. There is the realization that an intelligent audience of five to ten millions may be a better consumer prospect than one of twenty to thirty millions (which the sponsors and the agencies consider the minimum worthy of their attention), just as a magazine with a class circulation can sell more of a class product than a mass magazine with twenty times the circulation.

None of this discussion of commercials on television means that the newspaper is 100% virtuous on the score of advertising. Far from it. But there are important differences that place newspapers closer to the side of the angels (or further from the side of the devils) than television.

In the first place there is an obvious physical difference between advertising in the newspaper and on television. In the printed media, editorial matter and advertising are perforce clearly separated; the reader has no trouble distinguishing one from the other and he can take it or leave it. On television, however, editorial content and commercials are run one on the heels of the other and the viewer is often left to his own devices to tell where one ends and the other begins. This is even more pronounced on radio where only rarely is a commercial clearly identified by the announcer. In the second place, the newspaper is presumed to be primarily a medium of information and not, like television, a source of entertainment. Thus at its best the newspaper plays to a selective rather than a mass audience; its appeal is to the individual as a reader, not, as in television, as a consumer.

But if there are sponsor pressures on the television producer, there are similarly advertising pressures on the newspaper executive. As a general rule the larger paper, because it serves a considerable number and a great variety of advertisers, is better able than the smaller newspapers to resist the pressure of any one advertiser. However, this does not mean that many, even most, newspapers in such departments as fashion and travel do not keep in mind the special interests of the advertiser. As for the newspaper in a small community, it is unlikely that it would carry, in a prominent position the report of a fire in the only department store in town, unless the blaze was so conspicuous that it could not be ignored.

Yet in neither medium, electronic or print, is the commercialism as deeply ingrained as is often alleged. The big rub comes not in the plugging of products or the assertion of false claims (even though there is more than a modicum of such) but in the selection of programs or features that will attract audiences without regard for "the public interest." Again the analyst is led to the conclusion that until there are better audiences there will not be better television and until the readers reject them, bad newspapers will continue. Again we come back to the basic problem of education.

What the Audience Wants

Such then are the differences among the media—in controls, in techniques, in advertising approach, most of all in philosophy. What then are the audiences to which they appeal—or might appeal? What kind of fare do those audiences, huge and heterogeneous, want on their media menus? Specifically, because this is our main concern, what do they seek in the way of information on public affairs?

Distressingly, the general interest in news is far from high. In a survey of the TV viewing habits of some 2,400 adults, only 4% of listeners cited "regular news" as their favorite programs. The average viewer wants programs that provide pleasant relaxation rather than serious stimulation. He does not look to television for information.[6]

Television makes large claims for its news performance. The Television Information Office distributes a Roper survey of public attitudes toward television and other mass media which contains these assertions: (1) television is the primary source of news; (2) television is the most believable news medium, leading newspapers two to one; (3) television provides the clearest understanding of candidates and issues in national elections.[7]

As for Assertion No. 1, the question arises as to the kind of news television provides. The answer is that it is primarily a bulletin service, in contrast with the newspaper which is in a position to supply the essential facts plus background. Consider a Presidential press conference; viewers want to read about it, even though they may have seen it on television; also they look to the correspondent to set out the highlights and to the editor to discuss the validity of the Presidential arguments.

As for Assertion No. 2, obviously people are more likely to believe what they see than what they read. But it should be realized that, more often than not, television presents only segments and not the whole of a story. TV's assertions on the score of believability do not have more meaning or relevance than this.

As for Assertion No. 3, television has undoubtedly changed the political picture; unfortunately, because the television image is now probably the prime factor in politics. This is hardly progress; it means that voting is for shadows on the screen rather than for substance. In this same Roper study interviewees were asked repeatedly over a ten-year period which of the four basic media—newspaper, television, radio and magazine—they would prefer if they were confined to one source of the news. In its September 5, 1969 issue, *Time* published a Harris poll in which approximately the same type of question was asked. Both Roper and Harris reported that a majority designated television and only a third the newspapers.

However, when Harris put a follow-up question: "How upset would you be if your main source of news were to become unavailable for a month?," 44% said they would be "very upset" to lose their newspapers but only a third would be "greatly concerned" if their favorite TV news broadcast were not available. The newspaper, it seems, is a kind of "security blanket" for many readers; contact with it creates a strong identification which is lacking in television, where viewers switch from channel to channel.

Television will not, I believe, take the place of the newspaper, for these various reasons:

The newspaper is there when it is wanted, for the reader to peruse at his own time and speed; he is not required to tune in at an hour when there may be other becks or calls or to proceed at the pace set by the broadcaster, who may be too breath-taking or too snore-inducing.

The newspaper offers perspective, television does not. Every page in TV is the front page, with all items receiving almost the same vocal emphasis from the commentator, whether it be a report about an A-bomb explosion or news about the latest zyrations of Zsa Zsa.

The newspaper can supply interpretation of the news, but television rarely does, because of its time limitations and its demand for "hot copy." The news in the good newspaper is approximately complete; on television it is limited; even useful programs such as "Meet the Press" and "Face the Nation" run out of time before vital questions can be adequately answered or even discussed. And, of course, part of the newspaper's appeal is its variety, its capacity to serve diverse minorities with specialized news — from books and beauty aids to ships and sealing wax — in addition to the general coverage of events.

Finally, the newspaper supplies the written word in contrast with the spoken word. And the written word still carries more potential authority, if only because it is set down in type and it is there to be seen and pondered upon rather than snatched from the air waves.

Thus there is no doubt that the newspaper has a most definite future if editors will recognize that a newspaper has grave responsibilities as well as great opportunities and if publishers will acknowledge that while newsprint is important, what goes on newsprint is at least equally important.

*   *   *

In concluding this survey of the media, this fact should be kept firmly in mind: the American press has been looked upon as a vital instrument of democracy and, as such, has had special grants and privileges—most importantly the *First* Amendment, the most immediate, the most important amendment—guaranteeing freedom of the press, naming it second only to freedom of speech. Television and radio have had the enormous award of licenses, freedom at little cost to accumulate millions and the right to resell these franchises for staggering sums. The newspapers also have had their privileges in the form of lower postal rates.

Yet too often the press forgets that it has been accorded this exceptional status because of the profound belief that it has an urgent role to play, a large public duty. Consequently, there arise questions such as these:

• Is not television obligated, because of its grants, to provide much more than it does by way of public service?

• Are not the newspapers, even though they are not dependent on government franchise, also under the obligation of responsibility?

• Are the media providing space for dissenting views and access for the minority groups?

• In sum, are the media doing the essential job of providing the information on which enlightened opinion can be built?

These questions are discussed in the chapters that follow but before they are taken up it is useful to consider the basic question: What is "news"? An answer is assayed in the next few pages.

17: Definition of News

In less sophisticated days this was the classic definition: if a dog bites a man, it isn't news, but if a man bites a dog, it is. Wrong on two counts. If the bitten man happens to be Henry Kissinger or Richard Burton, or if the biting dog happens to be Lassie, this is decidedly news (of a kind). Moreover, the old formula will not do in these days of complex and global happenings.

"News" now means more than the factual coverage of spot events; it includes the broader trends, the recording and appraisal of the currents that run in the far-from-pacific ocean that is the world today. The factual reports that sufficed in the time of simple journalism are no longer adequate to provide understanding; interpretation—that is, *background:* survey of the past and analysis of the present; and *foreground:* illumination for the future—has become essential.

Interpretation: An Explosive Word

A setting down of facts without a statement of the meaning of these facts is almost useless for understanding. "Interpretation" is the key word. Without clues and background material the reader cannot be expected to arrive at reasoned conclusions about such subjects as Vietnam crises, nuclear testing, inflation or pollution.

There is a great to-do in journalistic circles about interpretation. Some see in it Great Peril, others Great Promise. The debate takes place in an atmosphere of confusion; there is no agreement on terms, little meeting of the minds and, most of all, there is failure to differentiate between interpretation and opinion.

I find no reason for these difficulties. Interpretation, in my view, is an objective (as objective as human judgment can be) judgment based on knowledge and appraisal of a situation—good information and sound analysis; it reveals the deeper sense of the news, providing setting, sequence, above all, significance. It is an indispensable ingredient in the reporting of national and international news—fields which are, in most newspapers and on most TV broadcasts, under-developed areas. Opinion, on the other hand, is a subjective judgment and should be confined to the editorial pages of newspapers and distinctly labelled on television and radio broadcasts. Recognition of the distinction between the two is of the utmost importance. To take a primitive example:

—*To report that Spiro Agnew attacks the press is news;*

—*To explain why Spiro Agnew makes the attack is interpretation;*

—*To assert that Spiro Agnew is a "radic-unlib" is opinion (even though that opinion may be justified.)*

The opponents of interpretation insist that to ensure "objectivity" the reporter must "stick to the facts"; that if he departs from "facts" and attempts interpretation, he inevitably moves into the area of opinion. In response, I ask: "What facts?" and I say there is no such thing as a totally "objective" news story. Consider the most "objective" of reporters. He collects, say, fifty facts and out of these fifty selects twelve as the important ones, leaving out thirty-eight. First exercise of judgment. Then he decides which of the twelve facts shall constitute the lead of the story; this particular fact gets prime attention because many readers do not go beyond the first paragraph. Second exercise of judgment. Then the news editor decides whether the story is to go on page one or on page twenty-nine; if it appears on page one it has considerable impact; if it appears on page twenty-nine, it may go unread. Third exercise of judgment.

So I ask the critics of interpretation: Is this "objectivity"? Is this "factual" reporting? Is the kind of judgment required for interpretation any different from the kind of judgment involved in the selection of facts and display of the news?

Now I am not in any way denigrating the ideal of "objectivity". Despite the difficulty of attaining it, objectivity must remain one of journalism's chief endeavors; there must be unflagging effort to prevent editorial judgment from influencing news play and to keep opinion out of the news columns in the form of "news analysis," "special correspondence," "exclusive stories." But I insist that interpretation should and can be as objective as a wholly "factual" presentation. (If there is to be crusading—and at times there should be—let it be done by the Knights of the Editorial Round Table.)

New Trend: The Trend Story

There is a broader area which should have increasing attention and to which interpretation should be especially applied—the trend story. To make the news comprehensible, long-range developments as well as daily happenings should be reported. The record should be set down, but the various elements must be pulled together so that there will be both synthesis and analysis. This means that reporters shall be expert researchers and that the deadlines for trend stories shall be set, not for tomorrow or for the day after, but for a time when the pertinent facts have been collected and the total situation has become clear and in turn can be clarified for the reader.

This type of story is usually the work of a team of reporters and editors who may spend weeks digging into records, conducting interviews, visiting areas in which developments have taken place or will take place—in short, providing a view of the forest instead of requiring the reader to piece the picture together out of the individual trees. Such a story might be one tracing the course of school desegregation under the Nixon Administration or describing the interaction between United States troop withdrawal from Vietnam and "Vietnamization" of the war or measuring progress in international negotiations toward the limitation of arms.

An excellent example of how a trend story can illuminate a subject for the general public is an article in the *Wall Street Journal* of May, 1970, which dealt with the Soviet Union's increasing involvement in the Middle East. The piece traced the course of Russian aid to the United Arab Republic—the military technicians sent to train the Egyptian forces, the installation of SAM missile sites, and Russian piloting of Egyptian planes. (Both the SAM's and the Soviet pilots, it was pointed out, jeopardized Israel's air superiority over the Arabs and threatened to upset the balance of power in the Middle East.) The Russians, it was suggested, in order to solidify their position in the vital area, were exploiting the preoccupation of the United States with Vietnam, thereby presenting a tough choice for Washington: on the one hand, aloofness, which could lead to further Israeli losses and strong political repercusions at home; on the other hand, increased aid for Israel, which could lead to escalation of the conflict and possibly to a U.S.-Soviet confrontation.

Another excellent example of a "trend story" is one that appeared in the *New York Times* four months after Prince Sihanouk had been ousted in Cambodia, and three weeks after American troops had been pulled out of the country. Ralph Blumenthal spent a week examining conditions there. Then, in a 2,000-word piece, he described the situation and appraised the future under the government of Premier Lon Nol. He found that, despite continued Communist attacks and disintegration of the economy, the Lon Nol regime was showing signs of growing self-confidence, stability and statesmanship that seemed to belie predictions that it would collapse. Political, economic and military conditions were discussed in terms of the American intervention, Communist control of many of the main transportation routes, development of the Cambodian Army and the presence of South Vietnamese troops. Looking toward the future, Blumenthal's article noted that the Communists dominated more than half the land and that the prospect of an early negotiated settlement between the Lon Nol government and the North Vietnamese was not bright.[1]

Raymond Anderson's article on the Arabs in the *New York Times* of July 28, 1970, is another example of an excellent job of perspective. It included a review of recent events, among them the defeat of the Palestinian rebels by King Hussein of Jordan; the sharp reaction of the leftist regimes in Iraq, Syria, Egypt and Libya, generally sympathetic to the Palestinians; the disclosure by President Anwar el-Sadat of Egypt of a plot to overthrow his government; the foiling of a coup by Army officers by King Hassan of Morroco, creating histility between Morocco and Libya, which had supported the rebels; and a few weeks later the Arab world was split again when leftist forces, supported by Iraq, overthrew the Sudanese government, Libya and Egypt intervened and restored the regime to power.

The Anderson piece provided a thorough analysis. It pointed out the new cracks which were emerging in the Arab world, not only the traditional ill will between the conservative and left-wing regimes, but new tensions in the left-wing camp. All this was undermining the Soviet role in the Mid-East and the Arab regimes were asserting their independence of Communist ideology. Even the common animosity toward Israel failed to bring a facade of unity to the Arabs.[2]

The *Wall Street Journal* is to be commended for putting emphasis on the trend article. Other newspapers, notably the *New York Times*

and the *Washington Post,* are now turning increasingly to this kind
of coverage. This means that less attention will be paid to spot news,
a good part of which is a statement of what is going to happen tomorrow and a good part more a restatement of what was printed
yesterday. The newspaper of the future, I am convinced, will put
heavy emphasis on the trend story.

The Large Issue: Truth

There is another objective of good journalism that has not had
sufficient attention in the mass media: unflagging effort, when conflicting statements are made, to discover and indicate what are the
facts. In these days of propaganda and of pressures of all sorts on
the press; of manipulation through the modern techniques of communication; of classification (concealment) and censorship, overt or
covert, it is not enough to present the news plus the meaning of the
news; it is also necessary to differentiate, wherever possible, between
truth and fiction. Questions:

• What do the reporter and the editor do when a United States
Senator (Joseph McCarthy) holds up a list which he says contains
the names of fifty-three members of the State Department who are
also members of the Communist Party?

• What do the reporter and the editor do if the President of the
United States (Mr. Johnson) says things are going well in Vietnam
when the editor has had reports from his correspondents at the
front indicating almost conclusively that things are going badly, both
at the front and in Saigon?

• What do the reporter and the editor do when a President (Mr.
Nixon) states that we are only peripherally engaged in Laos when
the paper's correspondents have reported that we are heavily engaged
with "advisers" and B-52's.

• What does a financial reporter do if he is told by high government
officials that the budget will show a considerable surplus when he
knows that the budget is precariously close to the red?

My answer is that the reporter and the editor should provide both
versions and attempt to indicate which is the true one. I concede
that this procedure is not always possible because deadlines often
prevent sufficient investigation. But the truth or the doubts should be

published as soon as possible, before opinion becomes cemented by falsehood, by juggling of fact or by concealment.

The answers, then, to the questions set out above are these: the first sentence of the McCarthy story should have stated the Senator's accusation, the second that he offered no proof of the charge; the first paragraph of the Johnson story should have reported his optimism about Vietnam, the second paragraph should have summarized the contrary reports of the correspondents; the first paragraph of the Nixon story should have contained the President's denial of involvement in Laos, the second paragraph should have stated that the dispatches from the Southeast Asia front indicated that we were on the way to becoming heavily committed in Laos; the first paragraph of the budget story should have reported the official optimism, the second the unofficial doubts.

There are editors with whom I have raised this question of truth-seeking who say that this is an ancient problem, that it was resolved long ago and that whenever it is at all possible to do so, they indicate what the facts really are. I disagree. I contend that only lip service has been paid to the concept of truth-seeking and that this phase of journalistic responsibility deserves much fuller exploration and much more frequent practice.

*   *   *

By this time the reader may have concluded that arriving at a definition of news is no easy chore. It isn't. Furthermore, the definition is often imprecise and often unobjective. On television the task of selecting and presenting information is a delicate and unscientific business; what is news is often dependent on what the camera sees or is able to see. As for newspapers, the definition may vary from day to day and place to place. Laurence Stern of the *Washington Post* cites this example: when three doves in the Senate announced their support of the antiwar demonstrations, this was "news" in the *Washington Post* and the *New York Times,* played on the first page. On the following day when it was announced that 355 members of the House had endorsed the President's position on Vietnam, this was considered lesser "news" and relegated to an inside page.[3]

How, then, to define news? Certainly the man-bites-dog formula won't do. Allowing for technical difficulties and human frailties, this might be at least the beginning of a definition: news is the report of a contemporary event or trend—a report that supplies background and explanation, that avoids partisanship and propaganda and that indicates, as far as possible, the truth.

And now, having approximately defined news, the discussion proceeds to the news media—the electronic media first, then the print media. We start with an analysis of television's performance.

18: Television's Performance: Dynamic, Massive, But Dubious

In any survey of the opinion process, few developments have been as dramatic and as significant as the evolution of the electronic media. First radio, with its immediacy, and then television, with its graphic power, have revolutionized the communications apparatus. Television has had tremendous impact in two directions: in supplying entertainment in great variety and in bringing events and personalities, in living color, into the nation's living rooms.

Commercial TV's primary concern, it is said once more, is entertainment; being commercial, it seeks maximum audiences for maximum sales. In its books the customer is always right; it caters to his desire for escape and makes only a lesser effort to inform him or elevate his taste.

Because the word "entertainment" cannot be clearly defined, it is difficult to estimate the amount of air time television allots to it. A survey of broadcast journalism made by an Alfred I. duPont-Columbia University task force indicates that the proportion of prime time—meaning the hours of maximum viewing: 7:30 to 11 p.m.—given to news and documentaries is only around 5%.[1] A spot check of New York City television stations in August, 1971, revealed that WNBC assigned 14 hours a week to public affairs, WCBS 15 hours, WPIX two and a half hours. Entertainment—or what purports to be entertainment—constitutes, it is estimated, 80% of TV's log.

A Large Effect On Opinion

Yet despite the preponderance of entertainment over public affairs, commercial television makes a considerable impact on opinion, largely through its live, on-the-spot news programs.

Possibly television's greatest influence in the public affairs area is in politics. The outstanding example is John F. Kennedy's 1960 debate with Richard Nixon, which opened the road to Presidential victory. The encounter gave the public a close look at the candidates

and placed Mr. Kennedy on a basis of equality with the better-known
Vice President. Perhaps attention was focused not so much on the
content as on Mr. Nixon's "5 o'clock shadow", and his unease, caused
by a recent illness and the overheat of the TV lights. (Mr. Kennedy
said to me: "I felt sorry for him, he looked so uncomfortable, so un-
convincing.") Mr. Kennedy was calm and confident; Mr. Nixon was
neither.

When Mr. Nixon ran in 1968 against Hubert H. Humphrey, he
remembered the lessons of 1960 and his television appearances were
meticulously planned and staged, an almost perfect job of "packaging."
There seems little doubt that an important reason for his victory was
the general feeling that it was "time for a change"; nevertheless television figured largely in the picture: the candidate's expert strategists
had succeeded in presenting a picture of a "new Nixon."

Another example of the "charisma" (that overworked word from
ancient Greece meaning charm, elegance, sex appeal, etc., etc.) that
television can convey was John V. Lindsay's political career, including
the attention he attracted when he announced his switch to the Democratic party. This appeal was apparent as early as 1969 when he won a
victory in New York's mayoralty race against political odds largely
because on television Mr. Lindsay looked like a mayor and Mario
Procaccino, rated as the front-runner, did not; the validity of their
arguments made little difference.

At the political conventions, television has prime attention. The
national committees issue behavior guides and even set up schools
designed to teach delegates how to keep their eyes and minds on the
cameras so that the proceedings will make a better show on the screen.
The duPont-Columbia survey revealed that a majority of Congressional and gubernatorial candidates felt that their TV appearances
were their most important media activities. "If your name is in the
paper, it's no big deal any more," a West Coast candidate said. "On
the other hand, people are quick to say 'Hey, I saw you on TV'." [2]

(Incidentally, the purchase by candidates of electronic time to
achieve exposure has raised a serious issue; the high cost of television
time gives an advantage to rich candidates or those with access to
wealthy backers. Free time for candidates, including those running for
state and local offices, seems the only solution.)

Another indicator of television's political impact is the increasing use of the medium by public officials for major policy statements. The most obvious examples are of course the Presidential messages; but other officials and public figures are frequent guests on the air. The Sunday interview shows are especially sought after because not only do the pronouncements made on them get an airing on the screen but they are likely also to have coverage in the Monday newspapers which usually are short on news.

Debits and Credits

Consider now the credits and the debits in the commercial television ledger. This is how, summarized, the entries might look:

IN ENTERTAINMENT—*Credits:* some good shows, such as dramatic presentations or the Kraft or Hallmark music hours; good movies, even late, late ones; some vivid moments on the Carson-Cavett-Frost circuits. *Debits:* many more poor shows, notably inane competitions like the "Newlywed Game"; cheap variety bits; stand-up comedians who should silently sit down; the sudsiest of soap operas.

IN PUBLIC AFFAIRS—*Credits:* vivid coverage of live events, such as the moon adventures or dramatic political confrontations; some excellent documentaries, such as "Hunger in America" and "The Selling of the Pentagon." *Debits:* failure to deal with some outstanding issues because of fear of offending advertisers or any group of listeners, even minimal ones; lateness in dealing with big problems; positing of public affairs discussions on Sunday afternoons, the non-primest of times.

Analysis of the entertainment aspect of commercial TV does not concern us in this book except of course to the extent that it curtails public affairs coverage. What is of larger moment is television's handling of news because of its effects on public opinion.

The News Performance

Admittedly the public, because of television, is getting more news reports than it did in the pre-electronic days. But this does not mean that the public, because more information is available to it, is better informed. There are limitations of time and space. In a 30-minute round-up—the period assigned to the evening newscasts—with about 8 minutes out for commercials, few events can receive thorough coverage and interpretation. A story without pictures is rarely assigned as much as three minutes.

No important story can be told in 180 television seconds any more than it can be presented in three paragraphs in a newspaper; clarification and explanation are needed. Also, there are situations that cannot be portrayed in graphic form, especially in complex areas such as economics.

Some years ago the nightly network news broadcasts were increased from 15 to 30 minutes. But the additional quarter-hour has provided little in the way of interpretation. Generally film clips have been added without too much regard to relevance; thus, instead of trying to explain the complex stories of the moment, there are likely to be various sequences that are concededly pictureque but remote from the day's news.

Richard Salant of CBS agrees that, despite increases in network news coverage, few stories are adequately told. "We can't give stories enough length or depth," he says, "things are always left out. We need an hour news show every night or an extra hour of prime time for news every week." [3]

As for the "specials" in public affairs, they are often marked more by color than by comprehensiveness. Moreover, the various panel programs—"Meet the Pressure Cookers," "Watch Spivak Scintillate," "Large Issues and Small Answers"—are placed in the Sunday Sahara hours. True, there are green interludes amid the desert stretches, but these are also periods when listeners are likely to be occupied with Sunday outings or Sunday innings of baseball or football or golf.

In direct, on-the-spot reporting, television obviously has an advantage over the newspaper in its ability to provide live, graphic coverage plus instantaneous transmission; it can break into any program with bulletins reporting an event hours before a newspaper can appear on the streets. But there are also definite disadvantages in television coverage. The camera must be on hand at the precise moment when events take place; unexpected occurrences often present difficulties. Moreover, television film coverage entails a mechanical operation which is still cumbersome and confining; heavy cameras, elaborate lighting and complicated connections are required.

Consequently the TV cameraman does not have the range of the reporter. At a political convention, for example, the camera can present speeches from the rostrum and interviews with the delegates and in general convey the circus-like atmosphere on the convention floor. But the camera cannot provide the behind-the-scenes story; it cannot cover the action in the "smoke-filled back rooms" and other political maneuverings.

The television reporter, it is true, like the newspaper reporter, can seek out stories which the TV camera cannot cover because of its physical limitations. But inasmuch as television is a graphic medium, the director more often than not will opt for film rather than for text. This obsession with pictures, often at the sacrifice of much more significant words, is one of the cardinal faults of TV coverage. The tendency is to play up stories for which the most interesting film is available, often without regard to the relative importance of the news. Thus, if films of an insignificant but colorful scene are available these are likely to be allotted minutes on the screen whereas a pronouncement by the Secretary of State may be given only seconds. One New York station led off its nightly news period with shots of a mentally unbalanced man climbing around the upper girders of the Queensboro Bridge; the second item was a State Department announcement that the Administration's Far Eastern policy was in process of change.

Play is given to the personality rather than the event, to situations involving the important and known persons rather than the unimportant and the unknown, to conflict rather than tranquillity. A demonstration is preferred to a speech, an airplane crash to a negotiating session.

The newspaper, of course, can be indicted on the same count: it, too, follows the credo that the news is not the normal but the departure from the normal and that good news therefore is no news. As one executive producer says: "All journalists assume that the Boy Scouts and the churches are operating normally; our job is to cover what goes awry."

Then there is the charge that selection in television often results in grave distortion or definite slant. For example, in November, 1969 there was a five-hour peace march at Berkeley; the procession was tranquil except for ten minutes during which a rock was thrown, hitting the wheel of a policeman's motorcycle and knocking him to the ground, his leg broken. This ten-minute segment had the play on television; this was action and action makes good visual presentation, peaceful scenes do not. Commenting on films taken by observers for the American Civil Liberties Union purporting to show "police brutality," Norman Frank, general counsel to the Patrolmen's Benevolent Association, said: "A picture is worth a thousand words only if it is accurate. A picture does not establish provocation. It does not show what preceded the event or what followed it. It can do a lot of tricks with a camera." [4]

Another example, frequently cited, of lack of objectivity is that found by investigators for the House of Representatives who made an exhaustive review of television's coverage of the 1968 Democratic Convention in Chicago. They suggested that the networks "had deliberately sought out to interview those with known biased feelings against the conduct of the convention and the city government" and "had deliberately withheld from the air film and videotape material which would have been derogatory to the demonstrators." The report added: "While many of the major commentators spoke at length concerning the shock they felt at what was happening to the demonstrators downtown, little or no comment was made concerning profanity, obscene signs and gestures, and physical abuse employed by the demonstrators to provoke the police." [5]

A certain amount of slant also results from the fact that it is difficult to append footnotes to pictures. Often an event is seen through the eye of a single camera that focuses on aspects selected by the cameraman or his director while other revealing angles are ignored.

Another count made against television is that at times it stages events. Two such episodes took place during the Chicago convention in 1968. A girl hippie with a bandaged forehead walked up to National Guard troops and shouted, "Don't hit me!" when a filming crew gave her the cue. A young man in Grant Park was asked by a camera crew to hold a bandage to his head for a filming even though he had no visible injury.[6]

Demonstrators on other occasions have been notified that if they arranged a sit-in or a shout-out at a certain hour, the camera crews would be on hand to record it; protesters have been asked to put on a show for the camera. This may all be done in the name of "graphic presentation," but it is wholly misleading and it should be strictly outlawed.

Testifying before the House Education Subcommittee, S. I. Hayakawa, president of San Francisco State College, spoke of the way in which television was used by dissidents on his campus. He suggested that radicals would go into their act before the cameras almost as though on cue, then would dash home to watch their "mugging, prancing and shouting" on the screen.

Allied to the charge of slant is the allegation that television often becomes part of the news itself. At the 1968 Democratic Convention the reporters and photographers were harassed and many of them could not get tickets of admission because of Mayor Richard Daley's tough prohibitions in the name of law and order. At one point, events outside the convention hall, disorders of various degrees, eclipsed events inside the hall. The television crews were caught in the middle of the action, so they took full advantage of the situation, and their films had prominent play on the home screens.

The duPont-Columbia survey contained this comment: "From observers, supposedly with professional privileges, they suddenly found themselves transformed into participants and finally into active antagonists—challenged not only on the streets and in the parks of Chicago and on the convention floor, but by a large segment of the viewing public as well. It wasn't that they were considered unfair in their presentation so much as that they were held somehow mystically responsible for the violence they reported. Ten weeks later, television's coverage of the street riots and what occurred later inside the convention hall was blamed by many Democrats for their defeat at the polls." [7]

There is no doubt that the mere presence of the camera often tends to change the character of a story and often encourages mischief or violence. Television thus not only transmits but also generates news.

The Network Dilemma

Network relations with their affiliated stations have an important bearing on commercial television's performance.

Under government regulations, each network may own and operate only five VHF (very-high-frequency) and two UHF (ultra-high-frequency) TV stations. These are in large urban areas and they are the principal outlets for network programs; the flagship stations of the three major networks—ABC, CBS, and NBC—are in New York

City. In addition there are about 200 local stations affiliated with but not owned and operated by networks. Control of scheduling for these stations lies with the individual owners.

This is the way the system works: the network sells air time to the sponsor; the greater the number of outlets the network can guarantee, the larger the fee. The network in turn pays its affiliated stations to present its programs, the amounts being set according to the market and ranging from $75 an hour for a small station to $10,000 an hour for a large one. The arrangements also vary from station to station; in some "package deals" stations are allowed to omit national commercials for perhaps 30 seconds and substitute local sales pitches. Thus if the network program is a popular one, the station can guarantee local sponsors a large ready-made audience for their commercials and charge substantial fees.

The system has two faults from the viewpoint of improvement of the opinion process: local stations are more likely to accept the networks' entertainment shows with their mass audience appeal than the news and public affairs programs; and many of the affiliates are reluctant to give up good time slots and local advertising revenue for a network presentation.

As William Whitworth has noted, "If local television is often bush league journalistically, it is strictly big-time financially." [8] An NBC affiliate in a Southern city will receive $453 a broadcast from the network for carrying the evening news program, but its own local news program can gross $8,500 a broadcast. Because of these factors, editorial and economic, news coverage on television is likely to be far from complete; there is little good investigative reporting except on relatively safe targets such as pollution and the abuse of drugs by teenagers; and there is shallow coverage of minority affairs.

Another point in dispute is whether television should provide editorials and commentary. For example, in its Vietnam coverage television portrayed the action but did little in the way of explanation and took no moral stand until very late in the day and then only in a sporadic way. Until recently the networks contended that because they served some 200 diverse affiliates, they should not be in the business of editorializing. I do not think this is a sound argument but rather a confession that the system ought to be changed. The networks should supply editorials and leave to the stations the decision as to whether they should be run or not. The public seems to want editorials; in a Roper study made in 1968, 63% of those questioned said they favored editorials and felt that even local stations should take positions on the issues of the day.

By Way of Confirmation

To obtain a cross-section of opinion on regional television performance, *Columbia Journalism Review* correspondents were asked to provide appraisals of stations in their areas. While the majority reported that more people acquire their news from the TV screen than from local newspapers, half felt that television news was, on the whole, unsatisfactory. The common complaints tend to confirm what has already been said in these pages: that TV news is a shallow "headline service," short on background and interpretation; that the news emanating from national news centers is much better than programs initiated locally; and that, in general, too little time is assigned to public affairs broadcasts. Here is a sample of comments:

Detroit: "Television news is utterly inadequate. It is superficial and devoid of background. It is little more than headline reading and film-chopping."

San Francisco: "The problem is not just the amount of time devoted to public affairs broadcasts, but the impact such programs have. The problem is to get public affairs integrated with the regular broadcast schedules, rather than in off-time periods for the already educated. I believe more people get their headline news from television than from newspapers, but I suspect that those who want any significant understanding of the news must turn to the newspaper."

El Paso: "You can tell those who get their news from television or radio because they generally only have a fraction of the story. Anyone depending wholly upon television news for his information is an uninformed person."

Austin: "On a local level, television's performance is pitiful. One station has gone all-color but it is so short on personnel that the broadcaster must do virtually all his own reporting, filming, writing and editing as well as appear on the air with the finished product. The station frequently sacrifices immediacy and good reporting in order to present only color programs." (Details of this survey appear in the Appendix.)

"In The Public Interest"

Concede that for the masses television is and always will be an entertainment medium; concede that informational programs, including those that illuminate current affairs, will never attract the audiences of a "Laugh-In" or "Sob-Out"; concede that the average viewer's non-working moments are largely dedicated to surcease from thought as well as work—concede all this and yet commercial television cannot escape the obligation to do more, much more, in the way of public enlightenment. Not only do the terms of its franchises call for such responsibility; in addition any real sense of social service would seem to demand it.

I am not advocating that NBC or CBS or ABC become educational or even semi-educational networks. I am suggesting only that, having captured their audiences with popular pablum, they systematically slip some doses of intellectual vitamins into their programs.

Television executives defend their entertainment-dominated schedules on the ground that they are "giving the public what it wants." They cite the duPont-Columbia survey: when, after four years of trying, Martin Agronsky was finally able to get Hugo Black, the senior Associate Justice of the Supreme Court, to sit for an hour-long television interview on CBS prime time, only 9% of the audience in New York tuned in; during the same hour, 44% were watching a Brigitte Bardot television special on NBC.[9]

There is a classic story on the same point. When Adlai Stevenson was campaigning for the Presidency, CBS pre-empted the Lucille Ball show for one of the Stevenson speeches. Whereupon the candidate received this wire: "We Love Lucy—We Like Ike—Drop Dead."

There has never been a cancellation of entertainment for public affairs, even for the Apollo flight, that did not light up the network switchboards with complaints. And so the television people ask how they can be expected to cover public affairs when the competition in the same periods is serving up enticing souffles. The answer might well be that the commercial broadcasters should be mindful that their grants are made "in the public interest," that maybe some day some valiant member of Congress will call this to the public's attention and that maybe there will result an F.C.C. mandate setting aside hours when all stations will be required to present programs designed to inform.

If public affairs programs are made dramatic, which they can well be, and if they are made relevant, meaning that their importance to the welfare of the listener is made fully clear, I believe that there will be discovered for them an audience of unsuspected dimension. Commercial TV might well try more experiments toward that end.

Also television executives can make important contributions to the essential process of communication. Because of the size of the TV audience, this is no easy assignment but there are ways of achieving it. There can be frequent programs in which significant issues of the day can be discussed—open forums in which representatives of the public would present their views, with ample provision for audience participation. Responses to editorials can be encouraged and a weekly half-hour or so given to excerpts from such letters—which would be the equivalent of the letters to the editor published in newspapers. In this manner, the remoteness can be at least partly overcome and a sense of participation fostered.

And What of Public Television?

Public Television (the word "public" has been substituted for "educational" because the latter seems to have forbidding implications, which is in itself a kind of reflection on the public viewpoint) could fill the void in coverage of public affairs, but thus far it has not done the job or demonstrated its ability to do it. There are various reasons for this failure. There is a lack of money; I estimate that at least $150 million a year is needed, whereas the Congress has granted about a fourth of that sum. There is the role played by the Ford Foundation, which provides some $20 million and calls many of the shots, some of them beside the true marks. There are few new approaches; many of the Public TV producers have come out of commercial television and think only in commercial television terms. There are about the whole enterprise an amateur touch, a shortage of imagination and a lack of a sense of humor.

Why has not Public TV made an important contribution to public affairs? Why has it not done a daily broadcast with its own teams of Cronkleys or Brinkites, with the accent heavily on interpretation? And an interpretative review of the week? And frequent documentaries that deal incisively with the paramount issues of the day?

Why? Because the Corporation for Public Broadcasting, set up and funded by the Congress, has become very wary of Congressional surveillance. And with good reason. The Congress is on the alert lest "slant" enter into public broadcasts. Recently I asked a Senator who has a lead role in television legislation: "When will public TV be free of Congressional scrutiny?" The answer: "As soon as it is no longer dependent on public funds." Which means certainly not in the immediate future. The Congress has been reluctant to grant funds for Public TV because it has an unwarranted fear of propaganda; "BBC" is a dirty term in the Congressional lexicon.

These Congressional doubts about Public TV were increased as a result of the "Woestendick Affair," a strange and significant story. William Woestendick, who has had a varied career in journalism, is hired at $50,000 a year as editor and moderator of "Newsroom," a new program inaugurated by Washington's Public TV station, WETA-TV, with funds supplied by the Ford Foundation and loosely supervised by the Corporation for Public Broadcasting. Then enters that lib lady of the right, Mrs. Martha Mitchell, wife of the Attorney General. Having had large notice in the public prints when, in the early hours of the morning, she called up the editor of the *Arkansas Gazette* and urged that he "crucify" Senator Fulbright for his opposition to various Nixon programs, she decides she needs a press secretary. And who gets the job? Mrs. William (Kay) Woestendick.

So William C. McCarter, then Director of WETA, fires Mr. W from his editorship, contending that Mrs. W's connection with Mrs. Attorney General raises serious questions of conflict of interest. The liberal "Elite" is upset and Congress is even more upset because it proves, in Congressional eyes, that Public TV can be wrongly "ideological," and needs to be watched. Thus Mr. McCarter succeeded in hitting two birds, one a Left-winger, the other a Right-winger, with a single stone. And so the corporation decides, not illogically, that it had better go easy in public affairs.

A letter written to WETA-TV by six Senators—Griffin, Cook, Dole, Dominick, Goodell and Hatfield—stated the consequences:

"Surely the quickest way to destroy public confidence in educational television is to permit political considerations to affect personnel decisions." The episode does not argue well for Public TV if it is dependent on government funds as it is likely to be for a long time to come.

But even if Public TV finally realizes its potential in the public affairs area, the commercial networks should also do their share, endeavoring to present the news in greater depth and with ample perspective, to offer editorial comment on a regular basis and to do much more in the way of background commentary. What are needed, in short, are more adult and fewer children's hours.

Above all, the broadcasters should keep always in mind or be forced to keep in mind that the Communications Act calls for performance "in the public interest, convenience and necessity" and that they receive grants of franchises worth millions for virtually nothing. Nothing, that is, except the assumption of a basic responsibility to the public.

Television, with its pictures and its approximately-living color, has had the media spotlight in recent years. Yet it has not displaced radio—far from it—as the next chapter demonstrates.

19: Radio: Still A Potent Sound In The Land

Radio generally is rated in the polls behind television and newspapers as a prime source of news and information about public affairs. It also scores lower than television in such categories as "thoroughness" and "trust." (Hearing is never as convincing as seeing.)

But radio does have special qualities that assure it a large and faithful audience. Obviously, unlike television or the newspaper, the radio does not require sole concentration. A man can tune in a radio broadcast while shaving or driving; his wife can absorb a soap opera while she irons or cooks; a youngster can snatch rock on a portable radio while he rolls to school.

There are two other aspects of radio that ensure its place as a vital medium: first, it has great impact among minority groups, in particular, blacks; second, there are times when radio is the only source of news, as was the case during the 1969 power blackout in the New York metropolitan area which put newspapers and television out of commission and radio alone provided information—and reassurance.

A study by the Brand Rating Research Corporation indicates that 95% of all Americans over 12 years of age listen to radio regularly and that the average American's radio set is tuned in more than two hours a day.

Some stations offer entertainment and music almost exclusively; some supply sob serials; some, much fewer in number, concentrate on news. Our concern here, as elsewhere in this book, is on performance in the news area.

News on the Radio

On most network-affiliated stations—that is, "majority-appeal" stations, in contrast with those that are "minority-oriented" — the "news" is a five or ten-minute spot broadcast sandwiched in between other programs. These news spots, covering national and inter-

180

national events, are prepared in network newsrooms for airing across the nation; primarily they consist of headlines, with virtually no commentary or analysis.

Local news is gathered by individual stations; its type and quality vary from station to station. Rural and suburban stations devote a great deal of coverage to local affairs, such as community meetings and organizational activities, and the weather reports for farmers, skiers and the like. The "news staff" of a smaller station consists of one or two persons; much of the national and international news it supplies is of the rip-and-read variety taken from the regional tickers of the wire agencies.

Suburban stations in metropolitan areas no longer try to compete with the big city stations; they cater more and more to the needs of their immediate communities. Some suburban stations in the New York City region—Long Island, Westchester County, parts of Connecticut and New Jersey — claim larger audiences than those of some metropolitan stations.

These are signs of the upgrading of radio in public affairs performance. *Broadcasting,* the business weekly of television and radio, reports a growing "community conscience" among the country's radio stations; it finds evidence of this trend in the increasing number of programs designed to bridge the communications gaps between the generations and between social strata and in the growing list of projects like "Call for Action," a community-involvement, problem-solving program done in conjunction with the Urban Coalition and volunteer groups.[1] Panel discussions, documentaries, educational series and editorials are increasing on radio and making a substantial contribution to the molding of public opinion. Less expensive than comparable programs on television and therefore done more frequently, they range over a wide variety of subjects.

An important development since the mid-1960's is the appearance of all-news stations with their own news staffs. Some of them broadcast news around the clock and others combine talk programs with newscasts. The first such station, WINS in New York City, began operations in 1965; within five years there was a second one in New York City, WCBS, and others sprang up in such cities as Los Angeles, Denver, Las Vegas, Sacramento, Boston, Philadelphia, St. Louis, Washington, Pittsburgh and Miami. But information stations seem definitely limited to metropolitan areas which have audiences large and interested enough to make such operations economically viable. At first these all-news stations were primarily headline-oriented, but now they are adding analysis, opinion and in-depth features.

WINS is a good example of the operation of this kind of station. It states its aim as this: "The packaging of news in such a way that any listener at any time of the day or night can tune in and know what is going on in the world very quickly." It breaks the news into half-hour segments which are repeated throughout the broadcast day. The first five minutes are devoted to the headlines, which are then followed by detail and analysis of the more important stories. Reporters, by-line commentators and feature writers are cut in regularly. Feature coverage is concentrated on stock market reports, business news, news for women, food and service reports, sports reports and commentaries, and reviews of movies and stage shows. On major continuing stories, such as Vietnam, race relations or the economy, the station frequently offers a series of analytic reports.

In politics radio is most effective in situations where television and newspapers are not easily accessible or particularly popular. John Lindsay utilized radio extensively in his mayoralty campaigns to reach the Negro, Puerto Rican and European-language minorities in New York City. Edward W. Chester says: "Whether Lindsay could have been elected mayor [in 1965] without employing radio as he did is highly debatable." [2] Eugene McCarthy, in his primary campaign in New Hampshire in 1968, used radio to spread his message among the voters of the largely rural state; in a three-week period 7,200 spot announcements were made over twenty-three New Hampshire stations.

Appeal For Minorities

Minority groups turn to radio because they consider it the medium least bound to the "Establishment." More than 500 stations direct a significant part of their programs to black listeners and more than 100 are aimed exclusively at Negroes. These stations play a great deal of "soul" music but they exert considerable influence by providing information and advice about such matters as local politics, business opportunities, school problems and race relations.

Since the assassination of Dr. Martin Luther King, most black stations have devoted themselves to the difficult task of keeping their communities cool. Some stations, like WLIB and WWRL in New York, offer programs during which black listeners can talk with the mayor and other city officials. In St. Louis, KXLW provides thirteen weeks of spot announcements for blacks seeking to start new businesses; WANG, in Atlanta, broadcasts job notices directly from the State Employment Office.

Nicholas Johnson, an articulate member of the Federal Communications Commission, praises the contribution of these stations: "Many institutions have tried to reach the destitute and alienated millions who seek a richer future in the hearts of our cities. The schools have tried. The Office of Economic Opportunity has tried. Newspapers have tried. Political parties have tried. But only one institution has consistently succeeded. That is Negro-oriented radio." [3]

The youth groups have also brought into being their own substructures in the radio world. In large metropolitan areas where television has little appeal for many in the 16-20 year-old group there has sprung up an "underground" radio system which uses the FM band and features such new varieties of music as "acid rock." Stations like WNEW-FM and WOR-FM in New York City probably exert a greater influence on the young than does television. The disc jockeys on these stations speak the language and know the concerns of the new generation. Certain AM stations have until recently had an appeal for youthful groups; despite their constant and shrill chatter, repeated time and weather information, and their high school approach, they filled a need. Now these stations have lost the contest to the new and sophisticated FM group.

Radio, then, is a force to be reckoned with because it provides quick news and community reports for the majority and, in addition, access for the minority. If news operations are expanded and if the "majority appeal" stations will pay more heed to the minorities, radio can be a really potent influence in the public opinion process.

Besides the electronic media, there are the print media, of which the newspaper is obviously the most important. In the next chapter the merits and demerits (or vice-versa) of the newspaper are discussed.

20: The Newspapers: Fourth—or Froth—Estate?

These, to my mind, are the tests of the genuine newspaper: that it is basically a *news*paper, a carrier of information, rather than merely a (news) paper, primarily given to features rather than news; that it presents the news objectively and understandably; that wherever possible it indicates what is false; that it expresses its own opinions forthrightly and forcefully and opens its columns freely to the opinions of others; that it applies to itself and newspapers generally the same vigilance with which it examines other elements of society; and that compensation for editorial work is commensurate with its importance.

How then do the newspapers of the country measure up to these tests? This chapter is an endeavor to find an approximate answer. The appraisal is based on my own experience, fortified or modified by the findings of two surveys conducted for the purposes of this book—an evaluation of press coverage in various parts of the country by correspondents of the *Columbia Journalism Review* and an analysis of news presentation in the 25 newspapers with the largest circulations in the country. The first will be referred to as "The Correspondents' Report," and the second as "The Eight-Day Survey." (Details of these inquiries and findings appear in Appendix II).

The assessment is made on the basis of the newspaper's effectiveness as supplier of sound information; as molder of opinion and crusader in the public interest; as guardian of journalistic ethics; as responsible and responsive employer.

As Purveyor of News

Even though the deeply yellow (and curious) press of the days of Hearst and Pulitzer is gone, traces of jaundice remain. Too many newspapers suffer from Tabloidemia—a plague which causes them to break out in strange rashes and to play up the sensational rather than the significant news; and from Triviallergies—addiction to a variety of non-news and irrelevant departments.

184

I do not hold that all newspapers should be good and grey and that entertainment should be ruled out. But when so-called *news*papers devote as much as 80% of their space to features, "funnies" and fluff, they have lost claim to the title; one is tempted to call them members not of the Fourth but of the Froth Estate.

Newspaper editors have expressed self-righteous indignation about television, charging that it thinks almost exclusively in terms of the dollar and neglects the main task of public enlightenment. But one wonders: Are not many newspapers guilty of the same malfeasance? Are they doing a sufficient job of turning our attention away from comfort and chrome toward recognition of our responsibilities as citizens? The answer to the first question is yes; to the second, no. With what warrant then do the editors indict television for trying to attract the advertising dollar by giving the customers what they want when they themselves follow the same formula? How, living in similar glass houses, do they dare to cast the first or any stones?

The picture that emerges from "The Correspondents' Report" is far from bright; many newspapers, according to these analysts, do at best a "barely adequate" job of news coverage; they neglect the essential task of interpretation; they permit intrusion into the news columns of opinion in the guise of "background." News staffs are often skeletal, only snippets of wire service copy are presented, publicity handouts are printed without charge. In general there are found a lack of initiative and imagination and a timidity about publishing any story that may disturb the status quo. The comments of a Portland, Oregon, correspondent are typical: "The newspapers here are not inclined to expend time, effort and financial resources on any investigative reporting—they do not have reporters with enough expertise to do any. Vital issues are not reviewed thoroughly or objectively."

There are, of course, important exceptions. The *New York Times* is rated as the "best newspaper"; the *Washington Post* and the *Los Angeles Times* are considered "good" to "excellent." The newspapers in Louisville and Boston are given high marks while dailies in Chicago, San Diego, Tucson and Rochester are applauded for their national and international news reports and for interpretative reporting. A few smaller dailies—in Geneva, New York, and Clarksdale, Mississippi, for example—are praised for their local reporting.

The correspondents were asked to rate the influence of the newspaper on the community. Twelve out of twenty-one considered the impact quotient of their papers as "fair," four as "good," two as "excellent" and three as "poor."

The second study—"The Eight-Day Survey"—largely confirms the conclusions of the correspondents. Twenty morning and five afternoon dailies were analyzed for eight days, from June 9 through June 16, 1969. Two tests were applied: the manner in which they presented the news and the perspective they applied to it.

Nationally and internationally, the period covered was one of significant happenings: the Midway Conference between Presidents Nixon and Thieu of South Vietnam; the French elections which followed General de Gaulle's decision to step down; the annual and important Congress in Moscow; the increase in the discount rate by the Federal Reserve Board, an action of considerable economic significance; the disorders on the country's campuses, and the debate in Congress over the Anti-Ballistic Missile system.

The manner of testing the papers was wholly subjective. Assuming that I was the news editor for this particular week, I indicated how I would have played the six stories and I posed certain questions which in my opinion needed to be answered if these complex events were to be made understandable for the average reader—questions such as these:

On the Midway Conference: What is the meaning of the withdrawal of troops from Vietnam?: How well prepared is the South Vietnamese Army to replace these troops? What did Midway accomplish in terms of Washington-Saigon relations? *On the French elections:* What is the relationship between Pompidou's policies and de Gaulle's? What is the meaning of the election for the United States? What effect might it have on the Common Market? *On the interest rate story:* What is the discount rate? What caused the rate increase? What impact will it have on inflation? How might it affect the consumer?

In coverage of these three stories, three newspapers out of the 25 rated 50% or over; two rated 25%, and the other 20 performed even more poorly.

But the three other "top stories" were barely covered, despite their importance. The Moscow conference was a significant non-happening; no business of note was transacted, apparently because the Kremlin's leaders had encountered so much discord in the Communist ranks that they decided not to raise any issues or hackles, and therefore to postpone the Congress for a year. The campus disorders were intensifying and merited close observation. The debate over the ABM was developing into a no-holds barred struggle between the friends and foes of the Pentagon. Yet these stories were almost wholly neglected. In general the performance was far from adequate, without depth and without consistency.

The second part of the survey dealt with "news play" — the importance the editor attaches to a story as indicated by its position in the paper. This is a vital element because the main news pages should provide a perspective on the day's events; if, for example, there is over-emphasis on the sensational, there will be a consequent distortion of news values.

(Incidentally, many newspapers have gone to a horizontal rather than vertical make-up, such as that to which the *New York Times* adheres. Vertical make-up enables the reader to obtain some idea of the relative importance of news accounts. When the lead story carries only a single column headline, the reader is being told that there is nothing of moment; a larger headline then has some meaning for him. But then the typographers are prone to sacrifice text and logic for appearance.)

This was the main question put in the survey; How many of the six stories included in the study were accorded the lead positions which in my opinion they merited? Of the twenty morning papers analyzed, three—the *New York Times,* the *Washington Post,* and the *Los Angeles Times*—compared favorably with the "ideal play" at least 60% of the time. Six met the test less than half the time; sensational or parochial local stories were displayed instead of the important news. (For example, the *Miami Herald* consistently played up weather stories in line with its unflagging endeavor to demonstrate that Florida is outranked only by Paradise. It overlooked the fact that Paradise does not have damp heat, sudden cloud-bursts, Portugese Men-of-War in its oceans or weather-wacky people.) Of the other eleven, none matched the "ideal" more than a quarter of the time; one, the *New York Daily News,* with the largest circulation in the country, did so less than a fifth of the time.

The evening newspapers fared badly; they displayed the six stories

25% or less of the time and their emphasis was on murder, the Mafia, statehouse corruption and the like. This is not surprising because generally evening newspapers have suffered greatly in competition with television and are making feverish efforts to entertain rather than inform.

Examination of the files of the Associated Press—a mutual organization serving some 1,700 newspapers—for the eight days of the test reveals that a great deal of material was sent out, but it was heavy on "who" and "what" and light on "why"; moreover, much of such interpretation as was supplied was cut by the newspapers. Few of the background questions were answered; two exceptions were the interest rate story and the story of the Moscow conference, on which the A.P. provided excellent dispatches; as for the remaining four stories, virtually no interpretation was supplied, the accounts consisting of bare recitals of events, news conference quotations, Congressional testimony, round-ups of reaction.

It can be concluded, then, that the Associated Press in these instances did an inadequate job of interpretation. The question may be raised: Is it the function of a wire service to provide interpretation when it is serving newspapers with widely differing viewpoints? It is. Inasmuch as most newspapers cannot afford to send reporters to Midway or to France to do perspective pieces and inasmuch as smaller papers are not staffed to do a proper job of analysis, the background task is decidedly one for the wire services.

The same 25 newspapers were rechecked in July 1971, to test whether the pattern of 1969 still existed. Again they were examined on the basis of performance in the two areas—the tasks of interpretation and of news display. The pattern apparently had not changed.

The story analyzed was the announcement that Mr. Nixon would visit China. The issues of July 16, 17 and 18, 1971 were examined to determine how well the news was reported and appraised on the first day and how good was the job of interpretation on the next two.

The same subjective method was used as that employed in the 1969 survey. The author acted as editor and put these six questions which he felt needed to be answered if the reader was to have any real grasp of the story: Why should Washington seek out an accommodation with China? Why should Peking consider an accommodation with Washington? What are the chances of reaching some kind of agreement? How does Russia fit into the picture? Can Mr. Nixon over-come the long anti-Communist tradition in this country (to which he heavily contributed)? Can Mao convince the Chinese that it is all right to reach an agreement or even consult with the "Imperialist Dogs?"

On the average, the newspapers answered three and a half of the questions; only the first was treated in any significant way by all; and only six answered five of the six. The only newspapers that made a genuine effort to serve both as recorder and analyst of events were the *New York Times,* the *Washington Post,* the *Boston Record-American,* the *San Francisco Chronicle,* the *Philadelphia Bulletin* and the *Miami Herald.* In most of the other newspapers, ample space was afforded the story but much of it was given to "human interest" side-lights such as a chronicle of "Ping-Pong" diplomacy, unimportant details of the announcement, and random interviews with men (and women, now) in the street.

The news services, the Associated Press and the United Press International, carried a considerable amount of interpretive and analytical material as well as full doses of trivia. But only approximately a quarter of the newspapers carried this material—indicating that the editors seem only casually interested in the all-important questions of why things happen.

As for news display, obviously all newspapers gave the story front-page position. Of the 25 newspapers, 19 published the wire service stories as their leads the first day; they made no attempt to do "specials" of their own. And the accent on local news was apparent there also. Some of the page one space that might well have been devoted to special angles—and there were many—of the China story was used for lesser unrelated pieces.

In sum, the 25-newspaper surveys indicated that while the major papers and the wire services do a fair job of presenting the facts about a big news story, they do a poor job of telling the reader what the facts mean.

My own conclusion is that a large majority of the American newspapers do not have sufficient news and editorial impact to qualify as genuinely effective informers of opinion.

There are doubtless editors who will question the validity of my "ideal first page"; also they will contend, with some justification, that no American newspaper is or can be a national newspaper and that, with rare exceptions such as the *Wall Street Journal* and the *Christian Science Monitor*, which make their appeal on general coverage, the newspaper must pay attention to local as well as national and international news.

In reply to the first of these criticisms, I can only say that this is the judgment of a single individual; how much weight should be given to that judgment obviously I am not the one to say.

To the second criticism my answer is that the local story does have its place on the front page, but it must not be, as it often is, trivial and it should never force off page one a significant world story. Because, in addition to its local and national roles, the press has an international role it must fulfill. At no period in history has there been greater need for a flow of true information among nations, so that there shall be understanding among peoples. In such exchanges, the day-by-day reporting by the mass media is the vital element. Yet the flow of the news at the present time is both polluted and insufficient.

We do not have accurate pictures of other countries, even of our allies; we still indulge in stereotypes when we attempt to present national images. Nor do other countries have accurate pictures of us. Hollywood and the Not-So-Great, Not-So-White Way get more of a play in many foreign newspapers than the significant news of the United States; our national aims and our international programs are unreported or misreported for readers abroad.

This is true of the exchange between the so-called developed countries—even between the United States and Great Britain, despite their common language and their unfettered press. In the case of the more remote areas, coverage is open to more serious question. For example, American coverage of Japan. Edwin O. Reischauer, former U. S. Ambassador to Japan, reports that of all the U. S. correspondents in Tokyo, only two speak the language, and he asks: "What would we think of a Japanese newspaperman who came to cover the United States and could not read the American press?" As for the underdeveloped or developing nations, the reporting is sporadic and lacking in depth even though these areas comprise two-thirds of the world and even though our future is heavily involved with them.

The Less Circulated Press

The smaller papers in the country do not have the scope of their larger counterparts but they can be potent influences in their own backyards. In more than a quarter of the 435 Congressional districts in the United States, the largest newspapers have circulations of less than 25,000. Moreover the small town daily usually does not face news competition from radio and television and so is the primary source of information about local matters.

But small town editors are too much concerned at times about antagonizing the "Elite" and/or the advertisers in their communities because they, much more than editors in large cities, are dependent on them either for prestige or commercial support. The *Wall Street Journal* has described the problem of keeping in right with the "right" people as the need "to balance the risk of offending their news sources against their professional duty to keep the public informed." More than sixty years ago, Warren G. Harding, then editor of the *Marion* (Ohio) *Star*, in a memorandum to his staff suggested this formula: "Bring out the good; never needlessly hurt the feelings of anyone; boost, don't knock."

Lately, such thinking has come under a certain amount of attack by those who contend that the press should take a more incisive look at its news coverage and be less protective of "establishment" figures. In the past much of this kind of criticism was directed at the way big-city papers reported hotly controversial subjects. Now the same sort of scrutiny is being directed at the coverage of the local scene by the small town paper.

The stage and screen image of the typical small town editor is that of a crusader; it is rarely true. "Whatever problems big city papers have in reporting local issues in a hard hitting way are magnified several times in the small town press," says Charles E. Hood, Jr., of the University of Montana journalism faculty, a close student of small dailies. "Small town papers typically are hampered by local provincial attitudes and a shortage of qualified people. In some towns, the major issues aren't even raised in the local press." [1]

Jack Gillard, who as state editor of the *Des Moines Register* leafs through dozens of small newspapers each day, agrees. "The distressing thing is their overriding concern about their town's image," he says. "When we uncover a small town controversy, the local editor has a big-time assignment and he can help the cause of journalism mightily by fulfilling it." [2]

As Molders of Opinion

The newspaper's obligation in the area of opinion is a two-fold one: the expression, frank and full, of its own views; and the presentation of the views of others, especially views opposed to its own— meaning that the newspaper columns should be readily accessible to outsiders.

Editorial pages, with rare exceptions, do not thunder as they did in the days of Horace Greeley, Charles Dana and William Allen White. There are newspapers with large circulations but little impact on opinion; many editorial pages do not reflect the views of the majority of the readers: some 75% of the country's publishers are Republican and express that Republicanism resoundingly in their editorials; yet most elections reveal how far they are from persuading the greater part of their audiences.

These sheets with little opinion impact are those that carry a minimum of news and instead merchandise slaughter and suicide and the products of the gossip gleaners, the love-lornists and the rest of the off-news-beat tribe. They make friends or rather customers but they influence few people.

Many newspapers have given up the editorial ghost and depend for opinion on columnists or editorials supplied by syndicates. In many instances the columnist has priority in the reader's mind over the editorial writer; people seem to require opinions for prestige reasons and many of their viewpoints are absorbed from favorite commentators who are certainly positive, even if, more than infrequently, inaccurate.

To a certain degree, the columns do supply enlightenment, but they cannot take the place of the vigorous editorial page, because they tend to be targeted at special audiences (such as the Lippmann-ese cerebral group, the Alsopian damn-the-torpedoes following or the large "inside-dope" contingent); because in the effort to attract attention they seek out special and exclusive angles of stories— a practice that frequently results in distortion; and because, being syndicated and therefore far-flung, they are written from a national rather than a community viewpoint. In contrast, the home-bred and home-nurtured editorial writer can take a much more intimate approach; he can consider complex issues in terms of immediate and local impact.

In addition to the forthright presentation of its own views, the newspaper should make ample provision for the publication of other opinions. This is the important issue of accessibility. A disturbing number of voices are raised in sharp protest against the press as an "instrument of the 'establishment,' " particularly, as indicated in the black and youth segments of the population. It is alarming that in the Negro ghettos there is little faith in either the metropolitan newspapers or the television networks; radio, as noted, has a somewhat less skeptical audience.

Hazel Henderson, an astute observer of the journalistic scene, believes that "the battle now shaping up over the public's right of access to the mass media may well be the most important constitutional issue of the decade. Until minority opinion groups are provided with a right of access to mass media and thereby society's group consciousness, they will continue to behave in any aberrant way necessary to get attention—in sit-ins, in demonstrations, even in violence." [3] Since such outbreaks lead to backlashes, counter demonstrations and counter violence, the result is chaos.

Paul L. Fisher and Ralph Lowenstein, editors of *Race and the News Media*, a book based on a conference held at the University of Missouri, come to this conclusion:

"The media have not studied and related events in the Negro revolution to issues such as urbanization, education, automation, the anti-poverty problem, the population explosion—all elements that have significant bearing on the position of the Negro today. In other words, they are not covering the Negro 'beat' full time or full measure . . .

"Speaker after speaker stressed the need to tell the whole story—to deal with de facto segregation, the difficulties encountered by Negroes in getting jobs and the bias that lies beneath the surface, shackling the Negro as painfully and with the same malevolent effect as the chains of overt discrimination. What is not a crisis is not usually reported, and what is not or cannot be made visual is often not televised." [4]

Some newspapers are trying energetically to correct the situation. One that has been relatively successful is the *Fort Worth Star-Telegram,* which has been commended by that city's Community Relations Commission for unbiased reporting and display of news about Negroes. What prodded the newspaper to re-examine its coverage, according to Jack Butler, its editor, was a comment he heard from a Negro boy who felt a story about a white bus driver shooting a black boy was distorted. "What did you expect?" the young Negro said. "A white man's newspaper sends a white reporter to interview a white cop about a white bus driver killing a Negro boy. Did you expect the truth?" This was Mr. Butler's reaction: "If 20 per cent of our population — the Negro community — felt that way about us, it was time for some soul-searching."

Regarding his paper's new approach to coverage of minorities, Mr. Butler says: "What they were concerned with was whether the *Star-Telegram* was fair to the kid charged with crime, whether we reported their sons in Vietnam or their daughters at the altar. We will keep on trying to find out whether their kids are getting an education and a chance at a job. But it seems to me that what the report [from the Community Relations Commission] cries out for is the human dignity of being treated as a person." [5]

Another example of attempts to give minority groups access to the media is the establishment of the Community News Service, which reports on New York City's black and Puerto Rican communities and covers stories that do not ordinarily get adequate coverage in the press. Negro and Puerto Rican reporters are used as much as possible. Philip Horton, who conceived the project, has received letters from other cities throughout the country indicating an interest in a similar service. Expansion is both desirable and essential.

There are various other approaches that can be made by way of correction. It has been suggested by Ben Bagdikian, a *Washington Post* executive, that newspapers should occasionally set aside a full page, prepared by skilled journalists, for presenting clearly and fairly the ideas of the most thoughtful experts on the solutions of specific public problems. "The editorial would still survive as the paper's own opinion, but the readers would be exposed to other opinions, presented in clear language, in a standard attractive format offering a series of answers." [6]

More space should be given to letters to the editor, to debates in which both sides of controversial issues are presented, to the re-printing of editorials from other newspapers. And more dialogue of consequence must take place between newspapers and citizens, especially the blacks, the young, and other members of minority groups which do not have any genuine access to the newspaper columns.

The process requires an open mind and a re-ordering of newspaper space. It is a chore many editors are reluctant to take on, because they like to believe they are almost always right and always cramped for editorial space.

As Guardian of Ethics

For some strange reason, most editors feel that they must appear omniscient—seeing all evil, hearing all evil, speaking no evil. They may make a heinous error on page one but in all likelihood the correction (unless, of course, a libel suit is involved) will appear on the ship news page or another back page. They do not seem to realize that if, now and then, they nod they are excused because they are human and not supermen. And so they resist both self and outside examination.

(It might be well for editors to keep in mind that the editorial "we" is pompous and misleading; as Bill Nye said: "There are only two people entitled to use the editorial 'we,' an editor and a man with a tape worm.")

The newspaper industry announces portentously every so often that it is doing a job of self-portraiture. But the eventual composi-tion is usually an abstraction that might be titled: "Whitewash on Whitewash." Television's efforts to view the press have succeeded to only a limited extent in penetrating the murky skies; the longer tele-scopes have been kept under wraps.

As for the common run of critics, they are likely to be too bitter, such as ex-editors (as a result of distressing encounters with journal-ism); or too indulgent, such as directors and professors in journalistic institutions, (because they are seeking subsidy or reassurance that they are part of the newspaper business). Most of the critics, in fact, deal with the fringe defects rather than the fundamental faults of present-day journalism. There are, to be sure, notable exceptions: critics such as Ben Bagdikian, Irving Dilliard, Edwin Diamond, the late A. J. Liebling of the *New Yorker*, and publications such as the *Columbia Journalism Review*. But these voices are few and heard only at intervals. The job has to be done by the press itself.

There are publishers' associations, and journalistic fraternities which profess dedication to the improvement of newspaper practices and content. They arrange conclaves to provide debate and illumination, but they fall, much of the time, on their typographical faces.

These two facts are revelatory of the general situation: the American Newspaper Publishers Association spends more than half a million dollars a year for research; most of it is assigned to mechanical or commercial inquiry and little for editorial betterment; the budget of the American Society of Newspaper Editors is $35,000 a year; nothing is allocated for research. There is obviously something wrong here.

The newspapers must be willing to submit to scrutiny by outside bodies. One such institution is that of the ombudsman, a person designated by the newspaper—the *Louisville Courier-Journal* and the *Washington Post* have them—to investigate complaints about the handling of the news. There is considerable merit also in the concept of a press council, local or regional or national. The model is the British Press Council, a most successful enterprise, composed of representatives of publishers, of editors and news staffs and of the general public; it passes judgment on complaints and hands down verdicts which, while they are non-binding, are published in the newspapers and have considerable impact.

The press council concept has become a matter of heated debate in American newspaper circles and it has now engaged the attention of the lay critics of the press. Not surprisingly, in their obsession that no outsider should look over their shoulders—the kind of obsession they condemn with polysyllabic adjectives where public officials are concerned—many editors and publishers vociferously oppose the press council idea or any proposal that even approaches it.

That attitude was revealed in a survey by the Associated Press Managing Editors' Association of 53 editors and public officials. More than 75% of the public officials favored establishment of local press councils, more than 50% of editors opposed it. Eighty-nine per cent of the public officials agreed that professional journalism organizations should set up permanent ethics committees with resources to investigate public complaints about newspapers and publish full reports of their findings; only 54% of the editors favored such bureaus.[7]

Editors and publishers should recognize that newspapers are at least semi-public institutions and they should apply to them the same scrutiny and standards they prescribe for any other public institution. They are not above the world, they are of it.

As Responsible Employer

Morale, meaning enthusiasm and team-work, is as important in a newspaper office as it is in almost any enterprise—more important perhaps, because in the news room and in the editorial sancta, the management is dealing with creative people who are likely to have more than a normal assortment of eccentricities and hang-ups. Involved here are the relations between reporters and editors and between editors and publishers.

A vital phase of the morale problem is the financial one. Average newspaper pay is lower than that for almost any other profession; starting salaries for engineers and pharmacists is about $9,000; for accountants $8,300; for journalists, $6,000. Thus many bright young men find the economic going so rough that they desert newspaper work for advertising, TV, and many, too many, for "public relations" (meaning press agentry). Penny-pinching in the editorial rooms is as unwise as it is unhumanitarian.

I do not accept the publishers' economic alibi that they cannot afford higher pay for the news and editorial departments. Editorial costs range from five to ten per cent of the total newspaper budget and surely cuts can be made in other areas so that the primary product, the news, can have the attention without which a newspaper is little more than newsprint.

Some of this false economy is due to the fact that publishers in general are too isolated from editorial problems. Often when a publisher is asked to allocate funds for editorial research, the reply might be something of this order: "You know we would not think of invading the editorial sanctum. God and Horace Greeley forbid!"

But the fact is that publishers do deal with editorial matters — in fixing the amount of editorial space, in setting the editorial budget, in making editorial policy, especially in political areas. Moreover, they *should* deal with editorial matters, for theirs is the over-all direction and the ultimate responsibility. And even as businessmen they should be vitally concerned with what is their basic merchandise, the editorial content of their newspapers.

There are, it is true, editors who are publishers and publishers who are editors. (You can't tell which came first, the chicken or the egghead.) But they are the exceptions; for the most part the two are neither identical nor twins. Most publishers insist on living in areas segregated from those of the editors, with ironic curtains in between. Certainly there has been improvement in the caliber of publishers since the 1920's, when William Allen White wrote this epitaph for Frank Munsey, large-scale buyer and burier of papers: "Frank Munsey contributed to the journalism of his day the talents of a meat packer, the morals of a moneychanger, and the manners of an undertaker. He and his kind have about succeeded in transforming a once-noble profession into an eight per cent security. May he rest in trust." There has been definite improvement in the managerial ranks but there is still a long way to go.

There is finally the question of the quality and morale of the staff. There must be done a better job in educating journalists, because in these times of complex news, there is great need of reporters who are capable of understanding and of conveying that understanding to the reader, reporters who are both knowledgeable and literate.

Journalism cannot be taught in the sense that law or most other professions can be taught. The essential newspaper "techniques" are not techniques at all but touches of talent. Instruction can be given in such matters as copy-styling, headline-counting, make-up and the like, but no man can be taught how to write or to edit; if he has latent abilities in these areas, they can be developed, but the capacity cannot be injected into him like so much vaccine.

A sound formula for the making of a good reporter might be this: a basic education which he shall ceaselessly broaden; a curiosity about all things and all people; an ability to sense and correlate events; a gift for describing them in simple yet vigorous prose, with an occasional dash of poetry.

As for the good editors, they are born not made. They do not edit according to surveys or polls. That is fatal; the sure formula for success is not easily come upon but the sure formula for failure is to try to please everybody. The real editor edits for himself; if he does not have the stuff no pollster can save him.

There are institutions that attempt the training of news personnel and others that offer seminars for journalists. But there are large gaps. Many so-called schools of journalism are little more than bargain basement outfits that offer unwary customers courses in almost everything. from press agentry through indoctrination in TV commercials to Don Quixotic freelancing. Institutes for practicing journalists perform a useful service in bringing together newspapermen in seminars, but some of the fundamental issues in journalism—such as the problems of interpretation and the proper coverage and presentation of international news—are dealt with only haphazardly. Moreover, the emphasis in the seminars is focused increasingly on the promotion, mechanical and accounting aspects of the newspaper, to the neglect of vital editorial issues.

*　　*　　*

There are, as indicated, formidable tasks that confront the newspaper business and/or profession. What, then, can be set down as the qualities of the true newspaper?

In my judgment the true newspaper reports the tides of events as well as individual happenings . . . It does the job of interpretation consistently and deeply, carefully drawing the line between interpretation and opinion . . . Even though complete and constant objectivity is a super-human goal, it keeps the ideal firmly in the foreground . . . It establishes good communication between newspaper and reader . . . It does not shirk the task of soul-searching . . . It looks upon itself not merely as a business but as an institution with a large social responsibility . . . It leads rather than follows; it molds opinion rather than being molded by it . . . And it does all this humanly and humbly.

As for the obsession with making newspapers entertaining, I contend that in this area they cannot compete with television, with its spectaculars, its stand-up and sit-down comics and its movies, early and late-late. Therefore, it seems good business as well as good ethics for newspapers to revert to their original assignment, the only assignment that justifies their existence, the publication of the news.

In the light of this performance of the press, what image does the public have of it? That question is discussed in the next chapter.

21 : Responsibility and Credibility Gaps

In two areas the press, in increasing degree, is challenged: on the issue of responsibility (questions of ethics and propriety and taste) and credibility (questions of accuracy or bias).

A canyon of mistrust has been evolving between the media and reader-listeners, who are saying in growing number, "I happen to know about that story and I know it's wrong," or "they shouldn't have printed that," or "the press slants things," or "the press is managed."

A recent Harris survey indicates that only 35% of readers believe that newspapers treat stories "fairly and impartially"; 55% feel newspapers are "sometimes unfair and slanted." Television fares better; 61% of its audience considers its news treatment "fair and impartial," but 33% feel it is "sometimes unfair and slanted." Further evidence of this scepticism about the press is found in the proliferation of the underground and minority newspapers whose main themes are attacks on the various "establishments."

Both the responsibility and credibility issues have of late been the subject of a great deal of concern. (Examples: the Nixon-Agnew-et-al attacks on the press and the sharp exchanges over the Pentagon Papers.) The two issues are in a way related in that doubts about press responsibility add weight to uneasiness about credibility. Both, however, are such important factors in the opinion process that they are treated separately in this chapter—first, the question of responsibility and then the credibility problem.

The Responsibility Issue

In rejoinder to those who criticize the press on the score of irresponsibility, many editors will assert that their assignment is to publish the news regardless of consequences. In effect they say: "It is a newspaperman's duty to print the news and to raise hell." (And, not incidentally, pick up circulation.) Privately, many TV editors endorse this credo, although publicly they are more cautious because their audience is wider and less knowledgeable.

I wonder. What news and what hell? Do you print all the facts for the sake of stirring up a storm without regard to consequences? I cannot believe that this is a responsible way of exercising the freedom guaranteed by the First Amendment.

The issue of press responsibility involves such sensitive matters as these: *Security:* Are there times when the media should withhold news in the public interest? To what extent should they be concerned about "national security?" *Fair Trial:* Do they respect the right of an individual to his fair day in court? *Yellowness:* Are they guilty of sensationalism and lack of perspective? Of want of a sense of proportion?

The Security Debate

The issue of "national security" is a delicate one. At the outset it is important that a differentiation be made between the two kinds of information involved: one, information the disclosure of which would endanger the nation's security; the other, information which is withheld solely because it may put the government in an unfavorable light. (There is no question about news in this second category; here there is no excuse whatsoever for withholding information.)

In the first area, the press as a whole has behaved with reasonable sensitivity. Of course there have been and will be exceptions. One conspicuous example involved the *Chicago Tribune*. A staunchly conservative paper, it had vigorously opposed American entry into the Second World War, and had been attacked in return by those who favored the Allied cause. But nothing the *Tribune* said in its editorials against our joining the war compared with its disclosure that the United States had broken the Japanese naval code. Breaking the code had been an enormous advantage to Washington in the war against Japan. But the *Tribune* lost us that advantage when it published stories alerting the enemy to the fact that its code was now known to us and thus clearly helped his war effort.

In the case of Vietnam, there have been demands that the Presidents—from Kennedy to Nixon — give the nation "more facts." Obviously, we cannot blueprint our military program for the American public without telegraphing our intentions to the enemy. And when there are secret diplomatic parleys under way we cannot disclose our ultimate terms without giving away our hand. There is no doubt that there has been too much concealment and too much misleading information by the government. But surely the government cannot be expected to divulge everything or even almost everything.

An outstanding case of withholding the news for the sake of "national security" involves the 1961 Bay of Pigs invasion of Castro's Cuba. The *New York Times* received information about the plans for the expedition, which was to be carried through by Cuban exiles trained and equipped by the U. S. There ensued among *Times* editors a sharp debate as to what should be done with the story. Some argued that it should be published on the ground that it was the newspaper's duty to throw full light on a questionable government action; others argued that the dispatch should be toned down or even killed in the interest of "national security." The final decision was to eliminate references to an "imminent invasion" and to CIA participation in the operation and to publish the story under a restrained headline.

Some years later, Clifton Daniel, an associate editor of the *Times*, reported that President Kennedy had remarked to Turner Catledge, then managing editor, that if the *Times* had printed all it knew about the preparations for the operation, the nation would have been saved from making a "colossal mistake."[1] James Reston, a vice president of the *Times* and a key figure in the decision, disagrees. "If I had to do it over," he says, "I would do exactly what we did at the time. It is ridiculous to think that publishing the fact that the invasion was imminent would have avoided the disaster. I am quite sure the operation would have gone forward."[2]

I agree with Reston; I do not think the *Times* should have published the full story. In a situation like this the newspaper does not have, as has the President, access to all the information bearing on the wisdom of this kind of operation and the prospects of its success. As for the Kennedy remark, I suspect it was quite casual and based on hindsight.

I recall a conversation with Mr. Kennedy at the time, in which he assumed all the blame for the failure, saying he had been misled by

the intelligence reports. But he believed that if the press felt free
to disclose secret operations without regard to the national interest,
no government could engage in such operations even though they
might be necessary to counter similar Russian undercover activity.

The case of the U-2 is another example of the withholding of news in
the national interest. For two years before the reconnaisance plane
was shot down over the Soviet Union in 1960 and the pilot, Francis
Gary Powers, captured, the *Times* knew that such flights were taking
place. It decided not to publish the fact, because, if it did, the
operations would be ended and an important source of information
about Russian military preparations cut off.

Our interventions in Laos and Cambodia raised similar questions
but the circumstances were different in that these were hardly secret
operations. For months correspondents at the front had been reporting that American "advisers" and planes had been active in these
areas, yet Washington would not confirm these reports. Finally, under
pressure from the press, Mr. Nixon admitted that we were involved
in both countries to an extent the public had not suspected. The impact was tremendous, much greater than it would have been if the
people had been informed about the need for the moves. In these
instances, I feel the newspapers acted in a responsible way in printing
the dispatches.

Government should recognize that secrecy and censorship in any
guise are dangerous practices and should be used with the utmost
caution. For its part, the press must be willing to sacrifice scoops
and sensations when the public interest is clearly involved. In this
connection, the case of the Pentagon Papers has special interest and
concern.

The Pentagon Papers Issue

The publication by the news media in July 1971 of the classified
Pentagon Papers was a spectacular episode in the conflict between press
and government and it raised vital questions that remain unanswered.
The case involves a whole series of issues, rather than a single and
simple one—issues of press freedom, of the "right to know," of national security, of classification of government documents, and, particularly, the issue of press responsibility.

In brief these are the facts. In the summer of 1967 Robert S.

McNamara, then Secretary of Defense, commissioned a massive history of United States involvement in Vietnam since World War II. The document was to be based mainly on the papers in the Pentagon files; the White House and State Department files were not available.

The team assigned to the study was a group of 36, composed of Pentagon personnel on a secondary level, army intelligence officers and some experts from the Rand Corporation; it was headed by Leslie Gelb, who had been in charge of policy planning in the Pentagon's Office of International Security Affairs.

To insure candor the authors were promised anonymity. One name that did emerge, however, and most prominently, was that of Daniel Ellsberg, who had been with Rand, served for two years in Saigon, and became a research fellow at the Massachusetts Institute of Technology. In his days in Vietnam Ellsberg had been a definite hawk; when he turned dove is not clear. In any case, by the time the study was completed he had become completely disenchanted with the war and was determined to do what he could to end it. In Ellsberg's eyes, the documents added up to a severe indictment of the conduct of the war and of those who conducted it.

Ellsberg sent these Pentagon Papers (as they came to be known) to the Senate Foreign Relations Committee in 1970 but they were ignored. He persevered and in February 1971, after the Laotian invasion, he offered them to various newspapers for publication. The *New York Times* (which did not reveal where it obtained the documents) began publication of excerpts on June 13, 1971.

The following day Attorney General John N. Mitchell asked the *Times* voluntarily to stop publication and to return the papers to the Pentagon on the ground that such publication would cause "irreparable injury" to the defense interests of the United States." He cited the Espionage Law of 1917 which stipulates that "whoever having unauthorized possession of, access to, or control over any document, writing, code book . . . or information relating to the national defense which information the possessor has reason to believe could be used to the injury of the United States or to the advantages of any foreign nation, willfully communicates, delivers, transmits . . . the same to any person not entitled to receive it, or willfully retains the same or fails to deliver it to the officer or employee of the United States entitled to receive it . . . shall be fined not more than $10,000 or imprisoned not more than ten years, or both."

The *Times* refused to stop publication. The Justice Department then obtained a temporary restraining order and filed a civil suit in the District Court for the Southern District of New York seeking a permanent injunction. When the court ruled in favor of the *Times,* the Attorney General went to the Court of Appeals for the Second Circuit which ruled on June 21 that the *Times* could resume publication but could not include any material the government considered likely to endanger national security. The *Times* then appealed the case to the Supreme Court, which on June 30 held that the *Times* should be allowed to resume publication.

The Supreme court's decision was hailed by the press as a "landmark" victory for freedom of the press and for the public's "right to know." But reading of the decision and the opinions, six concurring and three dissenting, leads to puzzlement as to what the verdict really settled.

The decision of the court was brief and based on a narrow area. Its ruling was confined to a statement that the court on previous occasions had held that "any system of prior restraints of expression comes to this court bearing a heavy presumption against its constitutional validity," that "the Government thus carries a heavy burden of showing justification for the enforcement of such a restraint" and that in this case the Government had not met that burden.

That was all: There should be no prior restraint unless the government could make a formidable case for such action. This was surely a restricted ruling and hardly a "landmark" decision. The Justices, however, each wrote individual opinions which encompassed a wide range of disparate issues, legal points and personal observations.

Justice Black, for example, with Justice Douglas concurring, contended that "paramount among the duties of a free press is the duty to prevent any part of the Government from deceiving the people and sending them off to distant lands to die of foreign fevers and foreign shot and shell." Justice Marshall observed that since Congress had twice in this century refused to pass censorship laws, even in wartime, the Supreme Court could hardly act as censor in the case of the "Pentagon Papers."

Four Justices—White, Stewart, Burger and Blackmun—made or concurred with the point that the court's refusal to grant an injunction prior to the publication of the Pentagon Papers did not mean that it might not have a good case for criminal prosecution after publication.

One further note should be added: the outstanding impression the public had out of its perusal of the newspapers' stories was that President Johnson was guilty of grave deceit when in his campaign against Barry Goldwater, he made a paramount issue of the Senator's hawkish intent as against his own dovish purpose.

These are the facts. But there are still a number of mysteries: What were Secretary McNamara's motives in ordering the study? (Did he, as reported, feel deeply that the war was wrong? Had he a sense of guilt about it and did he want the story told so the nation would not embark on another such "misadventure"?) Was the study team decisively against the war policy and thus made a slanted rather than an objective report? (Was it appointed, as alleged by some, because it had this viewpoint?) Why was so little attention paid to the document? (When Clark Clifford succeeded McNamara in the Pentagon the study was only casually mentioned to him; when it was completed in 1969 after Mr. Nixon became President and Melvin Laird Defense Secretary, why did no one in the higher echelons read it, instead of ordering it filed away in the secret documents vaults and distributing only a few copies?)

So much for the facts and the speculations. These are the issues as I see them: (1) Is there involved here an issue of national security? (2) Or an issue of press freedom and the people's "right to know"? (3) Or an issue of classification? (4) Or is it entirely an issue of press responsibility?

The first question, of security, is hardly involved; there are virtually no surprises in those parts of the papers that were published. Surely it was generally known that the war decisions were tough, that there was a lot of backing and filling, that the administration, even though it had said in the campaign that it would not escalate, soon began escalation, that Mr. Johnson's advisers were largely an aggregation of hawks (even though most of them have since turned dove.)

What is new about all this? The only newness, if any, arises out of the fact that the events of the mid-60's are being judged in the perspective of the early '70's, in other words out of historic context. The London *Economist* made this point in its issue of June 26, 1971:

"The evidence is not all in yet, and will not be for quite a time. But it is worth repeating what seemed to most people to be the case at the time, and still seems to be. This is that the war had been set in motion by a decision taken in North Vietnam; that North Vietnam was supplying the apparently decisive margin of men and guns; that the superb military efficiency of the Communists had brought the South Vietnamese army to the point of collapse; that the defeat of South Vietnam would have been followed by a similar process in Laos and Cambodia and possibly elsewhere; and that for ten years the world, not least the enemies of the United States, had been watching to see if the Americans would allow that to happen. This account of how things looked in 1964 may not be the final story; but it is important enough that it not be left out of the row about those documents. After all, it is why Mr. Johnson acted as he did."

Is there, then, an issue of "freedom of the press," of the people's "right to know" on which the press rested virtually the whole of its case? Now it is without question the duty of a newspaper to ferret out wrong-doing and to promote as vigorously as it can the national welfare. Nor is there any doubt that "freedom of the press" is a precious right that needs to be safeguarded with the utmost vigilance.

On the other hand, "freedom of the press" is not an absolute right, superior to the laws of the land, to the rights of individuals, to the canons of responsibility. (No one, as Justice Holmes pointed out in a famous aphorism about freedom of speech, has the right to falsely cry "fire" in a crowded theatre.)

In the case of the Pentagon Papers, it seems to me, the news media were asserting that the First Amendment gave them an unqualified prerogative to print classified material on their own authority. It is not a question as to whether the material should have been classified in the first place; it is wholly an issue as to whether an individual, whether he be butcher, baker, or even editor, has the right to judge what is a matter of national security and properly classified and what is not, and, if he decides the latter, to declassify it.

As for the third question—is the system of classification the issue?—

there is no doubt that the system needs a complete overhauling, but that issue is involved only tangentially. The principle stands: the government classifies and, if we are to have orderly and democratic procedure, only the government can declassify. If the system is abused the remedy is to change the system or the government or both, but not to assert and to implement recklessly a "right" that does not exist.

The answer to the final question—is the real issue one other than security or press freedom?—is indicated in what has been said above. My answer is yes; the basic issue, as I see it, is not the issue of security which the government raised or the issue of press freedom which was accented so heavily by the press; it is the issue of press responsibility—the question of the right to declassify government documents. This is not a legal but an ethical matter and on that score I think the news media can be faulted.

There is another sharp criticism of the media's conduct in the case. Much of the material, it was charged, had been prepared by reporters who had expressed strong convictions against the Vietnam war policies and it had been published in newspapers which had taken firm stands alongside the dissenters. Admiral U. S. Grant Sharp (retired), commander in the Pacific during the height of the war, made this argument in the *New York Times* of August 6, 1971:

"So what we have here is not necessarily an objective history, but rather a distillation of a large document written by people who have a definite point of view. We might also ask what is the point of view of the various historians appointed by Mr. McNamara to develop this history. As revealed by the history itself, a great many civilians in the Defense Department in the middle of 1967 were disenchanted with the war, convinced that the bombing of North Vietnam was ineffective and that we should get out of Vietnam as quickly as possible."

Admiral Sharp suggests that both the writers of the papers, Mr. Ellsberg and his group, and some of the media analysts who commented on the documents were both lacking in objectivity—in other words, that slant was piled upon slant.

Two other related questions arise: Were the disclosures important enough to justify the prominent play the news media gave them? And are the news media contending, as Justice Burger suggested in his dissenting opinion, that a newspaper has "the right to protect its sources but the government does not"? I would express strong doubts on both points.

The media won general applause for their "disclosures" in the press and among important segments of the public. It should be realized, though, that the press does have a Peter Zenger complex and every effort to defend the First Amendment, whether logical or not, is likely to get a tremendous hand. As for the public, obviously the critics of the war policy could have been expected to hail the publication with loud huzzas. But this again was emotion rather than reason; these critics had become convinced that this was a dirty, useless war and now their suspicions were further strengthened by revelations that purported to show that the enterprise had been conceived and nurtured in sin.

Yet there are indications that the public was and is somewhat confused about the issues involved. A Gallup poll (published in *Newsweek* on July 5, 1971) asked how those surveyed felt about the government's action in trying to prevent the publication of the papers. The was the result: approve, 33%; disapprove, 48%; no opinion, 19%.

This question was also posed: "Taking everything about the current situation into account, is the greater danger that the freedom of the press might be violated, or that the nation's security might be harmed by letting the information out?" The answer: freedom of press violated, 34%; national security harmed, 57%; no opinion, 19%. Finally, the pollsters asked: "Do you think the press is too quick to print classified information whether or not it might hurt the nation's security? "The answers: yes, 56%; no, 28%; no opinion, 16%.

It was suggested earlier that even though no formal violation of the Espionage Act was involved and no apparent damage done to security, nevertheless there are other unfortunate situations that might well result from the publication of documents such as the Pentagon Papers.

There is the danger that in the future no confidential memos will be written to chief executives or even lesser executives because sometime or other they may be made public, through thefts or leaks or otherwise. There is the danger that foreign governments will hesitate about dealing candidly with us; that happened in the case of the Canadian government when the opposition gave Premier Pierre

Trudeau a rough time, charging that he was an "errand boy" of the United States, citing as proof one of the "secret documents" in which Washington suggested his intercession with Hanoi. Finally, there has been so much distrust of government that the publication of any material which adds to that distrust should be treated with the greatest sensitivity.

As for the charges against President Johnson, the reply is made that the proposal to bomb North Vietnam, urged by the Pentagon before the election, was only one of several contingency plans but there is no evidence that Mr. Johnson had agreed to it before the election. Despite Mr. Johnson's penchant for intrigue I am inclined to believe this; I have always thought that he was on the whole an honest even though devious man.

Leslie H. Gelb, the coordinator of the Pentagon Papers team, lends support to this view. In an article published by *Life* September 17, 1971 he says that the *Times* "should have stated explicitly that President Johnson before the 1964 elections was not part of the general consensus in our government to bomb North Vietnam." And he adds, "Our studies depict him as quite resistant to this course."

As a result of the Pentagon Papers episode there has begun a re-examination of the whole classification system. But regardless of this over-hauling and regardless of any legal and constitutional questions arising out of the controversy, the problem of responsibility still confronts the press; only the editors and the broadcasters, not the courts, not the government, and not the public, can resolve it.

Free Press vs. Fair Trial

Another issue of responsibility arises out of the seeming conflict between the First and Sixth Amendments (the First a guarantee of freedom of the press, the Sixth a guarantee of fair trial). In the simple days when communication was slow and limited in range, this kind of clash rarely occurred. But coverage on television and by newspapers has become so detailed and so wide-spread that in certain dramatic cases it seems almost inconceivable that a fair trial could take place because virtually nowhere in the country could jurors be found who would not have read or seen reports about these cases.

There was, for example, the investigation into the Mafia operations in New Jersey in 1970. A federal judge released 1,200 pages of transcript and the logs of alleged Mafia conversations, all obtained years before through illegal wiretapping and bugging. The material, published in newspapers and aired on TV and radio, was clearly injurious to the reputations, perhaps the careers, of numerous persons who were the unknowing subjects of the conversations; all of it was hearsay and unproved allegation. Moreover, the FBI conceded that persons overheard may well have been name-dropping, boasting and exaggerating in an effort to impress one another.

Tom Wicker observed in the *New York Times:* "Not only have numerous persons suffered infringement of their rights and damage to their reputations, without a shred of proof being advanced that the allegations against them have merit; but if any of them ever should be charged with crimes even remotely linked to anything discussed in these transcripts, it would be most difficult to show that their cases should not be thrown out because of prejudicial publicity. So not only may innocent men be considered guilty, but guilty ones may go free." [3]

I agree. The Sixth Amendment should be respected even though some editors and broadcasters may consider it a restriction on the First; the Mafia transcripts should not have been released and, if released, should not have been published.

Another case which involves the question of the Sixth Amendment is the My Lai or Songmy incident in which American soldiers were accused of massacring Vietnamese civilians. When finally after an interval of sixteen months the story became known, the press quoted at length comments by Vietnamese civilians said to be survivors of the killings and by GI's who claimed to have been present at the time. The media likewise reported unsubstantiated statements about Lieut. William Calley, the platoon leader accused of killing more than 100 persons. Yet there was no uncontradicted evidence to support any of these allegations. The judge in the pre-trial hearings in the Calley case became so concerned about the publicity that he issued an order against further pre-trial interviews with potential witnesses. "This is not to be a trial by the press," he said.

Thus the question arose: Did these reports and interviews prejudice the right of fair trial for the American soldiers charged with taking part in the alleged massacre? I believe they did; the general story could have been told without disclosing the parts individuals played in the episode. (Incidentally, there was wide criticism of the way the story had been handled by the mass media. A Harris poll in December, 1969, indicated that 67% of those surveyed believed that the press should not have reported the statements made prior to the trial.)

A landmark case in this area is that of Samuel H. Sheppard, the Cleveland osteopath who was convicted of the murder of his wife after a trial conducted, as the U. S. Supreme Court later noted, in "a carnival atmosphere." On July 4, 1954, Dr. Sheppard's wife was found bludgeoned to death in her bed. Dr. Sheppard contended that she had been slain by a "bushy-haired intruder." From the beginning, the story was played sensationally by the three Cleveland newspapers. Before any arrests were made, the *Cleveland Press,* in a front-page editorial, urged that the police give Dr. Sheppard "the same third degree to which any person under similar circumstances is subjected." The *Press* ran such headlines as "Why Isn't Sam Sheppard In Jail? Quit Stalling, Bring Him In." When the defendant was arrested three weeks after the crime, other newspapers began to cover the story in equally sensational fashion.

Dr. Sheppard steadfastly asserted his innocence, but the jury convicted him and sentenced him to life imprisonment. Almost ten years later the conviction was upset in the United States District Court on the ground that the trial had been "a mockery of justice." The case went to the Supreme Court which in 1966 reversed the conviction—without ruling on the osteopath's guilt—on the ground that "inherently prejudicial publicity" had prevented the defendant from getting a fair trial. The action opened the way for a new trial — and Dr. Sheppard was acquitted.

This problem of prejudicial publicity is a complicated one. It is not a new issue, but in these days of wide coverage it has become acute. The American Bar Association and the U. S. Judicial Conference have adopted codes intended to correct the defects disclosed in the Sheppard case. But solutions are not easy, because in their ardent search for circulation some newspapers will print the news "regardless" of how prejudicial it may be to the rights of an accused.

Another Charge: Provocation

One recurring charge against the press is that it promotes violence, by presenting films and articles that vividly portray destruction and looting and thus encourage others to try their hands at similar forays. The same charge is made about coverage of civil disorders; for example, the study group on mass media of the National Commission on the Causes and Prevention of Violence, established by President Nixon, concluded:

"The press reports violence because violence sells the press. . . The press encourages violence because the violent seek the publicity that the press provides . . . The news media can play a significant role in lessening the potential of violence by functioning as a faithful conduit for intergroup communication, providing a true market-place for ideas, providing full access to the day's intelligence, and reducing the incentive to confrontation that sometimes erupts in violence. This is a subtle and uncertain mission . . . Too many news organizations fear social ideas and social action. As a result they stimulate backlash and arouse anxiety, only to fall silent, or limit themselves to irrelevant cliches, when thoughtful solutions are required." [4]

The President's Advisory Commission on Civil Disorders (1968) passed judgment on the reporting of the 1967 riots, the events leading up to them and the consequences. In answer to the question "What effect do the mass media have on the riots?", the commission arrived at three broad conclusions: "The portrayal of the violence that occurred last summer failed to reflect accurately its scale and character; the over-all effect was, we believe, an exaggeration of both mood and event; and ultimately most important, we believe that the media have thus far failed to report adequately on the causes and consequences of civil disorders and the underlying problems of race relations." [5]

On the whole I agree with this assessment; some of the press can be accused of irresponsibility because isolated incidents have been described out of context and some events staged for the cameras. But, what is most important, the press has done little, notably in the case of Watts in Los Angeles, to alert the communities to the inflammable situations in their ghettos.

The Credibility Problem

"Credibility gap" was a phrase invented by the press to describe the public distrust, first of the Johnson and later of the Nixon administration. Of late the press has been hoist by its own label.

Critics of the press add to their indictment counts of inaccuracy and distortion. The main reasons, in my view, for the credibility gap are these: the complexity of the news; inaccuracy and bias in both newspaper and television reporting; and the "crisis complex" that possesses both editors and broadcasters.

The Tough Job of Reporting

The news assignment has become increasingly difficult. Two examples: the USSR and the Middle East. In Russia, more than half a century after the Bolshevik Revolution, it is still almost impossible to penetrate the wall of secrecy. As Henry Shapiro of United Press International, who has been Kremlin-watching since 1933, puts it, "In Russia, it's the government that makes the news. A government official hands it out and possibly answers a few questions. You take it. If a fellow started moving around, talking to ordinary people — a real eager beaver — he'd be in trouble in no time at all." [6] Foreign newsmen do not have the kind of access to government offices they have in Western countries; they are generally confined to an area within twenty-five miles of Moscow.

Soviet censorship was "abolished" in 1961, but foreign correspondents are sharply watched by government officials and, if their dispatches are considered "too rough" by the press-watchers or even if their publications carry something displeasing to the Kremlin, they are expelled from the country, as Stanley Cloud of *Time* magazine and and John Dornberg of *Newsweek* were in 1970. This kind of post-censorship is more effective than pre-censorship, because a Damocles sword of uncertainty always hangs over the correspondent's head and he must be constantly on guard lest the blade descend.

So the Moscow correspondents are reduced largely to talking to one another, to Western diplomats and, occasionally and unfruitfully, to Soviet newsmen. Coverage becomes a round of cautious speculation, with no hard facts on any development which the Kremlin decides to classify. Classic examples of this were the downfall of Khrushchev in 1963 which was not predicted by any Western Kremlinologist; and the Soviet space shots, none of which was witnessed by a Western correspondent. Similar conditions exist, although not as stringently, in other Soviet-bloc countries. An Associated Press round-up of censorship in 1969 indicated, for example, that foreign newsmen in Poland and Czechoslovakia were subject to monitoring and phone tapping.[7]

(There is the story of a British diplomat who was being hard pressed by a correspondent at the UN. Finally, in exasperation, he said: "You are from Tass, I presume." The correspondent drew himself up and replied: "No, I am from Poland." Said the diplomat: "Oh, demi-Tass.")

Coverage of Middle East conflicts has also been frequently reduced to guesswork. Cairo and Jerusalem issued contradictory reports about the fighting and the terrorism and there was no way of confirming either version. Correspondents have not been allowed near the war zones, communications have been bad and censorship tough. Roy Essoyan, who covered the war for the Associated Press, has reported, "In Cairo itself you can be arrested if you flash a camera in the wrong places. Your telephones are tapped or at least spot-checked. And you can't file much beyond the official government announcements." [8] In Israel, correspondents have had more freedom and access to government officials, but military censorship has been strict and trips to the fighting fronts rare. Alfred Friendly of the *Washington Post* has said of his experience in Israel: "Outright falsification of facts is very rare indeed. But, naturally, the news sources tell it to you the way they see it or want it to be seen." [9]

Because of the complexity of the news and the difficulties of coverage, some inaccuracy is inevitable and the reader should, in all fairness, take this into account and recognize that these lapses, for the most part, are not the product of willful misrepresentation or dubious procedures.

Some of the difficulty lies in the very nature of reporting, which is a human assignment and subject therefore to human failings. Consider the problem of accuracy in observation generally. Twenty witnesses to an accident will have at least a dozen versions of how and why it happened. In confrontations between protesters and police, some observers will stress the provocations to which the officers were subjected, others will put the emphasis on police brutality. A reporter cannot write all that he sees and so he must make a selection among his findings; moreover his editor may decide to change the accent or even omit the entire story.

Nevertheless, conceding these difficulties, the astute reporter can overcome a good part of the handicap by wholesome scepticism and avoidance of too-positive conclusions. The newsman is not doing his job if he thinks only of building up a dramatic story rather than collecting the material which will explain the significance of events. There is too much obsession with "scoops" or achieving the front page or prime time on the screen. At times one wonders whether the old wire-service expression, "Get it first even if you have to get it right" does not still have some currency.

Some editors and broadcasters say that they are blamed for the blackness of the news: that they are somehow assumed to be the creators of that news rather than the carriers of it and that, just as kings in the Middle Ages ordered that the bearers of ill tidings be beheaded, so the reader-listener, in an effort to block out reality, psychologically decapitates those who make public the unpleasant facts about today's world. There is some substance, but not as much as is claimed, to this contention.

The Crisis Complex

There prevails among many editors and commentators what might be called the "Crisis Complex"—a frenetic search for headlines, a yen for the spectacular, a substitution of exclamation points for explanation. Here are five examples among hundreds:

• President Nixon's various reports on the economic situation. With unemployment rising concern about inflation and the elections of 1970 approaching, there were daily stories about Democratic criticism of the administration and pressures put on Mr. Nixon by Republicans who wanted him to try various means of restraining the economy.

Then on several occasions the White House let it be known that the President would make a major economic address. During the ensuing days, in breathless anticipation of the speech, the press would carry all manner of stories about Mr. Nixon's consultations with his advisers and about the conflict among economists on what should be done and, as the suspense grew, reports that the President would indeed resort to wage and price controls. Finally the President would deliver the long-awaited speeches. And to what effect? The basic policy, the President would announce, would remain unchanged. Mild stuff, indeed, in view of the build-ups.

And then, on August 15, 1971, came the blockbuster—the President's announcement of a "New Economic Policy," a wage-price freeze, a cut in taxes, import levies—a veritable Keynesian approach. And this time the press had virtually no hint that this eight-column news was in process; the "Crisis Complex" had missed its big chance.

• The Chilean election in late 1970. In the fall various pieces appeared predicting that Dr. Salvador Allende would become President in circumstances that promised one of the most tense periods in Latin America's history since the early years of the Cuban Revolution. There were reports of the possibility of intervention by the Chilean Army if Allende, the left-wing candidate, who had received a plurality but not a majority of the votes, were elected President by the Congress. Some correspondents warned of an economic collapse; almost all created the impression that violence was imminent as election day approached. When the day of reckoning came, Allende was formally chosen by the Congress to be President. The event did not produce an Army coup, a civil war, an economic collapse—or U. S. intervention.

• The William Rogers visit to the Mid-East in 1971. As soon as the Secretary of State announced that he would be visiting the major capitals involved in the Arab-Israeli conflict, newspapers began hailing the proposed journey as a "Mission for Peace." Mr. Rogers himself said nothing about the imminence of a break-through, and in fact was gradually sceptical, but press speculation was rife. Correspondents reported that agreement was soon to be reached between Egypt and Israel involving withdrawal of Israeli forces from the Suez bank and the re-opening of the Canal after three long years.

There were photos on the front pages of Mr. Rogers meeting Golda Meir, sitting down with Sadat, and of Assistant Secretary of State Joseph Sisco hurrying back to Cairo—but despite the hoopla, the break-through, it developed, was something for the future.

• President Nixon's pilgrimages to Europe (one soon after he entered the White House, a second in October 1970.) The television networks went hey-hey-wire; by satellite and in rainbow color, they showed All. And the newspaper reporters tried breathlessly to keep up. And what did we learn? Whom Mr. Nixon saw, what he wore, what he ate — little more. In reality it was the most preliminary of reconnaissances — an approach to a possible approach to a tentative summit meeting with the Russians. There were, to be sure, some fascinating personality shots and sketches but nothing of real significance emerged. But this did not curtail what was shown on the screen. When you bill a trip as a grand tour and deploy your cameras widely and expensively, when you shoot the works, you have to show some returns; and so, even if there is no real news, you make a fireworks display.

• The West German presidential elections in 1969. At intervals for more than a month, the unsuspecting reader or listener might well have believed that the holding of the balloting in West Berlin would surely bring on World War III. Der Tag arrived, the election was held, and nothing happened, as reported on page 10 or thereabouts in the papers and in ten seconds on the evening newscasts.

In contrast with—but just as harmful as—this tendency to overplay beforehand potentially important stories, there are the trivailities collected in the name of "human interest"—that category so beloved by the newspaper men of "The Front Page" and ever since.

An episode that took place in January 1970 illustrates how, in the breathless pursuit of "human interest," the press at times strains credibility. This was the story of Michael James Brody, the self-styled billionaire, who announced he was prepared to give his money away to promote "peace and love"; for a week, the New York press had a field day exploiting Brody's exploits. He was quoted at length without any real probing into his statements and the press made little or no effort to check the status of his bank account.

As a result, a number of poor and down-hearted persons came hundreds of miles in the hope of sharing in Brody's largess; some stood for days in the cold waiting for him to make an appearance. Finally, he did appear, but it was on the Ed Sullivan Show, playing the guitar and uttering not a word of apology or explanation.

Eventually Brody was exposed; his inheritance, it turned out, was less than a million dollars and there was not enough in his bank accounts to cover the checks he had issued. If Brody had had the idea of taking the public for a ride, the New York press had surely provided the vehicle.

Obviously overplay of the news, whether it be a trivial or a paramount issue, must be eschewed in the interest of credibility— and responsibility, too.

Basic Reasons for Doubt

These questions about responsibility and credibility call for stern examination by the press itself. But first the press will have to realize that it does not see itself as others see it.

This delusion was clearly revealed in a survey undertaken in December, 1969, by the Associated Press Managing Editors Association, an organization with considerable know-how and prestige. Responses to an elaborate questionnaire were received from twenty-eight editors and twenty-five public figures, the latter including members of Congress, mayors and college presidents. Interestingly, the public figures and the editors as groups expressed markedly varying views.

The public figures cited these as the reasons why newspapers are criticized: refusal to publicize corrections; failure to attribute sources of news; editorial slant in the news columns; the influence of pressure groups; over-emphasis on sensational news or news of violence; oversensitivity to criticism. On the other hand, the editors see these as the chief causes of public distrust: inaccuracies in reporting; bad copy-reading and headlining; public frustration over bad news; competition from other professions for young talent.

Especially to be noted are those questions about which there were the greatest differences of opinion: Is overplay of sensational news a major cause of public distrust of newspapers? Yes: public figures— 33%; editors—5%. Is the too-defensive attitude of the press a major cause? Yes: public figures—49%; editors—11%.

The second reality the press needs to face is the fact that it has some but not unlimited special rights, that it is the Fourth, not the First Estate.

Too many editors and publishers seem to have the idea that the First Amendment gives them the right to limitless access, to print without restraint and to invade places and privacy anywhere at any time; they fail to recognize the differences between liberty and license, between freedom and free-booting. The journalistic profession must abandon its belief that all that happens has only one ultimate purpose: to produce news; and that the end-all of government and of society in general is to supply "scoops."

A free press is essential to democracy but that is not enough; the press must be responsible and believable as well as free.

Part IV

CONCLUSION

In these two final chapters the author attempts to pull together the threads of the book, to restate his basic credo, and to review impersonally his personal history.

Questions such as these are put: Is "public opinion" more than a phrase? Can it ever be really informed? If it can be, what difference does it make? In sum, is democracy feasible?

22: Summary, Argument, Exhortation

These are the main findings of this book:

We are pledged to democracy, to government "of, by and for the people." But democracy will not truly work unless its citizens actively take part in the process, unless there is a broad and informed public opinion to guide the makers of policy.

Enlightened opinion cannot be achieved unless two conditions are met: the communicators must supply reliable information and the public must recognize the vital need of making use of that information.

At the present time, a large part of the electorate does not have the information and is too prone to emotion to make sound judgments. As a result, in many instances, it is left to the "Elite" minority to formulate opinion.

This indicates that the forces which mold opinion are not functioning as they need to function; that the nation's leaders and the media are not educating the ignorant and stirring the lethargic.

The polls have too much impact on the opinion process; they have their uses, but they should be regarded as soundings rather than conclusions. Yet many politicians regard them as mandates. That is not leadership; it is followership.

An informed and concerned electorate—a wise and inspired government—these are the marks of a genuine democracy. To achieve both is the nation's formidable task.

Ideological Interlude

There are those who would dispute the assumption that democracy has this fundamental dependence on public opinion. They hold that the public cannot possibly understand the complexities of most problems and we must therefore rely on the "Elite" for good judgments.

Walter Lippmann would look to "intelligence bureaus" (staffs of experts) to provide "illumination" for the decision-makers. "The purpose," he says, "is not to burden every citizen with expert opinions on all questions, but to push that burden away from him toward the responsible administrator." [1]

Gabriel Almond, Jr., a Princeton University political scientist, also questions the validity of the classical democratic theory. "The democratic myth is that the people are inherently wise and just and that they are the real rulers of the republic . . . There are inherent limitations in modern society in the capacity of the public to understand the issues . . . The function of the public in a democratic policy-making process is to set certain policy criteria in the form of widely held values and expressions . . . The policies themselves, however, are the products of leadership groups ('Elites') . . . In view of these considerations many of the moralistic exhortations to the public to inform itself and to play an active role in policy-making have the virtues and failings of evangelism." [2]

An additional and important element is added by Prof. de Sola Pool, who argues that the notion of rational leadership making for rational decision making is also a myth: "The information overload is such that nobody can possibly weigh all the facts or act in accordance with the myth of rational discussion. We have no doubt that the 'Elite' are better informed and sometimes smarter than the general public, but however well informed and intelligent they are, they still must act on the basis of prejudices and preconceptions."

These theories, it seems to me, imply almost a negation of democracy; their exponents concede that we should have a government "of" and "for" the people but they rate as virtually impossible government "by" the people. What is missing in their calculations is this foremost factor: that the ultimate decision, the decision as to who the decision-makers shall be, is made by the voter. Moreover, the "Elite," contemplating the world from their navel observatories or the experts closeted with their computers or the chosen ones in their seats of power are as divided in their viewpoints and in their counsels as the men in the streets; and the voter must choose among them—again the primary decision.

As for the theory that neither the general public nor the "Elite" is capable of arriving at wholly satisfactory decisions, all that is being said, it seems to me, is that human beings are fallible and that their judgments are likely now and then to be faulty (in other words, they are human). Therefore all you can expect of any system of government is that it will enable the people to muddle through. And, to put it in its minimum terms, of all the systems of government extant, democracy seems the most effective or surely the least undesirable.

The basic task then, it seems to me, is to educate the "Non-Elite" voter so that he will have sufficient knowledge to make sound appraisals of the "Elite" and their performances and to cast his ballot for logic and character rather than charisma. In this way the size of the informed minority can be increased in the near future and, in the more distant future, possibly become a majority.

If We Had Been Informed

At this point the doubters raise a second question: assuming that the information is available and the people make good use of it, what proof is there that the opinion process would be measurably improved and our decisions sounder? Obviously we have now entered the realm of speculation, but consider three or four of the cases cited in the preceding pages.

Vietnam provides a prime example. The public did not have sufficient information to reach any general conclusions about the war policies, due in large part to the government's failure to tell and the media's failure to explain; but also to the early disinterest of the voters and their later puzzlement over the rationale of entry into the war and the subsequent decisions.

If opinion had been informed, if there had been more facts, even unpalatable facts, and less false optimism, the origins and sequences of the war would have been better understood, the shock of such events as the Tet disaster would have been greatly reduced, and the credibility gap would have been avoided—a gap that eroded faith in the American government at a time when confidence was sorely needed.

In other areas of foreign policy—admittedly difficult areas for public understanding, because of their complexities and the frequent need of secret negotiations for the success of diplomacy—more information would have been of sizeable help. Our policies with the

Soviet Union and with Communist China would have been more
realistic and more effective if the government and media had done
more to educate the public toward understanding and to substitute
sophistication for slogans.

Consider the areas in which prejudice is deep-seated and evil—
civil rights disputes, campus disorders, emotion-dominated elections.

If greater effort had been made by government agencies at all
levels, by the mass media and opinion-influencing organizations
generally to bring about communication between blacks and whites,
the conflict might have been much less corrosive and the retreat
from integration to new forms of segregation avoided.

If both sides of the campus issue had been more faithfully reported
by the press, at least some of the heat might have been dissipated.
If effective dialogue could have been arranged between students and
parents and students and university administrators, the "generation
gap" might have been considerably narrowed. If the extent and
intensity of the racial feeling had been revealed in such elections as
those in Los Angeles and Alabama, the disclosures might well have
aroused more voters to counter-action and others, out of shame, to
repudiation of the backlash candidates.

If an effort were made by all elements concerned — government,
media, people—to use words precisely, opinion would be influenced
by facts rather than phrases. When the Left assails "Fascists" and
the Right indicts "Communists," the general public must learn, as Alice
learned, that to a partisan, as to Humpty Dumpty, a word means "just
what I choose it to mean, neither more nor less." Only if there is
this kind of discrimination will there be rational debate that leads
to sound conclusions.

Filling The Information Gap

Assuming then, as I do, that informed opinion *is* vital to the working of democracy, what can be done to bring it about? There are
four areas in which the opinion forces can help toward that end.

The government should provide informed and informing reports
on the state of the Union; it should avoid credibility and capability
gaps; it should fulfil the three basic functions of communication, enlightenment and inspiration.

The mass media should furnish accurate and illuminating reports of events; they should not permit a credibility gap of their own to develop; they should provide a forum to which the public has easy access and in which various viewpoints are presented "without fear or favor."

The educational systems should endeavor to make the campuses forums in which ideas can be communicated and debated rather than arenas of conflict; universities should graduate complete men and women rather than narrow specialists or laggard citizens; they should offer continuous and relevant courses in all the areas of education, adult as well as academic.

The public should demand better information; it should put that information to use so that its opinion shall have impact and its vote true meaning; it should realize that many complex issues which seem remote from the voter have a direct bearing on his present and future welfare.

Government, the media, education, all must contribute to the enlightment of opinion and thus the betterment of democracy. Unless the individual citizen plays his part "participatory democracy" will remain only a phrase.

Although we have had much talk about "New Deals," "New Frontiers," "A Great Society" and the like, the ideal state or its approximation remains remote. A truly great society will come into being not out of manifestos or legislation or manipulation, but out of belief; not out of cant or compromise but out of conviction. If there is to be a Great Society, there must be Great Debate.

We have not learned the way of the Great Debate. Our custom has been to leave it to the Man in the White House; we have been too prone to lay our concerns on the doorstep of 1600 Pennsylvania Avenue in the hope that we can proceed undisturbed with our domestic affairs and with our escapes: Bonanzas and Baseball, Peyton Places and Professional Mayhem.

Lately, it is true (and a most hopeful sign), there has been more engagement in public affairs, more speaking out by more persons, especially those of the younger generation and of the minorities. Yet the majority, when it *is* stirred, is likely to be aroused to backlashes and other counter moves and to react negatively rather than positively; usually its efforts are attempts to ensure that the status remains quo. Ignorance, prejudice, apathy—these are the dark forces that must be fought.

A Touch of Optimism

Because of the lethargy of many voters the question persists: How certain are we that democracy is the best system for us, or for any other people? I am convinced that democracy is the best form of government yet devised and that the American people have the capacity to make it work. There is in the nation an impulse to do the right and decent thing; somehow we have muddled through to the correct decisions; in the long run the Joseph McCarthys and the John Birchers have not prevailed.

There has been a tendency lately to denigrate American idealism, to downgrade the Great American Dream. I say the detractors are mistaken. Never in the history has there been a nation as unselfish and as charitable as we, to the point almost of naivete. Take Vietnam. We went into the war not to make a colony of the Indo-Chinese peninsula or to promote the interests of the Blank National Bank or the All-American Chamber of Commerce, but because, rightly or wrongly, we thought we were blocking Communism as we had blocked imperialism twice in Europe and once in Korea and because we had a assumed a prime world role and felt we could and should not default on our commitments. If later events proved these premises false, the motives at the beginning cannot justly be questioned.

*   *   *

But now there is a new kind of world, there are new challenges. Never before as today has the nation been confronted with as many and as huge problems, such formidable canyons of misunderstanding and division. If we are to meet these challenges, there must be understanding, tolerance, steadfastness.

There must be understanding of ourselves so that we shall be fully conscious of our responsibilities, always aware of our prejudices; understanding of others so that we shall not minimize their problems or bear false witness against them.

There must be tolerance so that we shall not be vulnerable to unfounded scepticism or hasty accusation.

There must be steadfastness and a shunning of compromise; as Benjamin Franklin said, "They that give up their liberty to obtain a little temporary safety deserve neither liberty nor safety."

The urgent task is to make the people aware; never was it so true that if the bell tolls for one it tolls for all. The responsibility is great; great also is the opportunity.

23: Postscript: Virtually Fit To Print

After some three score and five years of good, grey anonymity, the spotlight has been focused on the *New York Times* and the "inside story" is being told and discussed with raised and somewhat astonished eyebrows. The grande dame of West 43rd Street is being subjected to the kind of strip-tease and psycho-analysis that has in the past been reserved for the treatment of the lower order of media such as the tabloids and the other purple papyri.

In recent years three volumes about the *Times* have appeared— *Memoirs*, by Arthur Krock, for 21 years chief of the *Times'* Washington bureau and for 12 years thereafter Washington columnist (sale: close to 100,000 copies); *My Life and the Times* by Turner Catledge, for five years Executive Editor of the *Times* and now Vice President (several printings); and *The Kingdom and the Power* by Gay Talese, for 12 years a member of the *Times* staff and since then a dissecter of the current scene (sale: more than 100,000 copies.) The wide circulation of these books indicates the avid interest of the public in the tell-it-all, hushingly intimate story of a great and solemn institution.

There is no intention here of passing judgment on these volumes except to say that in addition to much solid material there is a plenitude of anecdote (and now and then gossip), leading the reader to believe that he is getting the "real dope" about an organization whose mystery has traditionally been matched by its austerity. In this chapter, I propose to review my years on the *Times* only in terms of the changing concept of newspapering as I have been seeing it over the span of almost half a century—a news analysis, as it were, of the *New York Times* from the early 1920's to the 1970's.

* * *

I came to the *Times* as Sunday Editor in 1923, at the age of 29. I had worked on the old *Tribune*, leaving shortly before it became merged into the *Herald-Tribune*. My assignments there had ranged from reporter to assistant managing editor, with eight other posts in between. On no other newspaper, I suspect, could a similar experience have been had, so adventurous and flexible was the old Trib. At the *Times*, I did the Sunday job forty-two years, then served as Associate Editor for five years and, among other assignments, inaugurated, edited and moderated "News in Perspective" on the Public Television Network.

After his days on the *Tribune* the newcomer to the *Times* in the 20's immediately sensed a startling difference in atmosphere. The *Tribune's* City Room was carefree, wholly informal; we used to play handball outside the managing editor's office, race-track "bookies" were frequent callers, poker was rampant. Symbolic of the spirit of the place was the lively Sunday magazine section edited by Franklin P. Adams, (the F.P.A. of that coruscating column, "The Conning Tower") and staffed by such future luminaries as Robert Benchley, Heywood Broun, Marc Connelly and Irwin Edman (future professor of philosophy and my brother-in-law.)

The *Times* City Room even then was solemn and business-like. Handball? Absurd. The farthest-out activity was bridge in which, seriously and quietly, the reporters engaged while waiting for assignments. The transition was from a leaping scarlet to a sedate grey.

The publisher of the *Times* in 1923 was Adolph S. Ochs, who had made a success of the *Chattanooga Times*, bought the *New York Times* in 1896 for $70,000, most of it borrowed, and survived and even prospered in difficult circumstances. Confronted when he arrived with the circulation circuses and the news extravaganzas staged by those two Yellow Kids, Hearst and Pulitzer, he was not intimidated. The Ochs approach was a strictly news one. In the beginning it was a matter of necessity as well as conviction. When the Spanish-American War broke out in 1898, Hearst and Pulitzer sent such journalistic stars as Richard Harding Davis to cover the story. Mr. Ochs did not have the money to hire this kind of talent and so he printed the copy supplied by the wire services—simple copy without flourishes, but stories that provided a clearer understanding of events than the elaborate pieces written by the stellar performers. Thus the *Times* acquired a reputation for publishing the news straight, unadorned, authentic. The lesson was not lost on Mr. Ochs and for the rest of his career he kept undeviatingly to the news path.

*   *   *

Mr. Ochs was extraordinary both as a person and as an editor. He moved almost wholly by intuition but it was intuition guided and moderated by analysis and logic. He was a kind of genius in the circulation and advertising fields—and on the news side, too. I was in charge of the feature sections of the Sunday paper, which eventually included the Magazine, the Book Review, the Review of the Week, the Arts and Travel Sections and any special supplements. In a sense this was a new enterprise for Mr. Ochs, whose almost sole concern had been the daily paper. Yet his interest in the Sunday edition was soon aroused; on Saturday afternoons, when the final Sunday section had gone to press, I would visit with him and he would set out his newspaper philosophy for the guidance of his youngish editor. Out of these visits I recall some episodes that illustrate the range and the originality of his editorial talent.

There was the week of Woodrow Wilson's death. Mr. Ochs asked me to come up to his office and tell him my plans for coverage in the Sunday paper. I went through the usual routine—various estimates of Wilson's contribution, quotations from his speeches and writings, a picture biography and the accustomed rest. Suddenly Mr. Ochs paused and said: "No. What we are going to do is to print the Covenant of the League of Nations. That was Wilson's great contribution." Clearly it was—and that is what we published.

In those days the *Tribune's* attitude toward news was almost as cavalier as the atmosphere in the city room. The writing was colorful and unrestrained and the coverage was decidedly limited. The *Daily News* was embarking, splashingly and sensationally, on its tabloid career. Meanwhile the *Times* was publishing much more straight news than the *Tribune*—"All the News That's Fit to Print"— or almost all. (I have yet to discover who was being quoted; I have always suspected that Mr. Ochs was quoting himself.) Yet I soon learned that the slogan was more than somewhat elastic; at times it was stretched to include what many of the more puritanical customers might have termed "unfit" copy.

I recall an episode in 1930 that illustrates the point. This was the year in which the Halls-Mills case broke—a story made to order for yellow journalism. No saffron editor could have devised a more fascinating plot and a more colorful set of characters: the Preacher, the Lady Choir Singer, the Pig Woman who witnessed this local Chatterly affair, the rendezvous in Lover's Lane.

The *Daily News*, to no one's surprise, was printing reams of copy about the case, but the *Times* day by day was printing even more. So one Saturday afternoon I said to Mr. Ochs: "I can understand about the *Daily News* coverage of the Hall-Mills case, but how about that slogan about 'Fit to Print'?" Mr. Ochs replied, with the hint of a twinkle, "Mr. Markel, you must understand this: when the *Daily News* prints this kind of thing, it is sex; when we print it, is is sociology."

Mr. Ochs insisted on absolute honesty in the presentation of news as well as advertising. When, early in my *Times* career, I remarked on this, he said, modestly but hardly accurately: "Mr. Markel, always remember that we can afford to be honest." I say "hardly accurately" because I am convinced that the same standards of integrity would have prevailed even if the *Times* had come upon hard times, because they did prevail in the days of his early struggles.

*   *   *

Mr. Ochs made the kind of newspaper he himself liked, proceeding on the principle that you cannot please everybody. (A good maxim, I believe. If you try to please everybody you are heading straight for bankruptcy and oblivion. As the old editor said: "You cannot scratch every man where he itches.") So Mr. Ochs edited for himself; if what he wanted was desired also by a considerable number of people, he was in; otherwise, he was out.

It soon became apparent that his kind of editing had definite appeal for the better educated, information-seeking reader—and so he was in. Yet he underestimated the potentiality of his brand of newspaper; he once told me that he did not expect the *Times* could ever attain more than 300,000 circulation. (Today the daily circulation is close to 900,000, the Sunday circulation in the neighborhood of a million and a half.)

Mr. Ochs read the paper from the first page to last, devoting some three hours a day to it and paying particular attention to the "agate sections," those departments set in smaller type and designed for special groups, such as the weather report, ship news, lists of arriving buyers, the appeal of which, added together, made up a large segment of circulation. It was a kind of department store of journalism; nobody was expected to read all of it but it was all there if anybody wanted to.

There was a story that went the rounds to the effect that Mr. Ochs had said that the Book Review was designed for people who wanted to talk about books without reading them. This was a canard circulated by the literary "establishment"; yet it had a kind of validity because of Mr. Ochs' insistence that his strict news formula be applied to all sections of the paper, Sunday as well as daily.

Mr. Ochs used to add to his formula this disavowal; "No comics, no features, no crossword puzzles." Early in my career as Sunday Editor, I became convinced that there was a large call for a crossword puzzle even among those addicted to a strict news diet. Mr. Ochs demurred for some years but finally I won consent by pledging that we would include in the puzzle at least a dozen words out of the current news. (Incidentally, the crossword puzzle proved to be one of the most popular features in the Sunday newspaper. It used to annoy me when, having labored all week on the Sunday paper, I would approach a news dealer and ask how the Sunday Times was selling; he would answer: "Great. How they love that crossword puzzle!")

The Review of the Week provides another example of Mr. Ochs' insistence on making his own kind of newspaper. Soon after I arrived at the *Times,* I began to advocate a weekly summary-plus-interpretation of the news. Mr. Ochs, because he read almost every line in the daily paper, felt no need for such a recapitulation. It was only when his eye-sight began to fail and he could not absorb all the daily paper that he consented to the idea of a Review—a section that tried to make clear the sequence and the meaning of the week's events, to pull together the news threads and to indicate their significance. The Review became one of the prime parts of the Sunday *Times;* known as Section Four, it attracted wide readership and in 1955 was awarded a Pulitzer Prize.

*   *   *

By 1935, when Mr. Ochs died, the world—and journalism with it—had greatly changed. World War I had marked the end of the old established order of things; under Wilson, a "new freedom" for the nation had been enunciated and a new world order proclaimed under the auspices of the League of Nations. But the country was not yet ready for such bold steps or, for that matter, for any further domestic experimentation. There came Harding and normalcy and finally the Depression.

The world was undergoing vast convulsions; it saw the beginnings of the revolutions sparked by Marx, Lenin, Freud and Hitler. In the making were the forces that produced World War II, the subsequent emergence of the United States as the Number One power and the promise (a false promise, as it soon turned out) of domestic peace and prosperity. Under Kennedy and Johnson, "new frontiers" were opened up, but the world currents were strong, various cataclysmic changes—economic, social, psychological—were already in process and there began the Age of Uncertainty, with an end nowhere yet in sight.

These changes required new approaches to journalism. To these Arthur Hays Sulzberger, Mr. Ochs's son-in-law and successor, applied himself, and under his leadership, the *Times* continued to grew. Mr. Ochs used to say that the life of a newspaper was one generation, "from shirtsleeves to shirtsleeves"; possibly he wanted to believe that only an Ochs could carry out the Ochs formula. But time has proved him wrong and the evidence is found in the continuing predominance of the *Times*.

Arthur Sulzberger was most modest about his role. When he was asked about his formula for success in the newspaper business, he used to say: "Work hard, don't watch the clock—and marry the boss's daughter." (He had wed Iphigene, Mr. Ochs' only child.) He had been educated at Columbia and then engaged in the family textile business; his career, up to the time of his arrival at the *Times,* was not marked with a single trace of printer's ink. Yet he developed an excellent news sense and a strict code of journalistic behavior. And he was altogether flexible in his approach to editorial problems; he used to say: "Always keep an open mind, but not so open that your brains fall out."

Arthur Sulzberger embraced fully and encouraged the implementation of the news interpretation concept. Events had become so complex that the reporting of the facts provided few clues to understanding; the meaning of the facts had also to be supplied.

This was possibly the most significant change in American journalism since the turn of the century. The Sulzberger period also saw the beginning of another important newspaper development: the evolution of the "trend story"—articles concerned not so much with the daily spot news but with the larger news currents.

News coverage was now significantly expanded; the vital element of interpretation was extended to the daily paper; new areas were added to the news assignment, notably in the fields of science and culture; the foreign staff was greatly increased so that the *Times* coverage of world news became more extensive than that of any other newspaper. Wire service stories were used largely as back-up material for *Times* "specials"; both in manner of writing and content, *Times* men were allowed much more latitude than the news agency staffs.

Arthur Sulzberger was greatly interested in the development of the Sunday paper; the definition of "news" was extended to include coverage of what men were thinking as well as what they were doing; the Magazine and the Review of the Week were further developed; the Arts Section and the Book Review were revised and expanded and an effort made to improve their literary quality.

*   *   *

Orvil Dryfoos, also a son-in-law (he married Marian Sulzberger, now Mrs. Andrew Heiskell) succeeded Arthur Sulzberger as publisher. Under his stewardship the news concepts enunciated and implemented by his two predecessors were continued. He too won admiration for his modesty and his integrity. Like Arthur Sulzberger, he had come out of an entirely alien environment (in his case it was Wall Street). Yet he too developed a sense of the news and recognized the responsibilities of newspapers in general and the *Times* in particular.

Orvil Dryfoos died in 1965, a victim of a prolonged strike, and was succeeded by Arthur Ochs Sulzberger, Arthur Hays Sulzberger's only son, youngest of his four children and known both to the family and to the staff as "Punch."

Under "Punch" there opened a period of experimentation, with innovations in coverage, concept and typography. The news tradition has been continued, but there has come about a debate over the definition of news—a debate involving basic newspaper philosophy, between those who adhere to the strict news-plus-interpretation approach and those who favor a looser news-plus-feature formula. (By "feature" I mean an article not directly related to the news or to news trends.)

I belong to the first group. I believe that the presentation and interpretation of the news and the publication of trend articles require all the space that a newspaper, even one as large as the *Times,* can economically provide, and that any non-news features or even pieces on the fringe of the news consume space that cannot be spared if the *Times* is to do a fully effective news job.

Even though the words have been used by certain critics in a pejorative sense, I contend that the *Times* must continue to be the "good grey *Times.*" When most readers apply the phrase, they mean that the newspaper is trustworthy, accurate, honest; if they ever abandon it, there will be reason, I believe, for the stockholders to repair to the nearest Wailing Wall.

This conviction of mine was expressed in an exchange I had in 1969 with Newsweek which had published this statement: "Markel has stubbornly adhered to his credo, that a newspaper's job is solely to inform and to interpret—not entertain." In rejoinder, I wrote: "I believe that the prime function of a newspaper is to provide the news and the background (or the interpretation, if you will) of the news in a comprehensible and palatable form. I do not believe it is the primary function of a newspaper to supply entertainment. Entertainment as such is the main business of television and the magazines; newspapers that put entertainment above information are not entitled to be called *news*papers.

"I believe that a newspaper can and should be interesting . . . ('interesting' is the right word, not 'entertaining'). It should provide the news of entertainment itself, it should present columns and other supplementary material based on the news and, most importantly, it should be written in an agreeable and digestible form. The Sunday *Times* has been made according to this concept. If the formula is as cockeyed as your reporter seems to suggest, then I am Horace Greeley and I ought surely to go West."

I did not go West. I remain East as a friendly critic on the hearth. I still consider the *New York Times* the best newspaper in the country, probably in the world. I am concerned, nevertheless, about signs of a possible shift in its news philosophy, mainly the tendency toward featurization. More power to the experimenters. But I trust they will always keep in mind that the assignment of the *Times* is to print all, or approximately all, the *news* that's fit, and sometimes unfit, to print, and to make that news understandable, so that the reader shall have and comprehend the facts without which public opinion is shallow and perilous.

I. A Biography of the Polls

The history of the modern poll really begins with the straw vote which originated in the nineteenth century and was used by newspapers as a circulation come-on. The press did a haphazard job of it, with most uncertain results. Newspapers printed ballots to be returned by readers, but it was soon discovered that such polls could be easily stacked by ardent partisans who sent in large numbers of ballots for their candidates. Consequently, the system was generally discarded. (The *New York Daily News* continued for a while to use it but it now also utilizes "scientific sampling.") Some newspapers tried man-in-the-street interviews and house-to-house surveys but these methods also proved very hit-or-miss.

In 1916 the *Literary Digest* entered the field with a great hullaballoo. It "quantified" the process, overwhelming the public with the sheer size of its operation. In 1920 it mailed out 11 million ballots; in 1924, 16.5 million, in 1932, 20 million. For sixteen years the forecasts proved fairly accurate. But in 1936 the *Digest* came a cropper; it predicted that Alfred E. Landon, the challenger, would win easily and that Franklin Roosevelt would receive only 41% of the popular vote in that year's presidential elections. In the greatest landslide up to that time in American political history, (only Lyndon Johnson surpassed it—in 1964 with 61.4% of the vote) Roosevelt won 60.8% of the popular vote; Landon with 36.5% carried only Maine and Vermont.

The *Digest* poll was kaput. Its gigantic error was due primarily to the composition of its mailing list, which was made up of names taken from its subscription rolls, from the telephone directory and from automobile registration files—a list certain to contain a disproportionate number of persons in the middle and upper income groups. Moreover, there was no attempt to determine who planned to vote and who did not. (The *Digest* poll's earlier successes could be attributed to the fact that there were no close elections between 1920 and 1932 and few issues divided voters along income lines.)

In the years in which the Digest was riding toward a fall, some advertising men were perfecting, as a guide to marketing, a new technique of measuring popular taste and reactions. They had become convinced that from a small, but carefully selected, sample of the population, a picture of the whole could be projected, on a regional and even national scale. Three members of the group—George Gallup, Archibald Crossley and Elmo Roper — concluded that the same methods could be applied to forecasts of election results. In 1936, the year of the *Digest* debacle, they predicted that Roosevelt would win by a substantial margin. Roper was right on the nose, largely due to luck. The other two were correct about the outcome even though their percentages were off. Modern polling was on its way to general acceptance.

To ensure more representative samples, the pollsters prepared quotas of population groups according to the divisions of the nation's voting population as revealed by the census. Gallup's sample was based on the same proportion of men and women, blacks and whites, Catholics and Protestants as that of the general population. In the elections of 1940 and 1944 these quota polls proved remarkably accurate. In 1948, however, they suffered a major setback when they predicted that Thomas Dewey would easily defeat Harry Truman.

The error made by the poll-takers in 1948 was overconfidence. Roper, announcing that only a "political convulsion" could keep Dewey out of the White House, had stopped issuing regular reports on the campaign early in September. Also, defects in the sampling methods were revealed.

The leading poll-takers decided then to add a "probability factor" to their procedures, meaning that interview areas were picked in a mathematically random manner rather than being left to the discretion of the interviewers. The effectiveness of the new methods is attested to by the fact that since 1948 Gallup's average margin of error in national elections has been 1.6%.

Yet polls are still imperfect in several respects, mainly because in some of the key processes accuracy depends on the competence and the perspicacity of human beings. The pollsters are engaged in persistent efforts to ensure accuracy and to counter the human errors. But it is no simple task and it must be a continuous assignment.

The Criticisms

Of the three elements of a poll—the sample, the questionnaire, and the interview—the first is the one most often questioned by the general public: "How is it possible to interview only 1,500 persons and reach a sound conclusion about how a nation of 200 million feels about a particular issue?" Yet this procedure is considered sound mathematically provided that it is a "probability sampling."

The process can be likened to that of throwing into a hat the names of all persons in the United States and picking out 1,500 at random. This is "probability sampling," meaning that each person in the population has an equal chance of being selected. In the effort to achieve a representative sample, the pollsters use procedures designed to include all important groups in the population and to cover rural, urban and suburban areas.

What is questioned is not the basic sampling method but the deviations from it. Gallup, for example, uses "probability sampling" only down to the block level; he does not select beforehand the individuals to be interviewed; instead he instructs the interviewer to start at the house next to the house on the corner of the block and, if no one is at home there, to go to the next house.

Some university researchers, on the other hand, designate the precise individuals to be sampled; they will make up to four callbacks in an attempt to reach all the people included in the sample, on the theory that the more callbacks you make, the more accurate the results will be. Yet, even with multiple callbacks, complete sampling is rarely achieved even by the most painstaking researchers. (An 84% return is a top figure.) Gallup and most other commercial poll-takers contend that the increased accuracy is not worth the cost of the callback procedures.

Another criticism made is of the use of "subgroupings," divisions of the whole sample into segments according to race, education, income, age and so forth. A pollster will decide to report not only the sentiments of the population as a whole, but also the views of a part of it, say of the black voters. Since Negroes constitute approximately 10% of the population, the sample is likely to consist of only 150 interviews—a sample surely subject to far greater error than one of

1,500. Obviously, in any such procedure, the sample size should be considerably increased.

The questionnaire itself presents large problems. Great care must be exercised to avoid ambiguity, bias and, especially, generalities in the wording. Differences in phrasing may bring completely different answers. For example, if Northern whites are asked: "Do you support civil rights legislation aimed at bettering the Negro position in the nation?" they are likely to register general agreement. But if they are asked: "Would you like a black as a neighbor?" the answer in all probability will be a resounding negative.

In judging poll results, it is important to know whether the person interviewed answered the questions in his own words ("open-ended questions") or whether he selected one of several answers already on the questionnaire ("multiple-choice questions"). "Open-ended questions" allow more freedom of expression and thus provide more information, but because they are difficult to classify they are employed only infrequently.

The amount of time allotted for each interview is another critical factor. Gallup does a survey every three weeks and issues two releases a week; in every survey, in addition to the public affairs questions, he includes queries designed to aid commercial clients. Irving Crespi, one of Gallup's chief executives, believes that a questionnaire should run about thirty minutes. Harris says his average interview runs about an hour; he is likely to put twice as many questions as Gallup and he does not, he says, include marketing research questions in his current affairs surveys. This strikes me as sound practice because otherwise the persons polled may conclude that this is polling for private, not public ends.

Informational questions, designed to reveal how knowledgeable an interviewee is about a subject, should be an absolute requirement for any poll. Many opinion researchers do use some form of "filter" question designed to identify the uninformed, but they do not always report the results. Elmo Roper, believing such questions to be essential to surveys on major issues, urges that the results be published in two columns, one setting out informed, the other uninformed opinion. The late Hadley Cantril, a polling expert, also emphasized the importance of informational questions: "On a complicated issue, first of all, find out how well informed the person is, then ask a series of questions that put the original question in a different context . . . to give people choices or alternatives."

Questionnaires are also inadequate if they do not measure the intensity of sentiment; it is important to discover whether people feel strongly enough about issues to implement their convictions because it enables the poll-taker to sort out those who are likely to act from those who are not. If all opinions are counted equally, there are no clues as to the number of persons who will vote or take part in a campaign or a demonstration. Such information is most useful to the lawmaker or administrator who is trying to determine the public's interest in an issue. Such in-depth questioning is used by the major university researchers and by most commercial pollsters when they are commissioned to do special studies; it should be the rule for almost every poll.

The capacity of the questioner is another factor to be considered. Unless the interviewer has a news background, persistence and perspicacity, plus psychological insight, his reports are likely to be superficial.

The manner in which surveys are presented to the public is another area of criticism. Much of the press is guilty of sensationalizing poll results, of putting out biased reports to promote particular points of view and of failing to alert the reader-viewer to potential inaccuracies. According to Oliver Quayle, "There are all kinds of problems with the American press. They are the biggest culprits in the misuse of polls. Reporters will take anything that is a poll without even finding out who did it." But the pollsters are also at fault. In many press releases they do not include such vital information as the size and composition of the sample, the time of the survey, or the method of interviewing.

The mass media are criticized for treating all polls alike, as if there were no differences in scientific validity among them. "Polls, like politicians, newspapers and other groups, range from good to poor," says Gerhard Wiebe, Dean of Boston University's School of Public Communications.[10]

Philip Meyer, a correspondent in Washington for the Knight newspapers and a journalist with a background in sociology, has long been concerned about the quality of poll reporting. He believes that any code of poll ethics is of little use so long as reporters and editors are ignorant about polling techniques. He suggests that news organizations have their own experts in opinion research who could interpret poll findings and conduct their own surveys when required.

The British Elections

The heaviest blow in recent history to the pollsters was their miscalculation of the British elections in June, 1970. With a single exception, they forecast a Labor victory. The Gallup Poll (*Daily Telegraph*) predicted that Labor would win by 7.1%, with a majority of 100 seats in the Commons; the Harris Poll (*Daily Express*), Labor by 2%, with a majority of 30 seats; the National Opinion Poll (*Mail*), Labor by 4.1%, with a majority of 60 seats; and the Marplan Poll (*The Times*), Labor by 9.6%, with a majority of 150 seats. Only the Opinion Research Center (*Evening Standard*) predicted a victory for the Conservatives—by 1%, with a majority of 20 seats. The actual result was a victory for the Conservatives by 2.4%, with a majority in the Commons of 30 seats.

The polls seemed to dominate the election. The forecasts were accepted unsceptically by the media and, the evidence suggests, by the voters also; the London *Economist* of June 9, 1970 characterized the coming election as a "routine affair," and added "the most rational Conservative hope must be to keep Mr. Wilson to a majority of 30 or less, and no longer to dislodge him altogether." Harold Wilson also seems to have had total faith in the surveys. His campaign was run in low key on the theory that victory was in the bag.

What had been the impact of the polls on the voter is difficult to gauge. Some commentators concluded that complacency had also possessed the average Labor Party adherent, especially the younger ones who, at eighteen, were voting for the first time. Election day was a lovely English Thursday in June and one suspects that many of these younger voters, assured by the polls of a Labor victory, went to picnic on the river instead of going through the bother of actually casting their ballots. A turn-out of 75% of the electorate had been expected; only some 70% voted.

This question of turn-out seems to have been the critical one, as it is in most elections—whatever the reasons, many voters stay away from polls, be it from complacency, or as a protest against the policies of both parties. Yet this question was virtually ignored by all the pollsters, with the exception of the Opinion Research Center.

Dr. Gallup attributes the error to the failure of the British poll-takers to use the checking methods adopted by Americans after the false prediction in the Truman-Dewey election, notably the check on turn-out and the up-to-the-last-minute surveys. In comments prepared for this book he says: "The failure of the polls to predict the defeat of Wilson and his Labor party in Great Britain raises anew the issue: can the polls be trusted? The answer, unfortunately, has to be an equivocal yes and no. It is all a matter of the degree of accuracy expected.

"The press reported that the polls pointed to a certain Wilson victory. But to the individual who is knowledgeable in polling development, this was not the case at all. All the major polls, except one, showed Wilson leading by seven percentage points or less. Actually, in the British way of reporting poll results, emphasis is placed on the spread between candidates rather than on the actual percentages; this doubles the error factor.

"The British press should have reported poll findings something like this: 'Poll results show that neither party is winning a higher percentage of the vote than the margin of error that must be taken into account in interpreting their findings. Consequently, no firm prediction of the winner is possible; the range is from a relatively narrow Conservative victory to a fairly wide Labor victory.'

"One of the most difficult problems in all polling is to screen out non-voters. In the United States only about half of all adults vote in Congressional elections; in the last Presidential election only 61 percent voted. This means that allowance for the non-voter must be made and to do this requires highly sophisticated procedures.

"The 'no opinion' vote is always a possible source of error, since into this category go those people who have not made up their minds and those who have made their minds up but do not want to disclose their voting intention. Various techniques, including the secret ballot, must be used to reduce the number of 'don't knows' to the minimum possible."

Louis Harris, in an explanatory piece published in the *New York Post* of June 29th, says the Harris Poll recorded the sharp drop in Wilson's appeal five days before the election and noted the increase in the number of those who felt that an economic crisis, a wage freeze and continued high prices would occur in the fall. "The Tories pounded hard on the economic issue and swung the house-wife vote over to their side decisively." He admits that his people failed to pay sufficient attention to the question of turnout.

As for the effect of this gaffe on the business of polling, Mr. Harris says: "What happened to the polls in Britain is probably a healthy thing . . . the polls must stop claiming precision-like infallibility, as though they were a kind of decimal point gospel. Nor is it good for polls to dominate an election as they did in Britain. Polls will be accurate in the future within limits of error—when they are run right. In a way, too much has been expected of the polls as crystal ball gazers and too little as reporters of what people really think and how they make their decisions in an election."

So there is agreement among almost all concerned, including the pollsters, that the process of election polling should be subject to severe re-examination.

II: The Newspaper Surveys

Reports From Regional Correspondents

In an effort to obtain a national assessment of the quality of media performance, an extensive questionnaire was sent to 21 regional correspondents of the *Columbia Journalism Review*. The *Review* depends on these correspondents for keeping abreast of journalistic developments around the country. The replies provide useful insights into the difficulty of producing informed public opinion.

The correspondents reported from the following places:

Boston	Detroit	Albuquerque, N.M.
Springfield, Mass.	Madison, Wisc.	Tucson, Ariz.
Seneca Falls, N. Y.	Minneapolis	Portland, Ore.
Lexington, Ky.	New Orleans	San Francisco
South Bend, Ind.	Austin, Tex.	San Jose, Calif.
Peoria, Ill.	Dallas	Los Angeles
Chicago	El Paso	San Diego

In general the performance was rated as "fair"; the rating "excellent" was rarely applied—nor for that matter was "very poor." (It might be remarked that "fair" would be considered by most observers inadequate in view of the important assignment of the press.)

Among the criticisms were these: lack of vision, imagination and enterprise; and editorial bias in that news is slanted either in play or writing to conform to local taboos, management opinion or advertiser wishes; and an insufficient effort to interpret the news.

Question: How would you rate the thoroughness and accuracy of these newspapers in their coverage of: (a) international news; (b) national news; (c) local news? *Answer:*

	International	National	Local
Excellent	0	1	0
Good	7	6	6
Fair	10	10	10
Poor	4	4	5
Very Poor	0	0	0

Question: How would you rate the over-all quality of the interpretative material provided by the newspapers? *Answer:*

	International	National	Local
Excellent	1	1	0
Good	5	5	2
Fair	9	10	12
Poor	4	4	6
Very Poor	2	1	1

Question: How would you rate the efforts of the newspapers to present a variety of viewpoints both in their news columns and editorial pages?

Answer: Excellent—0; Good—5; Fair—10; Poor—5; Very Poor—1.

Question: How would you rate the kind of job the newspapers are doing in terms of the minority groups, specifically the young, the students, the blacks, women. *Answer:*

	Young and Students	Blacks	Women
Excellent	0	0	0
Good	3	2	6
Fair	9	10	10
Poor	8	9	5
Very Poor	1	0	0

Question: Do you feel that newspapers generally slant or shape news stories to conform with local taboos, tastes and sensitivities or to the management viewpoint? *Answer:* Often—9; Occasionally—10; Seldom—2.

Question: How would you rate the impact of the newspapers in your area? (By impact we mean the extent to which a newspaper can affect the knowledge, opinions and actions of a community). *Answer:* Excellent—2; Good—4; Fair—12; Poor—3; Very Poor—0.

Appraisal of "Play" and Perspective

In an effort to measure the performance and the impact of newspapers, the 25 newspapers with the largest circulations in the country —20 morning and five evening newspapers—were examined from June 9 through June 16, 1969, eight days of important news. Two tests were applied: first, how the papers "played," that is, displayed, the outstanding news stories; second, what kind of job they did by way of interpretation and perspective.

The newspapers included in the survey—(e) indicates evening— are listed below in order of circulation:

New York Daily News	Philadelphia Inquirer	Miami Herald
Los Angeles Times	Wall Street Journal	Kansas City Times
New York Times	San Francisco Chronicle	St. Louis Globe-Democrat
Chicago Tribune	Washington Post	Houston Post
New York Post (e)	Chicago News (e)	Des Moines Register
Philadelphia Bulletin (e)	Long Island (Jamaica)	Portland Oregonian
Detroit News (e)	Press (e)	Pittsburgh Post-Gazette
Chicago Sun-Times	Boston Record American	Minneapolis Tribune
Detroit Free Press	Cleveland Plain Dealer	

The manner of testing was wholly subjective. I assumed that I was the composite news editor for these eight days. For the first test I indicated how, for each of the days, I would have displayed the outstanding news stories, compared the play in each newspaper with the "Markel First Page" and converted the comparison to a percentage basis. In the second test, I selected the seven stories which seemed to me the most important, posed for each a series of questions which I felt needed to be answered if the news was to be made understandable, analyzed the performance of each paper in meeting this "Markel Interpretation Test" and again converted the results to percentages.

News Play

On news display this was the method: There were 32 stories on the "Markel First Page" list—four top stories for each of the eight days. A point was awarded for the display of any story that appeared on my list; thus a newspaper which played 16 of the 32 stories during the eight days would be given a rating of 50%.

This is how the newspapers scored:

New York Times	67%	San Francisco Chronicle	42%
The Los Angeles Times	67%	Chicago Sun-Times	40%
The Washington Post	65%	Philadelphia Inquirer	40%
Minneapolis Tribune	46%	Miami Herald	40%
Pittsburgh Post-Gazette	43%	St. Louis Globe-Democrat	39%

Cleveland Plain Dealer	37%	Philadelphia Bulletin	22%
Boston Record American	36%	Long Island Press	22%
Kansas City Times	35%	Portland Oregonian	22%
Houston Post	32%	Des Moines Register	21%
Chicago Tribune	25%	New York News	18%
New York Post	25%	Detroit News	18%
Detroit Free Press	25%	Chicago News	18%

None of the dailies surveyed gave top play, on the average, to as many as three of the four "Markel First Page" stories each day. Three newspapers—the *New York Times,* the *Los Angeles Times,* and the *Washington Post*—averaged between two and three stories a day; eleven papers averaged between one and two; and ten averaged one story a day or less. The *New York Times* played all four "Markel stories" one day, three out of four on three other days. The *New York Daily News,* on the other hand, played none of the top stories on three days and only one on four other days. The afternoon papers, the tabulation shows, made low scores.

(The *Wall Street Journal* was not included in this part of the survey because of the specialized nature of its reporting.)

Perspective

In evaluating the job done in supplying interpretation, I selected these six stories as the outstanding ones during the eight days of the test:

The Midway conference between President Nixon and President Thieu of South Vietnam; the French elections, in which M. Pompidou was elected President; the increase in the prime interest rate by the Federal Reserve Board, an action of considerable economic import; the conference of Communist leaders in Moscow; the increasing disorders on the country's campuses; and the growing debate in Congress over the antiballistic missile (ABM) defense system.

For each of these stories, I prepared a list of questions which I felt required answers if the news was to have meaning for the average reader. The newspapers were then analyzed to determine how many of these questions had been answered satisfactorily by each newspaper. The number of satisfactory answers was then converted into a percentage of the total questions on the Markel list. Thus a newspaper which provided six of the eight answers for questions posed on a particular story would be rated 75 per cent on that story.

These were some of the criteria applied in determining the performance in interpretation: treatment in depth of each question at least once in the course of the eight-day period; integration of the interpretation into the factual stories, without the intrusion of opinion; in general, perspective enough to bring understanding to the average reader.

This then is the record of performance on each of the seven stories.

The Midway Conference

The Questions: What is the meaning of the troops withdrawal? How well prepared is the ARVN (South Vietnamese Army) to replace the U. S. troops? What has Midway accomplished in terms of Washington-Saigon relations? What is the meaning of the new provisional NLF (National Liberation Front) government? What are the effects — realized and potential—of Midway on the Paris peace talks? What was Hanoi's reaction to Midway? What was Moscow's reaction to Midway? What was U. S. Congressional reaction to Midway?

The Score: 76% to 100%—4 newspapers; 51% to 75%—9; 26% to 50%—7; 0% to 25%—5.

Only one newspaper out of the 25 evaluated—the *Los Angeles Times* —covered satisfactorily each of the eight questions posed; the *Washington Post*, the *Philadelphia Evening Bulletin*, and the *Miami Herald* covered seven; the *New York Times*, the *Chicago Daily News*, the *Detroit News* and the *Houston Post* covered six of the eight. Half of the 25 top circulation papers failed to provide adequate interpretation. Of the eight top papers, only four provided consistent day-to-day in-depth analysis and interpretation—*Los Angeles Times, Washington Post, New York Times,* and the *Chicago Daily News*.

Some interesting names were recorded at the bottom of the coverage spectrum. The *Chicago Tribune*, for example, failed to deal with any of the questions in depth despite the fact it had correspondents in many areas of the world. The evening papers generally did a good job of covering the news, but failed almost totally in the interpretation test.

French Elections

The Questions: Is there any in-depth backgrounding to prepare the reader for the coming elections? What are the projected policies of Pompidou? What is the relationship between Pompidou's policies and those of de Gaulle? What is the meaning of the election for the United States? What effect might the election have on the European community? What problems does Pompidou face?

The Score: 76% to 100% — 2 newspapers; 51% to 75% — 2; 26% to 50% — 3; 0% to 25% — 18.

The papers by and large failed to offer any in-depth analysis or interpretation of an event which clearly marked the beginning of a new era in French politics. Few saw fit to devote space to the elections before the day of balloting, and after the results were in, rarely discussed the issues as they were clearly reflected in Pompidou's victory.

Of the 25 papers assessed, all but two prominently played the French election story on their front pages Monday, June 16th. But only four of these papers probed even half the questions we thought important to an understanding of the meaning of the elections, and this lack was made all the more apparent because of the prominent play the story received. A large number of newspapers relied almost exclusively on the rather skimpy AP and UPI stories describing who had won the election and by how much, quoting bits and pieces of Pompidou's victory speech, and sketching inadequately the projected policies of the new government.

Prime Interest Rate

The Questions: Is there an explanation of what the prime interest rate is? What is the PIR hike? How will the PIR increase affect inflation? How might the rate increase affect the average reader (consumer)? What is the relationship of the PIR to the surtax extension bill?

The Score: 76% to 100% — 8 newspapers; 51% to 75% — 7; 26% to 50% — 4; 0% to 25% — 6.

Such a complex and specialized issue demanded particularly lucid explanation, background and analysis, especially since the nation was greatly concerned with inflation then. But only a very few of the papers consistently provided this material.

One reason for the mediocre performance on this story was the apparent feeling among some newspaper editors that the prime interest rate increase had only specialized news value; therefore they relegated most of their coverage to the financial section. This inability to make relevant to readers news that, on the surface, seems distant from daily concerns is one of the prime failures of the press.

The initial announcement of the hike was greeted with frantic front page coverage, but in the days following, all too many of the newspapers minimized their coverage to include only a few inconsequential tidbits.

Curiously, the *New York Times,* the *Los Angeles Times* and the *Washington Post* omitted any analysis of the question dealing with the surtax. The *Post,* as usual, added to its normal coverage of events analytical pieces. The *New York Times'* coverage was noteworthy for both its comprehensive approach and for its lucidity of presentation. The best over-all coverage came from the *Wall Street Journal* which, of course, specializes in financial news.

The evening papers all ranked near or at the bottom of the list. Some vindication for poor coverage can be found in the fact that for many of them the stock market closes after their publication deadline and, for this reason, the morning papers are the only ones in a position to cover breaking economics stories adequately.

The Moscow Conference

The questions were these: Why did the Russians call the Communist summit conference? What is the impact on the conference caused by the absence of China? What is the state of the world Communist movement? What is the significance of the criticism of Soviet policy by delegates at the conference? Can Moscow enforce its solidarity pact? How does the conference relate to U. S. foreign policy?

No boxscore was justified on this story because of the uniformly

slim coverage and the lack of interpretation. The Russians elaborate-
ly choreographed the meeting to minimize political confrontation and
they tightly controlled press conferences. This was a case in which
the "news" was the non-news; the decision to soft-pedal the proceedings indicated there was internal trouble which the Politboro wanted
to conceal. (One is reminded of the newspaper man, assigned to
cover a wedding, who reported to his city editor: "There's no story;
the bridegroom didn't show up.")

Campus Unrest and the ABM

Though these issues were considered of importance by the author
for the period of the testing, they received such scant coverage that
neither questions nor boxscores were warranted. On the campus issue,
none of the papers offered interpretative material during the period
of the test, although some provided factual reports on the policy
statement by the National Commission on the Causes and Prevention
of Violence, and on the Congressional debate over the Nixon Administration's proposed college anti-riot legislation. Similarly on the ABM,
there were factual reports on the debate on Capitol Hill, but no
interpretation was offered. It should be noted in extenuation that the
campus unrest and the ABM issues were stories that had been running over a long period of time, rather than single events like the
other stories.

III: Surveys of Congress

In an effort to shed light on the part public opinion plays in a Congressman's decision-making, and on the relationship between constituent and representative, questionnaires were sent to all the members of the Senate and House of Representatives. Replies were received from 15 Senators and 94 Representatives; in addition, 16 Senators and 11 Representatives were interviewed in depth. The result is a representative sample, both geographically and politically. What follows are the questions put in the questionnaire and a tabulation of the answers. (The results differ numerically in various instances because some Congressmen either did not answer certain questions or did not indicate rank in their replies.)

Question: What factors determine your voting decisions? Please number in order of importance the following factors:

Senators	*Rank*		
	1st	*2nd*	*3rd*
Your own viewpoint	14		
Polls, national or otherwise		1	4
Opinion in your constituency	1	10	2
Opinion of the "Elite"			2
Party considerations			4
Arguments of lobbies			2

Other factors mentioned: research, study, national interest, state interest, hearings, mail.

Representatives	*Rank*		
	1st	*2nd*	*3rd*
Your own viewpoint	82	17	
Polls, national or otherwise	8		19
Opinion in your constituency	34	49	8
Opinion of the "Elite"		6	4
Party considerations	4	3	26
Arguments of lobbies	1	1	4

Other factors mentioned: research, national interest, colleagues who specialize in the subject to be voted upon.

Question: How do you determine public opinion in your own constituency? Please number in order of importance.

Senators

	1st	2nd	3rd
Local polls	1		1
Your own polls	3	1	2
Personal contacts	15	3	3
Local editorial opinion	3	2	
Your mail	3	8	4
Local opinion leaders	3	1	2

Representatives

	1st	2nd	3rd
Local polls	7	4	7
Your own polls	27	17	6
Personal contacts	62	16	12
Local editorial opinion	6	3	16
Your mail	28	33	15
Local opinion leaders	5	14	19

Question: Do you take your own poll?

Senators		*Representatives*	
Yes	10	Yes	76
No	7	No	27
"If yes, how often?"		"If yes, how often?"	
Annually	1	Annually	59
Twice a year	3	Twice a year	11
More often	6	More often	6

Question: How accurately do you think the national polls—Gallup, Roper, Harris—reflect public opinion?

Senators		*Representatives*	
Very accurately	3	Very accurately	13
Fairly accurately	13	Fairly accurately	83
Inaccurately	3	Inaccurately	3

Question: How informed do you consider the public?

Senators		*Representatives*	
Well informed	5	Well informed	12
Fairly well informed	10	Fairly well informed	67
Generally poorly informed	4	Generally poorly informed	31

Question: How well informed do you consider the Congress?

Senators		*Representatives*	
Well informed	6	Well informed	50
Fairly well informed	8	Fairly well informed	42
Generally poorly informed	1	Generally poorly informed	4

Question: On what do you depend to keep informed? Please number in order of importance.

Senators

	Rank		
	1st	*2nd*	*3rd*
Newspapers	11	1	2
Television	1	2	4
Other media	1	4	2
Briefings		2	1
Hearings	3		4
Talks with others	1	6	1

Other factors mentioned—research, government publications, committee reports.

Representatives

	Rank		
	1st	*2nd*	*3rd*
Newspapers	63	15	6
Television	11	13	14
Other media	11	17	11
Briefiings	8	11	13
Hearings	29	13	9
Talks with others	16	16	19

Other factors mentioned—research, government publications, committee reports.

Question: How often do you differ with your constituents' majority viewpoint?

Senators		*Representatives*	
Often	2	Often	14
Occasionally	13	Occasionally	60
Seldom	4	Seldom	29

Question: When you disagree, how do you endeavor to persuade them to your view?

	Senators	Representatives
By newsletter	12	52
Through newspapers	11	63
By television	13	40
By speeches in person	15	64
By mail	—	13

Other factors mentioned—personal visits, through local leaders.

Question: What do you consider the duty of an elected official?

	Senators	Representatives
To vote as your constituents desire	2	9
To vote according to your own judgment	10	46
To vote as a mix of the two	12	60

Two aspects of the Congressional process are of special importance: how the members of the Congress gauge public opinion; and the factors which influence their votes.

In answering the question—"How do you determine public opinion?" —as the tables indicate, most of the Congressmen cited their background and personal knowledge of the districts or their states, personal contact, the mail they receive, particularly individual letters of concern rather than form mail, newspapers, editors' opinions, and periodicals. Here are some specific comments—

Rep. Melcher (D-Mont.) : "I do what I think is best. I'm part of public opinion. I'm not divorced from it. I'm part of the group that is public opinion."

Sen. Cranston (D-Calif.) : "You develop antennae, although people tend to agree with you in personal conversation. We consider carefully what the leaders are thinking; we try to identify the leaders. Leadership in a growing, mobile state like California is less evident."

Rep. Findley (R-Ill.) : "I pay attention to polls. I try to do my own poll each year. It's helpful in showing me whether I'm in a halfway accordance with my constituents or not. The people who answer it represent those who have an interest in public affairs. Frankly, this poll is my primary tool for finding out what my constituents think."

Sen. Spong (D-Va.) : "There are three disturbing things about public opinion: (1) There are so many special interest groups that generate mail; this distorts the picture. (2) In this era of the pitchman and the public relations experts, it's easier to mold public opinion; this must be weighed. (3) Public opinion is at best a transient thing. It can be one way one week and another way the next week. You must wait until all the returns are in."

Sen. Hansen (R-Wyo.) : "Newspapers give a reflection of public opinion. There's also what I hear on the streets. I have good friends in Wyoming . . . and they give me their sensing of public opinion. As for mail, you can't just weigh or count letters. I differentiate between generated mail and self-prompted expressions of concern."

Rep. Bolling (D-Mo.) : "I have the most advanced intelligence network of anyone in western Missouri. I see to it that I cultivate channels into all elements of the community, especially into areas that are politically active. It gives me the lead on the intentions of my opposition months before."

Rep. Conyers (D-Mich.): "My district is overwhelmingly Democratic in disposition, in the heart of a major industrial center. I was born and raised there. I can almost tell automatically what they're thinking."

When asked whether they relied on polls for their assessment of public opinion, all but a few said the polls were helpful in pointing out areas of general concern, in suggesting guidelines or in persuading people toward a particular viewpoint; but that the polls are often too broadly worded and geographically spread to be truly informative, and generally they fail to provide analysis in depth. Some of the comments:

Sen. Church (D-Idaho): "I don't rely too much on polls because they're not limited to my state. Somtimes they provide guidelines. They're of marginal importance."

Sen. Yarborough (D-Tex.): "I don't let polls influence my vote to any appreciable degree. People change their positions. If a legislator lets the polls tell him, then he's not voting his convictions—and he ought to resign."

Rep. Hawkins (D-Calif.): "I tend to discriminate against polls because I think we should be a little ahead of what the people are thinking rather than following it."

The second question was, in effect, this: "Do you vote according to your constituents' wishes or according to your own judgment?" This question necessarily deals with how well-informed the public is and on the overall role Congressmen feel public opinion should play in decision-making. Congressmen varied in their estimate of their constituents' knowledge of political affairs and policy; many feel that people are aware only of those issues which directly affect them and that they tend to ignore more general problems. Others believe that the news media, particularly television, have brought a greater understanding of the government of the individual. Several Congressmen mentioned the large amount of technical and classified information available only to the legislature and not to the voters as a whole.

In general, it can be said that while Congressmen generally consider the views of their constituents, most of them vote according to their own best judgment and then let the public evaluate their performance at election time. Here are some typical comments:

Sen. Church (D-Idaho): "Congress shouldn't decide questions of great moment on the basis of the currents of public opinion. There would be no need for Congress then—just a computer to add up the figures and present a consensus. Our system rests on the underlying principle that men are elected to represent and use their best judgment. They're exposed to more information than is available to the public. They are supported or opposed at election time on the basis of the general record they have made and their general impression.

"As for changing my opinion because of public opinion, some things come along on which for one reason or another, opinion is absolutely and wholly formed. To oppose that opinion is to invite political defeat. Then you must weigh its importance. Is an issue of such importance to the country that I should take a stand and take defeat, or should I reflect the viewpoint of my constituents, recognizing the facts of life?"

Sen. Sparkman (D-Ala.): "I consider the issue, the best I can, from facts presented in the committee reports and on the floor of the Senate. I vote the way I think is best . . . Members of Congress ought not to be led around by what they believe the people think. They ought to offer leadership to the people and help them to shape their thinking."

Rep. Burton (D-Calif.): "I have a responsibility to vote my own conscience. My constituents can weigh my candidacy when I seek re-election and it is their duty to reject me if they think my performance is not in the public interest."

Sen. Cranston (D-Calif.): "It's the responsibility of leaders in the executive and legislative branches to inform the public—to seek to guide opinion in their district . . . Public opinion necessarily counts for less on a highly technical issue."

Sen. Spong (D-Va.): "I don't come to any decisions exclusive of what I think the prevailing mood of the state is. A few times I was guided by actions I don't think the public was aware of. I haven't yet reconsidered an issue because of public opinion. I would not be a representative if I were not mindful that public opinion *could* force my hand on some issues."

Sen. Yarborough (D-Tex.): "Public opinion in a democracy should theoretically control the course of government. Burke pointed out that he asked his constituents to judge his qualifications for office and once they elected him it was his duty to study the issues and make the decisions. After all, a member is elected not for the purpose of thwarting the will of the public, but to express the public will. But he also sees often that the information the public has is one-sided and slanted, so he might feel his duty is to try to provide accurate information for them."

Rep. Buchanan (R-Ala.): "Too much is bias from the press. The people have no chance to see things as they are. The most difficult part of my job is, first, figuring out how to vote on my own judgment, and second, figuring out what is right to do after taking public opinion into mind."

IV. The Underground Press

As a footnote and as a commentary, too, on the state of the "establishment" press there is the story of the growth of the (one resists the temptation to dub the two the "elevated" and the "subway" press) "underground" press. It is "underground" only in the sense that it does not have the exposure and the circulation of the "above ground" media; the better analogy is "off Broadway" as distinguished from "on Broadway." Its editors, however, assert that the more accurate designation is "all-around press."

In the last few years, some 250 to 300 newspapers in this group have sprung up, plus about 175 newspapers around the country designed exclusively for black audiences; the total circulation of these various publications is estimated to be more than three million.

Many of these papers come and go, but a dozen or so are permanent institutions. The *Village Voice,* one of the first of the breed, can no longer be reckoned as properly belonging in the group, because in format and appeal it is closer to the "establishment" than to the dissident press. (Not that it is not radical in viewpoint, but it does deal, in its own way, with the kind of stories with which the "establishment" press concerns itself.) Of the others, the most important are the *Los Angeles Free Press,* established in 1964, with a circulation of 70,000, the *Berkeley Barb,* established in 1965 and now with a circulation of 60,000, the *National Guardian,* twenty years old with a circulation of 20,000, and the *East Village Other,* established 1965, circulation 68,000.

In the beginning most of these newspapers were reflections of the hippie and psychodelic movements, echoing the "love" and "peace" slogans which began to have currency at the time, and indicating a kind of disenchantment with formal politics. But certain events and factors combined to bring about a change in viewpoint: notably the political developments of 1968 culminating in the Democratic convention in Chicago, the influence of the politically oriented youth movement abroad and the legal difficulties which arose over the use of drugs. As a consequence many "underground" papers have turned to coverage of national events and to muck-raking, some of it clean muck-raking, some of it far from spotless. In general, the "underground press" makes its appeal to the alienated groups who look with disbelief and scorn on the "establishment" press.

This is the way Art N. Kunkin, editor of the *Los Angeles Free Press,* sees it: "This growth of the 'underground press,' is, in my opinion, due to the combination of the new offset technology, plus the vacuum in modern American politics, plus the creation of new community interest groups including black and brown minorities, students, urbanites and the new youth class. These groups were voiceless and desperately wanted voices. They needed information and communication that the empty weekly neighborhood shopper and the metropolitan daily with its ad pages surrounded by wire releases, high society sections and already established business and political entanglements, would not and probably could never satisfy. It is this journalistic vacuum that called the 'all-around press' into existence."

A reading of these papers discloses striking similarities in style and content. One reason is that they exchange news copy; another is their common use of the Liberation News Service, which has 600 subscribers to whom it supplies packets of "anti--establishment" copy twice a week and which is admittedly a doctrinaire left-wing organization with a staff that looks upon objectivity as neither possible nor desirable and sees itself as an important revolutionary force.

Emphasis is put on stories that demonstrate "American imperialism" and "oppression," police harassment, economic exploitation abroad and at home. Politics to a considerable extent has replaced drugs, art, sex, dress and music as dominant themes. Jaakov Kohn, editor of the *East Village Other,* says that his paper "reports on the new life style which is usually ignored or distorted in the establishment press." The basic concept is "revolution," which to some means the armed overthrow of the state, to others the cultivation of the inner life or the freeing of the mind so that it will be "utterly indifferent" to the "oppressive" American climate.

(Incidentally the advertising in these newspapers is likely to be unrestrainedly concerned with sexual matters. Mr. Kunkin says, "We are often dismayed at the sexual content of much of our display advertising, because this distracts from our journalistic efforts. However, if there is any basic principle to the paper, it is anti-censorship.")

The expansion of the "underground press' is one of the striking phenomena of recent journalism and in a way a challenge to the "above-ground" press because it indicates there are important minorities which the "establishment" press does not reach.

BIBLIOGRAPHY

Public Opinion

Albig, William. *Modern Public Opinion*. McGraw-Hill, 1956.

Almond, Gabriel A. *The American People and Foreign Policy*. Harcourt, Brace, 1950.

Bailey, Thomas. *The Man in the Street: The Impact of American Public Opinion on Foreign Policy*. Macmillan, 1948.

Berelson, Bernard and Janowitz, Morris (eds.). *Reader in Public Opinion and Communications*. Free Press, 1965.

Bryce, James. *American Commonwealth*. Macmillan, 1893-1895.

Bryce, James. *Modern Democracies*. Macmillan, 1921.

Buchanan, William and Cantril, Hadley. *How Nations See Each Other*. University of Illinois Press, 1953.

Campbell, Angus, *et al. The American Voter*. John Wiley, 1960.

Campbell, Angus, *et al. The Voter Decides*. Row, Peterson, 1954.

Cantril, Hadley and Free, Lloyd A. *The Political Beliefs of Americans: A Study in Public Opinion*. Rutgers University Press, 1967.

Childs, Harwood L. *Public Opinion: Nature, Formation and Role*. Van Nostrand, 1965.

Choukas, Michael. *Propaganda Comes of Age*. Public Affairs Press, 1965.

Christenson, Reo M. and McWilliams, Robert O. *Voice of the People: Readings in Public Opinion and Propaganda*. McGraw-Hill, 1967.

Cohen, Bernard. *Citizen Education in World Affairs*. Princeton University International Studies, 1953.

Dexter, Lewis A. and White, David Manning (eds.). *People, Society and Mass Communication*. Free Press, 1964.

Doob, Lonard W. *Public Opinion and Propaganda*. Arehon Books, 1966.

Hero, Alfred O. *Americans in World Affairs*. World Peace Foundadation, 1966.

Katz, Daniel, *et al. Public Opinion and Propaganda*. Holt, Rinehart & Winston, 1954.

Key, V. O. *Public Opinion and American Democracy*. Knopf, 1961.

Key, V. O. *The Responsible Electorate: Rationality in Presidential Voting 1936-1960*. Harvard University Press, 1966.

Lane, Robert E. and Sears, David O. *Public Opinion*. Prentice-Hall, 1964.

Lasswell, Harold D. *Democracy Through Public Opinion*. Bantam, 1941.

Lazarsfeld, Paul F., *et al. The People's Choice*. Duell, Sloan and Pearce, 1948.

Lippmann, Walter. *Essays in the Public Philosophy*. Little Brown, 1955.

Lippmann, Walter. *The Phantom Public*. Harcourt, Brace, 1925.

Lippmann, Walter. *Public Opinion*. Macmillan, 1922.

Lipset, Seymour M. *Political Man: The Social Bases of Politics*. Double-day, 1960.

Lowell, A. Lawrence. *Public Opinion and Popular Government*. Longmans Green, 1913.

Markel, Lester (ed.). *Public Opinion and Foreign Policy*. Harper, 1949.

Nelson, William H. and Loewenhein, Francis L. *Theory and Practice in American Politics*. University of Chicago Press, 1964.

Pool, Ithiel de Sola, *et al. Candidates, Issues and Strategies. A Computer Simulation of the 1960 and 1964 Presidential Elections*. MIT Press, 1964.

Robinson, John P., *et al. Measures of Political Attitudes*. Survey Research Center, Institute for Social Research, University of Michigan, 1968.

Robinson, John P. *Public Information About World Affairs*. Survey Research Center, Institute for Social Research, University of Michigan, 1967.

Schramm, Wilbur L. *The Science of Human Communications*. Basic Books, 1963.

Schettler, Clarence H. *Public Opinion in American Society*. Harper and Row, 1960.

Smith, Charles W. *Public Opinion in a Democracy*. Prentice-Hall, 1939.

Steinberg, Charles S. *The Mass Communicators: Public Relations, Public Opinion, and Mass Media*. Harper and Row, 1958.

Wolfinger, Raymond E. (ed.). *Readings in American Political Behavior*. Prentice-Hall, 1966.

Weisbord, Marvin. *Campaigning for President*. Public Affairs Press, 1964.

Public Opinion Polls

Cantril, Hadley. *Gauging Public Opinion*. Princeton University Press, 1944.

Cantril, Hadley. *The Human Dimension: Experiences in Policy Research*. Rutgers University Press, 1967.

Deming, W. Edwards. *Some Theory of Sampling*. John Wiley, 1950.

Ernst, Morris and Loth, David. *The People Know Best: The Ballots vs. The Polls.* Public Affairs Press, 1949.

Gallup, George H. *Public Opinion in a Democracy.* Princeton University Press, 1939.

Gallup, George H. and Rae, Saul F. *The Pulse of Democracy: The Public Opinion Poll and How it Works.* Simon & Schuster, 1940.

Hansen, Morris H., *et al.*, *Sample Survey Methods and Theories.* John Wiley, 1953.

Hyman, Herbert H. *Survey Design and Analysis.* Free Press, 1955.

Meier, N. and Saunders, H. (eds.). *The Polls and Public Opinion.* Holt, Rinehart & Winston, 1949.

McClosky, Herbert. *Political Inquiry: The Nature and Uses of Survey Research.* Macmillan, 1969.

Parten, Mildren B. *Surveys, Polls and Samples.* Cooper Square Publishers, 1950.

Rogers, Lindsay. *The Pollsters: Public Opinion, Politics and Democratic Leadership.* Knopf, 1949.

Roper, Elmo. *You and Your Leaders.* William Morrow, 1957.

Stephan, Frederick F. and McCarthy, Philip J. *Sampling Opinions: An Analysis of Survey Procedure.* John Wiley, 1958.

Structure of Society

Baltzell, E. Digby. *Philadelphia Gentlemen.* Free Press, 1958.

Barber, Bernard. *Social Stratification: A Comparative Analysis of Structure and Process.* Harcourt, Brace, 1957.

Bendix, Reinhard and Lipset, Seymour (eds.). *Class, Status and Power: A Reader in Social Stratification.* Free Press, 1966.

Blau, Peter M. and Duncan, Otis D. *American Occupational Structure.* John Wiley, 1967.

Graham, Hugh and Gurr, Robert. *The History of Violence in America: A Report to the National Commission on the Causes and Prevention of Violence.* Bantam Books, 1969.

Kahl, Joseph A. *The American Class Structure.* Holt, Rinehart & Winston, 1957.

Kerner, Otto (Chairman). *Report of the National Advisory Commission on Civil Disorders.* Bantam Books, 1968.

Laumann, Edward O., *et al.* *The Logic of Social Hierarchies.* Markham Publishing Co., 1970.

Rose, Arnold. *The Power Structure: Political Process in American Society.* Oxford University Press, 1967.

Rosenau, James N. *The Attentive Public and Foreign Policy: A Theory of Growth and Some New Evidence*. Center of International Studies, Princeton University, 1968.

Rosenau, James N. *National Leadership and Foreign Policy: A Case Study in the Mobilization of Public Support*. Princeton University Press, 1963.

The Presidency

Austin, Anthony. *The President's War*. Lippincott, 1971.

Binkley, Wilfred E. *President and Congress*. Knopf, 1947.

Burns, James MacGregor. *Roosevelt: The Lion and the Fox*. Harcourt, Brace, 1956.

Burns, James MacGregor. *Presidential Government: The Crucible of Leadership*. Houghton Mifflin, 1966.

Chase, Harold W. and Lerman, Allen H. *Kennedy and the Press*. Crowell, 1965.

Cornwell, Elmer. *Presidential Leadership in Public Opinion*. Indiana University Press, 1965.

Corwin, Edward S. *President: Office and Powers*. New York University Press, 1957.

Coyle, David Cushman. *Ordeal of the Presidency*. Public Affairs Press, 1960.

Deakin, James. *Lyndon Johnson's Credibility Gap*. Public Affairs Press, 1968.

Hirschfield, Robert S. *The Power of the Presidency*. Atherton, 1968.

Hyman, Sidney. *The American President*. Harper, 1954.

Hyman, Sidney (ed.). *The Office of the American Presidency*. American Academy of Political and Social Science, 1956.

Johnson, Walter. *The American President and the Art of Communication*. Oxford University Press, 1938.

Kelley, Stanley, Jr. *Professional Public Relations and Political Power*. Johns Hopkins Press, 1966.

Koenig, Louis W. *The Chief Executive*, Harcourt, Brace, 1968.

Koenig, Louis W. *The Invisible Presidency*. Holt, Rinehart & Co., 1960.

Koenig, Louis W. and Corwin, Edward S. *Presidency Today*. New York University Press, 1956.

Kraft, Joseph. *Profiles in Power: A Washington Insight*. New American Library, 1966.

Landecker, Manfred. *The President and Public Opinion: Leadership in Foreign Affairs*. Public Affairs Press, 1968.

Michener, James. *Presidential Lottery: The Reckless Gamble in an Electoral System.* Random House, 1969.

Neustadt, Richard E. *Presidential Power: The Politics of Leadership.* John Wiley, 1960.

Pollard, James E. *The Presidents and the Press.* Macmillan, 1957.

Pollard, James E. *The Presidents and the Press: Truman to Johnson.* Public Affairs Press, 1964.

Reedy, George. *The Twilight of the Presidency.* World Publishing Co., 1970.

Rossiter, Clinton. *The American Presidency.* Harcourt, Brace, 1960.

Salinger, Pierre. *With Kennedy.* Doubleday, 1966.

Sidey, Hugh. *John F. Kennedy, President.* Atheneum, 1964.

Sundquist, James L. *Politics and Policy: The Eisenhower, Kennedy and Johnson Years.* Brookings Institute, 1968.

Warren, Sidney S. *The President as World Leader,* Lippincott, 1964.

White, Theodore. *The Making of the President 1968.* Atheneum, 1969.

White, William S. *The Professional: Lyndon B. Johnson,* Fawcett, 1964.

Congress

Bailey, Stephen K. *Congress Makes a Law.* Columbia University Press, 1950.

Berman, Daniel M. *In Congress Assembled.* Macmillan, 1964.

Bolling, Richard. *House Out of Order.* Dutton, 1965.

Bolling, Richard. *Power in the House: A History of the Leadership in the House of Representatives.* Dutton, 1968.

Burns, James M. *Deadlock of Democracy: Four-Party Politics in America.* Prentice-Hall, 1963.

Clapp, Charles L. *The Congressman: His Work as He Sees It.* Anchor Books, 1963.

Dahl, Robert A. *Congress and Foreign Policy.* W. W. Norton, 1965.

De Grazia, Alfred (ed.). *Congress: The First Branch of Government.* Doubleday, 1967.

Deakin, James. *The Lobbyists.* Public Affairs Press, 1966.

Eberling, Ernest. *Congressional Investigations.* Columbia University Press, 1928.

Galloway, George B. *The Legislative Process in Congress.* Crowell, 1953.

Gross, Bertram. *The Legislative Struggle: A Study in Social Combat.* McGraw-Hill, 1953.

Kefauver, Estes and Levin, Jack. *Twentieth Century Congress*. Greenwood Press, 1969.

MacNeil, Neil. *Forge of Democracy: The House of Representatives*. McKay, 1963.

McGeary, Martin N. *The Development of Congressional Investigating Power*. Columbia University Press, 1940.

Polsby, Nelson. *Congress and the Presidency*. Prentice-Hall, 1970.

Taylor, Telford. *Grand Inquest: The Story of Congressional Investigations*. Simon & Schuster, 1955.

Wright, Jim. *You and Your Congressman*. Coward-McCann, 1965.

The Press—General

Bagdikian, Ben H. *The Information Machines: Their Impact on Men and the Media*. Harper and Row, 1971.

Baker, Robert and Ball, Sandra (eds.). *Mass Media and Violence: A Report to the National Commission on the Causes and Prevention of Violence*. U. S. Printing Office, 1969.

Balk, Alfred, and Boyle, James (eds.). *Our Troubled Press*. Little, Brown, 1971.

Boorstin, Daniel J. *The Image or What Happened to the American Dream*. Atheneum, 1962.

Cater, Douglass. *The Fourth Branch of Government*. Random House, 1959.

Commission on Freedom of the Press. *A Free and Responsible Press: A General Report on Mass Communication*. University of Chicago Press. 1947.

Coons, John E. (ed.). *Freedom and Responsibility in the Mass Media*. Northwestern University Press, 1961.

Fisher, Paul and Lowenstein, Ralph (eds.). *Race and the News Media*. Praeger, 1967.

Gillmor, Donald M. *Free Press and Fair Trial*. Public Affairs Press,

Gross, Gerald. *The Responsibility of the Press*. Fleet, 1966.

Hero, Alfred. *Mass Media and World Affairs*. World Peace Foundation, 1963.

Hocking, William E. *Freedom of the Press: A Framework of Principle*. University of Chicago Press, 1947.

Klapper, Joseph. *The Effects of Mass Communication*. Free Press, 1960.

Lacy, Dan. *Freedom and Communications.* University of Illinois Press, 1965.

Leigh, R. D. (ed.). *A Free and Responsible Press.* University of Chicago Press, 1947.

Lippmann, Walter. *Liberty and the News.* Macmillan, 1920.

Mott, Frank L. *American Journalism: A History.* Macmillan, 1941.

Rivers, William L., *et al. The Mass Media and Modern Society.* Holt, Rinehart & Winston, 1971.

Rossi, Peter and Biddle, Bruce (eds.). *The New Media and Education: Their Impact on Society.* Aldine, 1966.

Rucker, Bryce W. *The First Freedom.* Southern Illinois University Press, 1968.

Schramm, Wilbur (ed.). *Communications in Modern Society.* University of Illinois Press, 1948.

Schramm, Wilbur (ed.). *The Process and Effects of Mass Communication.* University of Illinois Press, 1960.

Schramm, Wilbur (ed.). *Responsibility in Mass Communication.* University of Illinois Press, 1948.

Seldes, Gilbert. *The New Mass Media.* Public Affairs Press, 1968.

Siebert, Fred S., *et al., Four Theories of the Press.* University of Illinois Press, 1965.

Steinberg, Charles S. *Mass Media and Communication.* Hastings, 1966.

The Press—Newspapers

Agee, Warren K. (ed.). *The Press and the Public Interest.* Public Affairs Press, 1968.

Berdes, George R. *Friendly Adversaries: The Press and Government.* Center for the Study of the American Press, 1969.

Bleyer, Willard G. *Main Currents in the History of American Journalism.* Houghton Mifflin, 1927.

Bradley, Duanne. *The Newspaper: Its Place in a Democracy.* Van Nostrand, 1965.

Daniels, Jonathan. *They Will Be Heard: America's Crusading Newspaper Editors.* McGraw-Hill, 1965.

Emery, Edwin. *The Press and America.* Prentice-Hall, 1962.

Gerald, James E. *The Press and the Constitution, 1931-47.* University of Minnesota Press, 1948.

Gerald, James E. *The Social Responsibility of the Press.* University of Minnesota Press, 1963.

Glessing, Robert J. *The Underground Press in America.* Indiana University Press, 1970.

Haseldon, Kyle. *Morality and the Mass Media.* Broadman Press, 1968.

Hohenberg, John. *Free Press/Free People: The Best Cause.* Columbia University Press, 1971.

Howe, Quincy. *The News and How to Understand It.* Simon & Schuster, 1940.

Ickes, Harold. *America's House of Lords: An Inquiry Into the Freedom of the Press.* Harcourt, Brace, 1939.

Kornbluth, Jesse (ed.). *Notes from the New Underground.* Viking Press, 1968.

Lee, Alfred McClung. *The Daily Newspaper in America.* Macmillan, 1937.

Liebling, Abbott J. *The Press.* Ballantine, 1961.

Lindstrom, Carl E. *The Fading American Newspaper.* Doubleday, 1967.

Lofton, John. *Justice and the Press.* Beacon, 1966.

Lyons, Louis M. (ed.). *Reporting the News.* Harvard University Press, 1965.

Markel, Lester (ed.). *Background and Foreground.* Channel Press, 1960.

Mott, Frank Luther. *American Journalism: A History, 1690-1960.* Macmillan, 1962.

Peterson, Theodore. *Magazines in the Twentieth Century.* University of Illinois Press, 1964.

Reston, James. *The Artillery of the Press.* Harper and Row, 1967.

Rivers, William M. *The Opinionmakers: The Washington Press Corps.* Beacon, 1967.

Schlesinger, Arthur M. *Prelude to Independence: The Newspaper War on Britain, 1764-1776.* Knopf, 1958.

Snyder, Louis L. and Morris, Richard B. (eds.). *A Treasury of Great Reporting.* Simon and Schuster, 1962.

Starr, Louis M. *Bohemian Brigade: Civil War Newsmen in Action.* Knopf, 1954.

Television

Arons, L. and Way, M. (eds.). *Television and Human Behavior.* Appleton Century Crofts, 1963.

Barrett, Marvin (ed.). *The Alfred I. DuPont-Columbia University*

Survey of Broadcast Journalism 1968-1969. Grosset & Dunlap, 1970.

Barnouw, Erik. *The Image Empire: A History of Broadcasting in the United States.* Oxford University Press, 1970.

Blakely, Robert J. *The People's Instrument.* Public Affairs Press, 1971.

Bogart, Leo. *The Age of Television: A Study of Viewing Habits and the Impact of Television on American Life.* Ungar, 1958.

Brown, Les. *Television: The Business Behind the Box.* Harcourt, Brace, 1971.

Carnegie Commission on Educational Television. *Public Television: A Program for Action.* Bantam Books, 1967.

Chester, Edward W. *Radio, Television and American Politics.* Sheed & Ward, 1970.

Cronkite, Walter. *Challenges of Change.* Public Affairs Press, 1971.

Efron, Edith. *The News Twisters. Nash,* 1971.

Friendly, Fred W. *Due to Circumstances Beyond Our Control.* Random House, 1967.

Johnson, Nicholas. *How to Talk Back to Your Television Set.* Little Brown, 1970.

Kendrick, Alexander. *Prime Time: The Life of Edward R. Murrow.* Little, Brown, 1969.

Levin, Harvey J. *Broadcast Regulation and Joint Ownership of Media.* New York University Press, 1960.

MacNeil, Robert. *The People Machine: The Influence of Television on American Politics.* Harper & Row, 1968.

Minow, Newton. *Equal Time: The Private Broadcaster and the Public Interest.* Atheneum, 1964.

Morris, Norman. *Television's Child: A Report for Parents.* Little, Brown, 1971.

Shayon, Robert L. *The Eighth Art: 23 Views of TV Today.* Holt, Rinehart & Winston, 1962.

Skornia, Harry J. (ed.). *Television and the News: A Critical Appraisal.* Pacific Books, 1968.

Skornia, Harry J. *Television and Society.* McGraw Hill, 1965.

Smead, Elmer E. *Freedom of Speech by Radio and Television.* Public Affairs Press, 1959.

Steiner, Gary A. *The People Look at Television: A Study of Audience Attitudes.* Knopf, 1963.

Summers, Robert F. and Summers, Harrison B. *Broadcasting and the Public.* Wadsworth, 1966.

Thomson, Charles A. H. *Television and Presidential Politics*. Brookings Institute, 1956.

Wilson, Hubert. *Pressure Group: The Campaign for Commercial Television in England*. Rutgers University Press, 1961.

Government Information Practices

Barth, Alan. *The Government and the Press*. University of Minnesota Press, 1952.

Brucker, Herbert. *Freedom of Information*. Macmillan, 1949.

Chaffee, Zechariah. *Free Speech in the United States*. Harvard University Press, 1946.

Chaffee, Zechariah. *Government and Mass Communications*. University of Chicago Press, 1947.

Cooper, Kent. *The Right to Know: An Exposition of the Evils of News Suppression and Propaganda*. Farrar Straus, 1956.

Cross, Harold. *The People's Right to Know: Legal Access to Public Records*. Columbia University Press, 1953.

Ernst, Morris L. *The First Freedom*. Macmillan, 1946.

Goulden, Joseph. *Truth Is the First Casualty*. Rand McNally, 1969.

Goulding, Phil G. *Confirm or Deny, Informing the People on National Security*. Harper & Row, 1970.

Hudon, Edward G. *Freedom of Speech and Press in America*. Public Affairs Press, 1962.

Ladd, Bruce. *Crisis in Credibility*. New American Library, 1968.

Levy, Leonard W. *Legacy of Suppression: Freedom of Speech and Press in Early American History*. Harvard University Press, 1960.

McCamy, James L. *Government Publicity*. University of Chicago Press, 1939.

McGaffin, William and Knoll, Erwin. *Anything But the Truth: The Credibility Gap—How the News is Managed in Washington*. Putnam, 1968.

Mollenhoff, Clark R. *Washington Coverup*. Doubleday, 1962.

Nimmo, Dan. *Newsgathering in Washington*. Atherton, 1964.

Powledge, Fred. *The Engineering of Restraint: The Nixon Administration and the Press*. Public Affairs Press, 1971.

Raymond, Allen. *The People's Right To Know*. American Civil Liberties Union, 1955.

Rourke, Francis E. *Secrecy and Publicity: Dilemmas of Democracy*. Johns Hopkins University Press, 1961.

Schnapper, M. B. *Constraint by Copyright: A Report on Official and Private Practices*. Public Affairs Press, 1960.

Stein, M. L. *Freedom of the Press: A Continuing Struggle*. Messner, 1966.

Summers, Robert E. (ed.). *Federal Information Controls in Peacetime*. H. W. Wilson, 1949.

Thayer, Frank. *Legal Control of the Press*. Foundation Press, 1962.

Wiggins, James R. *Freedom or Secrecy*. Oxford University Press, 1964.

REFERENCES

CHAPTER 2

1. Walter Lippmann, *Public Opinion* (Free Press, 1966), p. 18.
2. V. O. Key, Jr., *Public Opinion and American Democracy* (Knopf, 1964), p. 14.

CHAPTER 3

1. Seymour M. Lipset, "A Private Opinion on the Polls,' *New York Times Magazine*, April 30, 1965, p. 65.
2. James Bryce, *The American Commonwealth*, Vol. II (Macmillan, 1910), p. 358.
3. Burns Roper, in a paper delivered at the American Association of Public Opinion Researchers meeting, Bolton Landing, New York, May 17, 1969.
4. Bryce, *op. cit.*, p. 560.

CHAPTER 4

1. U. S. Department of Labor, Bureau of Labor Statistics, *Study of Consumer Expenditures, Savings and Incomes*, 1950-1951, 1960-1961, and 1964-1965.
2. *Time*, January 5, 1970, p. 10.   3. *Ibid.*, p. 11.
4. *Wall Street Journal*, January 12, 1970.
5. Jean Gottmann, *Megalopolis: The Urbanized Northeastern Seaboard of the United States* (Twentieth Century Fund, 1961), pp. 4-16.
6. Wolf von Ekhardt, *The Challenge of the Megalopolis* (Macmillan, 1964), p. 13.
7. Arnold Hano, "East is East and West is Second—Or Is It?" *New York Times Magazine*, March 16, 1969, p. 33.

CHAPTER 5

1. Alfred O. Hero, *Americans in World Affairs* (World Peace Foundation, 1959), p. 6.
2. Lloyd A. Free and Hadley Cantril, *The Political Beliefs of Americans: A Study of Public Opinion* (Simon & Schuster, 1968), p. 61.
3. James Michener, *Presidential Lottery* (Random House, 1969), p. 43.
4. Details of this survey can be found in the Appendix.
5. Richard Neustadt, *Presidential Power: The Politics of Leadership* (John Wiley, 1960), p. 97.
6. *New York Times*, December 28, 1969.
7. Hugh Davis Graham and Ted Robert Gurr, *The History of Violence in America: A Report to the National Commission on the Causes and Prevention of Violence* (Bantam Books, 1969) pp. 794-97.

CHAPTER 7

1. Harwood L. Childs, *Public Opinion: Nature, Formation and Role* (Van Nostrand, 1965), p. 141.

2. Survey Research Center, University of Michigan, 1958, as quoted in V. O. Key, Jr., *Public Opinion and American Democracy* (Knopf, 1964), pp. 302-303.

3. *Ibid.*, p. 315.

4. Joseph Klapper, *The Effects of Mass Communication* (Free Press, 1960), p. 19.

5. Key, *op. cit.*, pp. 323-327.

6. Malcolm S. Knowles, "Adult Education," in *The New Media and Education: Their Impact on Society*, edited by Peter H. Rossi and Bruce J. Biddle (Aldine, 1966), p. 309.

CHAPTER 8

1. Theodore White, *The Making of the President, 1968* (Atheneum, 1969), p. 147.

CHAPTER 9

1. *New York Times*, July 20, 1950.   2. *New York Times*, May 10, 1970.

3. George Reedy, "Does the U. S. Need a King?" *Look*, March 10, 1970, p. 33.

4. *Ibid.*, p. 32.   5. *New York Times*, May 6, 1970.

6. *New York Times*, May 14, 1970.

CHAPTER 10

1. *New York Times*, August 24, 1970.

CHAPTER 11

1. *New York Times*, June 14, 1970.   2. *New York Times*, August 26, 1969.

3. *Editor and Publisher*, May 16, 1970, p. 38.

4. Stuart Symington, "Congress's Right to Know," *New York Times* Magazine, August 9, 1970, p. 7ff.

5. *New York Times*, August 11, 1970.

6. Abraham S. Goldstein, "Newsmen and Their Confidential Sources," *New Republic*, March 31, 1970, pp. 13-15.

7. *Wall Street Journal*, April 10, 1968.   8. *Congressional Record*, May 1, 1970.

9. *New York Times*, November 14, 1969. 10. *New York Times*, November 22, 1969.

11. *Washington Post*, May 26, 1970.

CHAPTER 12

1. James Deakin, *Lyndon Johnson's Credibility Gap* (Public Affairs Press, 1968), p. 17.

2. *New York Times*, May 23, 1970.

CHAPTER 13

1. James Madison, *The Federalist, 51*, ed. J. E. Cooke (Wesleyan University Press, 1961), pp. 348-349.

2. Nelson Polsby, *Congress and the Presidency* (Prentice-Hall, 1971), p. 134.

3. *Ibid.*, p. 137.

4. Meg Greenfield, "Why Are You Calling Me, Son?", *The Reporter*, August 16, 1962, p. 30.

5. *New York Times,* May 5, 1970.
6. *New York Times,* January 28, 1970.

CHAPTER 14

1. *New York Times,* January 19, 1970. 2. *Congressional Record,* June 8, 1969.
3. Jim Wright, *You and Your Congressman* (Coward-McCann, 1965), p. 185.
4. Warren Miller and Donald Stokes, "Constituency Influence in Congress," in *American Political Science Review,* March 1963, p. 47.

CHAPTER 16

1. Nicholas Johnson, *How to Talk Back to Your Television Set* (Little, Brown, 1970), p. 13.
2. *Network Programming Inquiry: Report and Statement of Policy,* Federal Communications Commission Report No. 60 of July 29, 1970, p. 970.
3. Newton Minow, *Equal Time* (Atheneum, 1964), pp. 91-92.
4. Fred Friendly, *Due to Circumstances Beyond Our Control* (Random House, 1967), p. 300.
5. On the CBS program "Face the Nation," September 14, 1969.
6. Gary A. Steiner, *The People Look At Television.* (Knopf, 1963), pp. 231-232.
7. Burns W. Roper, *A Ten-Year View of Public Attitudes Toward Television and Other Mass Media* (Television Information Office, 1969), pp. 3, 4, 10.

CHAPTER 17

1. *New York Times,* July 26, 1970.
2. *New York Times,* July 28, 1971.
3. *Washington Post,* November 19, 1969.

CHAPTER 18

1. *The Alfred I. dupont-Columbia University Survey of Broadcast Journalism, 1968-1969,* edited by Marvin Barrett (Grossett & Dunlap, 1969), p. 5.
2. *Ibid.,* p. 87.   3. *Ibid.,* p. 16.
4. *New York Times,* April 15, 1968.   5. *Washington Post,* November 5, 1969
6. *New York Times,* March 2, 1969.
7. *Alfred I. dupont-Columbia Survey, op. cit.,* pp. 23-24.
8. William Whitworth, "An Accident of Casting," *The New Yorker,* August 3. 1968, p. 58.
9. *Alfred I. dupont-Columbia Survey, op. cit.* p. 14.

CHAPTER 19

1. "Local Radio's Voice for a Better Tomorrow," in *Broadcasting Magazine,* June 30, 1969, p. 44.
2. Edward W. Chester, *Radio, Television and American Politics* (Sheed & Ward, 1969), p. 62.

3. "A Little Respect: Radio Power and the Public Interest," speech given at the Negro and Spanish Speaking Market Radio and Today's Urban Crisis Conference, New York, May 16, 1968.

CHAPTER 20

1. *Wall Street Journal*, December 4, 1969.   2. *Ibid.*
3. Hazel Henderson, "Access to Media: a Problem in Democracy," *Columbia Journalism Review*, Spring 1969, p. 5.
4. *Race and the News Media*, edited by Paul L. Fisher and Ralph Lowenstein (Praeger, 1967), p. 5.
5. Jack Butler, *American Association of Newspaper Editors Bulletin*, March, 1969, p. 5.
6. Ben Bagdikian, "The American Newspaper is Neither Record, Mirror, nor Herald of the Day's Events," *Esquire*, March 1967, p. 124.
7. Courtney R. Sheldon, "Do Newspapers Have a Serious Credibility Gap?" *Associated Press Managing Editors Red Book*, 1969, p. 146.

CHAPTER 21

1. Clifton Daniel in a speech to the World Press Institute, St. Paul, Minnesota, May 30, 1966.
2. *New York Times*, June 1, 1966.   3. *New York Times*, January 11, 1970.
4. *Mass Media & Violence: A Report of the National Commission on the Causes and Prevention of Violence*, Robert K. Baker and Sandra J. Ball (U. S. Government Printing Office, 1969), pp. 151 and 156.
5. *Report of the National Advisory Commission on Civil Disorders* (Bantam, 1968), p. 363.
6. Henry Shapiro, *Editor & Publisher*, February 14, 1970.
7. *New York Times*, January 4, 1970.
8. Roy Essoyan, *American Association of Newspaper Editors Bulletin*, March 1970, p. 8.
9. Alfred Friendly, *American Association of Newspaper Editors Bulletin*, March 1970, p. 9.

CHAPTER 22

1. Walter Lippmann, *Public Opinion* (Free Press, 1965), p. 250.
2. Gabriel Almond, *The American People and Foreign Policy* (Praeger, 1950), pp. 4-9.

INDEX

Adams, Franklin P., 233
Advertising, 153-55
Aerospace Industries, Assn., 138
AFL-CIO, 137, 141
Agency for International Development, 83
Agnew, Spiro: popularity, 23; on Middle American, 22; press relations, 96 et. seq., 114
Agronsky, Martin, 176
Allende, Dr. Salvador, 218
Almond, Gabriel, Jr., 226
American Assn. of Public Opinion Research, 17
American Bar Assn., 213
American Civil Liberties Union, 97, 172
American Medical Assn., 137
American Newspaper Publishers Assn., 196
American Society of Newspaper Editors, 196
Amherst College, 53
Anderson, Raymond, 163
Anti-Ballistic Missile, 41, 42, 46, 138
Archibald, Sam, 85
Associated Press, 188, 189, 216
Associated Press Managing Editors Assn., 196, 220

Bagdikian, Ben, 194, 196
Bagehot, Walter, 110
Bartlett, Ruhl J., 116
Bay of Pigs, 59-61, 203
Bayh, Birch, 120
Bendiner, Robert, 126
Bentham, Jeremy, 8
Berkeley, Cal., 171
Berkeley Barb, 264
Birch Society, 55, 230
Black, Hugo, 176, 206
Black Panthers, 55, 85, 88
Black Power, 43
Black studies, 53

Blackmun, Harry A., 207
Blumenthal, Ralph, 163
Bolling, Richard, 132, 134-135, 260
Boston Record-American, 189
Bradley, Thomas, 43
Brewer, Albert, 43
Britain: public information, state of, 32; education, 50; 1970 elections, 246-48
British Press Council, 196
Broadcasting, 181
Brooke, Edward, 11
Brown, Rap, 95
Bryce, James, 8, 15, 19, 107
Buchanan, John, 263
Buchanan, Patrick J., 73
Bunker, Ellsworth, 103
Burch, Dean, 99, 122
Burger, Warren, 151, 207, 209
Burton, Philip, 133, 262
Butler, Jack, 194
Byrd, Harry Jr., 129, 133

Calley, William, 212
Cambodia, 44, 46, 62, 69, 94, 105-06, 118-21, 163, 204
Cantril, Hadley, 27, 30, 244
Carmichael, Stokely, 95
Carswell, G. Harold, 111-12, 119, 137
Catledge, Turner, 232
Censorship, 86 et. seq.; 215-216
Central Intelligence Agency, 83, 203
Chamber of Commerce, 137, 142
Chattanooga Times, 233
Chester, Edward W., 182
Chicago Daily News, 253
Chicago Tribune, 153, 202
Childs, Harwood, 47
China: Russian relations, 44-45; U. S. relations, 44-45, 62-63
Christian, George, 83
Christian Science Monitor, 190
Church, Frank, 43, 103, 118, 133, 261
Citizens Crusade Against Hunger, 141

282